Affluent Workers Revisited

Privatism and the Working Class

FIONA DEVINE

EDINBURGH
EDUCATION AND SOCIETY
SERIES

General Editor: Colin Bell

EDINBURGH UNIVERSITY PRESS

© Fiona Devine, 1992

Edinburgh University Press
22 George Square, Edinburgh

Set in Linotron Palatino
by Koinonia Ltd, Bury, and
printed in Great Britain by
Robert Hartnoll Ltd, Bodmin

A CIP record for this book is available
from the British Library

ISBN 0 7486 0370 0

FOR MARTIN

CONTENTS

TABLES

ACKNOWLEDGEMENTS

I should like to acknowledge the support of a number of colleagues and friends who helped me complete this research. First and foremost, I should like to express my gratitude to the interviewees who participated in the study. Their willingness to be interviewed, and the hospitality which I received when I visited their homes, made my stay in Luton a very pleasant one. I should also like to thank those people who, in an individual or offical capacity, helped me contact Vauxhall workers and their families in Luton.

My greatest debt goes to Gordon Marshall, who supervised my doctoral thesis on which this book is based. His encouragement and advice, which he willingly gave at all stages of the research, made the study far better than I would have thought possible. I should also like to thank other members of the Department of Sociology at the University of Essex, particularly David Lee, David Lockwood and David Rose, who guided me through my undergraduate and graduate career.

Other people also helped me along the way. Thanks must go to Graham Crow, who meticulously read a number of drafts of the thesis, and who also gave a great many helpful suggestions in the preparation of this book. Andy Davies commented on the draft from the perspective of a social historian. Ken Roberts kept a watchful eye over me while Colin Bell, as editor, provided overall guidance on the manuscript. Finally, Ceridwen Roberts and Susan McRae gave much needed support and encouragement.

Thanks should also go to my family for their support over the years. My interest in the *Affluent Worker* study grew when I discovered that my parents nearly moved from London to Luton in the mid-1960s. Of Irish descent, they were going to follow some friends to Luton who worked at Vauxhall. However, the sale of the house fell through and I, along with my sisters and brother, grew up in Bournemouth instead. My first interviews were with a family who had just returned from their holiday at the seaside resort. They wished they lived there!

Sadly, my father died suddenly three days before I was awarded the doctoral thesis. He never knew that it would become a book, but I know that he would have been very proud. Finally, I should like to acknowledge my heartfelt thanks to my husband, Martin Smith, who supported me throughout the completion of this research.

FIONA DEVINE
Liverpool

1

INTRODUCTION

One of the main debates within British class analysis since the Second World War has centred on the demise of the working class as a demographic formation and, more importantly, as a distinctive socio-political entity.[1] In the late 1950s and early 1960s, for example, proponents of the British version of the embourgeoisement thesis (Abrams *et al.* 1960; Butler and Rose 1960; Mogey 1956; Young and Willmott 1957; Zweig 1961) argued that working-class families had adopted middle-class norms and values as they achieved relatively high incomes and standards of living in the post-war period of prosperity. Affluence generated and sustained life-styles which centred on the individual home and family, fuelled individual consumer aspirations and led members of the working class to vote for the political party which would best meet those individual consumer aspirations. In other words, the 'traditional' working-class occupational community and associated proletarian solidarism of the first half of the twentieth century had given way to working-class instrumentalism, privatism and individualism. The class structure had changed, and the working class was no longer distinct from the middle class.

In the 1980s and early 1990s numerous sociologists and political scientists (Crewe 1987, 1989; Dunleavy 1980; Dunleavy and Husbands 1985; Saunders 1990a, 1990b) have charted the advance of working-class instrumentalism, privatism and individualism still further. The continued rise in affluence – of increased standards of living, high levels of consumption, extensive home ownership, opportunities for social mobility and so forth – across social classes has changed working-class life-styles and aspirations. Moreover, increased individual consumption within mass society has undermined old class divisions and political allegiances. Members of the working class no longer see themselves at the bottom of an unchanging class-based society nor feel the need to align themselves with the vehicles of working-class support, namely, the trade unions and the Labour Party. While little reference is made to the adoption of middle-class norms and values among members of the working class today, the revival of all or part of the embourgeoisement thesis, as others have noted (Heath *et al.* 1985, 1991; Hill 1990; Marshall *et al.* 1988), continues to emphasise a shift in the values of the British working class.

A distinct working-class socio-political identity, it has been claimed, has all but disappeared.

Thus, the thesis of working-class instrumentalism, privatism and individualism has retained its popularity over a considerable period of time. The account of the shift of the socio-political proclivities of the British working class has remained unchanged despite the uneven economic climate of the last forty years. The strength of this prevailing view is somewhat surprising, since the early version of the embourgeoisement thesis was refuted over twenty years ago by John Goldthorpe, David Lockwood, Frank Bechhofer and Jennifer Platt in the *Affluent Worker* series (Goldthorpe *et al.* 1968a, 1968b, 1969).[2] Indeed, the main findings of the *Affluent Worker* study have been incorporated into the wide-ranging theory of economic, social and political change since the Second World War, especially in the work of political scientists like Crewe (1989). By implication, therefore, the central findings of the Luton team remain the source of controversy as well.[3]

The principal aim of the *Affluent Worker* study was to test the embourgeoisement thesis (Goldthorpe *et al.* 1968a: 1).[4] Conducted in the early 1960s, the empirical study consisted of interviews with manual workers and their wives living in Luton. Luton was chosen on the expectation that a group of people prone to embourgeoisement could be contacted for the research. As Goldthorpe and his colleagues stated:

> In this way, we would, on the one hand, gain the best chance of being able to study workers who were actually in course of changing their class situation; while, on the other hand, if in the case in question this process was *not* in evidence, we would then be in a position to claim a *fortiori* it was unlikely to be occurring to any significant extent within British society at large (1969: 31, emphasis in original).

It was to be a critical case study of the embourgeiosement thesis.

Goldthorpe and his colleagues firmly rejected the embourgeoisement thesis. They found little evidence to suggest that the working class had been assimilated to the middle class. Nevertheless, they went on to argue that 'traditional' working-class norms and values had adapted in the post-war period of prosperity. Favourable economic circumstances had fuelled 'new' aspirations for individual material well-being among members of the working class. In turn, these aspirations had engendered an instrumental orientation to work, the desire for a home and family-centred life-style, and collective support for the trade unions and Labour Party which was directed towards individual ends. Members of the working class were identified as 'privatised instrumental collectivists'.[5] Rather than assimilation, a 'much less dramatic process' of normative convergence was occurring between some sections of the working class and some white-collar workers. Summarising their position, the Luton team explained:

In other words, we suggested that the major ongoing modifications in manual–non-manual differences were occurring at the level of values and aspirations, rather than through any radical reshaping of status hierarchies and relationships in either work or community life; and further, that these modifications resulted from shifting orientations among white-collar as well as among manual strata (Goldthorpe *et al.* 1969: 26).

Most importantly, the Luton team concluded that their respondents were 'prototypical', more representative of the future than the present working class or the 'traditional' working class of the first half of the twentieth century. Speculating on the 'wider significance' of their findings in the concluding chapter to Volume 1, the Luton team surmised:

As we stated at the outset, our sample is not one on the basis of which any far-ranging generalisations of a direct kind can safely be made: on the contrary, it was expressly devised so as to represent a special, critical case. And, as we have repeatedly tried to show in course of the monograph, the attitudes and behaviour of our respondents appear often divergent from those of most other industrial workers who have been studied in different, more 'traditional' contexts. Nevertheless, while these contrasts are, of course, central to the argument of the monograph, we have at certain points found reason to speculate that our affluent workers may perhaps be revealing a pattern of industrial life which will in the fairly near future become far more widespread (Goldthorpe *et al.* 1968a: 174).

That is, the Luton team expected an instrumental orientation to work, a privatised social life and the vigorous pursuit of material aspirations to characterise the working class of the next few decades. They argued:

In these several ways it is our view that the subjects of our Luton enquiry will prove to be more typical of the future than they are of the present time. But it need scarcely be added that the foregoing paragraphs should in no way be understood as implying unconditional predictions about the future course of events. They are intended rather as an attempt at outlining, in the light of our research, some probable consequences for working-class economic life of already observable trends of change within British society at large. Such trends may, of course, be checked or reversed in ways which cannot be foreseen; and it is only on the condition that they continue that our analysis can stand (Goldthorpe *et al.* 1968a: 177–8).

These claims to 'prototypicality' and predictions about the future have remained the source of controversy since publication of the series in the late 1960s. As Platt (1984: 186) later conceded, one of the most valid criticisms was T.H. Marshall's (1970) methodological critique of the study. A critical case study, he argued, may have been appropriate for the 'negative' finding that embourgeoisement was not taking place.

However, it was not the best means of establishing the 'positive' finding that the working class was changing in the post-war period of prosperity. The choice of Luton as the locality for the study and the design of the sample to include affluent workers was not an adequate base from which to claim either typicality or prototypicality. On the basis of their findings, the Luton team could not conclude that the social changes which they described were more than transitional, or applied to other members of the working class (Marshall 1970: 416).

More recently, criticism of the claims of typicality and prototypicality has been elaborated upon by Grieco (1981, 1987). In her study of the role of family networks in shaping employment chances in the steel town of Corby, Grieco stumbled across people who had been recruited to Luton by Vauxhall in the 1950s and 1960s. It appeared that Vauxhall had actively recruited workers from Scotland and the North East, where peripheral sectors of the economy were in decline and unemployment was far higher than the national average. It was in these uncertain economic circumstances that families with little experience of mass production methods moved to Luton. In other words, these people were not typical workers, and it was not instrumental orientations to work which led them to move in search of jobs. This finding, Grieco argued, implied that working-class norms and values were not necessarily changing as the Luton team claimed.

Furthermore, Grieco argued that Goldthorpe and his colleagues paid scant attention to the role of family networks in facilitating migration in search of jobs, especially over long distances. Information on kin within Luton was limited and information on sociability between kin in the workplace in particular was absent from the series. The trend towards privatised life-styles had been over-stated. She argued that the 'shaping of the workforce' by the company and role of family networks should

> give us cause for concern about to what extent the workforce was indeed representative of the solidary working class. Given the recruitment strategy at Vauxhall, their workforce cannot be understood as being typical of the working class. Far from being the vanguard of the working class, a significant section of the work force has to be understood as labour peripherally recruited and therefore untypical. Prototypicality, given this finding, would be an even more unsubstantiated claim (Grieco 1987: 128).

Like Marshall, Grieco questioned the extent to which the 'disrupted and attenuated kin and community ties' found in Luton were permanent, or were merely transitional changes and the result of recent migration. A later account of people's lives might find a regrouping of families in a new locale. Both of them cast doubt on the Luton team's account of social change and their characterisation of the working class of the future.

Against this background, this book re-examines the Luton team's central conclusions on instrumentalism, privatism and individualism and the claims of prototypicality. The research is based on intensive interviews with sixty-two Luton residents, either Vauxhall workers or their wives. Interviewed separately at home, the men and women were asked to discuss different facets of their daily lives. Topics of conversation included geographical mobility, work histories, sociability with kin, neighbours and fellow workers, conjugal roles, leisure patterns, consumer aspirations, class identities, and industrial and political attitudes and behaviour. In other words, the topics were broadly similar to the issues covered in the Luton team's interview schedule.

The research focuses on issues surrounding working-class life-styles and socio-political values in the 1980s. Have the Luton team's predictions stood the test of time? Do working-class people lead home– and family-centred lives as Goldthorpe and his colleagues found among their sample over twenty-five years ago? Or do their life-styles now take a communal form more usually associated with the 'traditional' working class? Do their aspirations centre on the desire for material well-being in general and domestic comfort in particular, or do they hold other ideals? Are their social and political perspectives shaped by individual consumer aspirations or do working-class collective identities still inform their political attitudes and behaviour? In what ways do people's daily lives shape their aspirations, social, industrial and political perspectives. It is, therefore, a study of the relationships and interconnections between different aspects of people's everyday lives.

The research is not a 're-study' of the *Affluent Worker* series *per se*. The aim of this research is different: the object of this study is to examine the Luton team's central conclusion on 'privatised instrumental collectivism' in-depth. It is not a study on embourgeoisement, which was the principal objective of the *Affluent Worker* study. Nor does this research consider the wide range of other debates in the fields of industrial sociology – including issues such as the impact of technology on the workplace and orientations to work, which were contemporary debates in the late 1950s and early 1960s. It was these controversies which the Luton team sought to address when they began their research in the early 1960s. In contrast, the primary interest of this research with issues of instru-mentalism, privatism and individualism are of importance in the 1980s and 1990s.

Furthermore, the methods of this research are different from the methods employed by the Luton team. This study is based on intensive interviews with sixty-two Luton residents, all either Vauxhall workers or their wives. In contrast, Goldthorpe *et al.* conducted a survey drawing on a tightly defined sample of affluent workers across three different industrial settings in the town for their study over two decades earlier. My research was designed to explore the different facets of life-styles and socio-political perspectives in particular detail. Some of the in-depth issues could be tackled only very briefly in the highly-structured survey conducted by Goldthorpe and his colleagues. Hence, rather than repeat the *Affluent Worker* study, the current research goes further to re-examine some of the central conclusions and predictions of the series. In the following chapter, the theoretical debates which Goldthorpe and his colleagues sought to address and the findings of their empirical research in Luton are considered. Reviews and criticisms of the *Affluent Worker* study and subsequent research on the working class are also examined. It will be argued that the central findings of the series remain strongly contested, not least because the main conclusions are not unlike a cautious account of the embourgeoisement thesis which the Luton team sought to refute. Moreover, current attempts to locate privatism among the nineteenth–century working class have effectively drawn attention away from the question of whether the concept of privatism adequately describes working-class life-styles and socio-political proclivities in the late twentieth century.

Chapter 3 describes the way in which this study was undertaken, and introduces the men and women interviewees. Attention centres on the diverse origins and the varied, often less than favourable, circumstances in which the interviewees came to live and work in Luton compared with the Luton team's repondents in the early 1960s. It will be seen that the interviewees were not instrumental in the search for highly-paid manual work in affluent Luton as Goldthorpe *et al.* argued. On the contrary, they were geographically mobile, in search of paid work and affordable housing *per se*. The circumstances in which they moved invariably meant that they followed, or were followed by, kin. They were not always physically separated from them but regrouped in the town.

The main empirical chapters explore the issue of privatism further. Chapters 4, 5 and 6, which focus on patterns of sociability with kin, neighbours and fellow workers, consider the extent to which the interviewees' lives could be described as family-centred. Chapters 7 and 8 focus on the extent to which their lives were home-centred by exploring the interviewees' domestic roles and patterns of leisure. It will be argued that while the interviewees' lives centred on the immediate family in the home, their life-styles also encompassed sociable contact with kin, neighbours and fellow workers as well as leisure pursuits beyond the home. They were not privatised. More often than not, the extent of sociability with friends and leisure patterns varied between the men and women interviewees according to paid and unpaid work roles across the family life-cycle. These opportunities and constraints, rather than working-class norms and values, shaped the interviewees' life-styles. Their norms and values invariably legitimised the structural patterning of their daily lives.

Chapters 9 and 10 go on to examine the socio-political perspectives of the sample. Chapter 9 is specifically concerned with the aspirations and social perspectives of the interviewees, while Chapter 10 explores their industrial and political perspectives. The evidence will show that the interviewees' aspirations were based on increased standards of living in general and individual domestic well-being in particular, but these ideals were an important aspect of their collective working-class identity. Their individual consumer aspirations, therefore, did not preclude them from collectively identifying with other working-class households aspiring to material affluence. On this basis, the interviewees aligned themselves with the trade unions and the Labour Party as vehicles of working-class collective action, although their support was tempered by their poor evaluation of the successes of these two organisations in fulfilling both collective working-class and individual family interests. Self-interest and individualism did not reign supreme.

In other words, the Luton team's account of social change and the primacy which they attached to changing working-class norms, values and aspirations has been found wanting. The interviewees did not lead an exclusively home – and family-centred existence, nor did they have a firm preference for such a life-style. The extent and processes of cultural change are more complex issues than the Luton team supposed. This theme is considered further in the concluding chapter, where the findings of the research are summarised. In the context of the empirical findings, sociological accounts of the changing nature of the working class as a distinctive socio-political entity are re-evaluated.

Of course, Britain's economic performance has been uneven since the Second World War (Gamble 1990; Green 1989). When the *Affluent Worker* study was conducted in the early 1960s, Luton and the wider economy were booming. Thriving manufacturing industries, like the Vauxhall car manufacturing plant, were the main source of prosperity in the locality. There were seemingly unlimited employment opportunities for semi-skilled and unskilled manual workers, with the prospect of relatively good wages. By the mid–1980s, when this research was completed, the town's economic fortunes had collapsed, and the wider economy was in recession. Despite a short boom in the late 1980s, general economic advancement did not continue as the Luton team anticipated. In other words, 'revisiting' Luton entailed revisiting a town with a different economic and social structure from the structure previously described by Goldthorpe and his colleagues. If the life-styles, aspirations and socio-political attitudes of the interviewees of this study are to be understood in the context of the economic climate of the last two decades, it is important to describe the changes in the economic fortunes of Luton and its main employer, Vauxhall, over this century.

Before the arrival of manufacturing industries, Luton had been associated with the hat trade, which depended on a predominantly female workforce (Mark-Lawson 1988). The growth of the town occurred in the latter half of the nineteenth century as the hat industry expanded. It was the sole industry of the town. But, by the early twentieth century, the hat trade began to wane. As a result, the local Borough Council, in liaison with the Chamber of Commerce, formed a New Industries Committee in 1899 extolling the virtues of Luton. The overall aim of the initiative was to attract other industries to the locality as a way of establishing a new and more diverse industrial base (Holden 1983). The Committee was successful in attracting manufacturing industries primarily because Luton enjoyed close proximity to London and good transport links with the capital. The Vauxhall car company was one such manufacturer which moved from London to Luton in 1905.

With a manufacturing-based local economy, the town grew in the 1920s and 1930s, escaping the brunt of the depression and the high levels of unemployment of the inter-war period. It was the 'new' manufacturing industries which attracted migrants from South Wales, Scotland and the North to the town in search of work. As Canon Davison recalled:

> People were coming to Luton from depressed areas all over the country, from North East England, South West Scotland and South Wales as well as the surrounding districts. Luton was not hit by the depression of 1929–31 as much as elsewhere because of the diversity of industry. As the hat trade began to shrink so such newer industries as Vauxhall, Skefco and Electrolux and Laporte's chemicals filled the gap and needed recruits. It is hardly an exaggeration to say that men travelled to Luton as though the streets were paved with gold (1977: 93).

Needless to say, the industry shift also witnessed a change in the character of town's workforce (Mark-Lawson 1988). Female employment in the hat industry declined and was replaced by male employment in semi-skilled and unskilled manual jobs in manufacturing industries. Luton became one of the few manufacturing towns in the South East.

The rapid growth and prosperity of Luton continued after the Second World War, when manufacturing industries, geared to the production of consumer goods, thrived. Vauxhall, for example, was taken over by General Motors, an American multinational company, in 1925 and began the mass production of cars in the 1930s (Holden 1983: 232). The real growth in production, however, occurred after the Second World War. Demand in the domestic market alone was high and to meet this demand companies like Vauxhall needed labour to keep the 'track running'. The size of the workforce was expanded considerably, drawing upon local recruits and migrants from other parts of the country. As a consequence, Luton's population continued to grow and there was extensive house building to cater for the influx of people (Goldthorpe et al. 1968a: 150–1). Workers enjoyed high wages and new, privately owned housing, which contributed to a comparatively high standard of living among members of the working class.

By the early 1960s Vauxhall employed over 20,000 people. Between 1962 and 1964 the company increased its workforce from 23,600 to 32,800.

The majority (over 22,000) of its workforce lived in Luton and neighbouring Dunstable, while the rest of its employees worked at Ellesmere Port, a Merseyside plant opened in the 1960s (The *Luton News*: 6 August 1964). Many of its employees were attracted from outside Luton and the company used a variety of means to recruit new members to the workforce, as Grieco (1981, 1987) highlighted. The help of the workforce itself was enlisted on a number of occasions to attract new workers. In 1965, for example, the company required 750 workers to meet demand, and over 500 potential workers queued for work after an appeal to the workforce was made. As the local newspaper explained:

> The rush of applicants followed Vauxhall's offer in a pay packet leaflet distributed to employees on Thursday of a £5 tax-free 'bounty' to any employee able to introduce a suitable recruit to the company (The *Luton News*: 6 May 1965).

The 1950s and 1960s, then, were a period of considerable population growth, and Luton was a 'boom' town. Indeed, Luton attracted migrants well into the 1970s. The relatively new arrivals in the late 1960s and 1970s came from the New Commonwealth. They migrated from Indian South Africa, Pakistan, Bangladesh and the Caribbean Islands, establishing themselves in the centre of the town. Many of them were employed by Vauxhall as well. In other words, immigrants from the New Commonwealth were almost the last chapter of substantial geographical mobility into a town with a long history of in-migration.

Evidently, the expansion of the town was tied very closely to the fortunes of Vauxhall. Unwittingly, Luton had almost become a one-industry 'company town' once again. Zweig (1961), who derived some members of his sample of affluent workers from the Vauxhall plant at Luton, described Luton as a 'rapidly expanding' and 'prosperous' town but a town, dominated by one employer. He noted: 'The preponderence of Vauxhall in the Luton labour market has meant that the population of Luton has grown mainly in response to Vauxhall's labour requirements and the prospects of Vauxhall still condition the fate of Luton to a large extent' (1961: 236). Despite these observations, neither Zweig nor the Luton team envisaged a time when these manufacturing industries would decline or the wider economy would enter a recessionary period. The consequences for Luton, as a town largely dependent on Vauxhall for employment, were not considered at all.

The late 1960s, however, saw the beginning of an economic downturn and the restructuring of manufacturing industries in Britain (Gamble 1990). Domestic demand for cars began to fall away as the market saturated (OECD 1983). Moreover, throughout the 1970s, other car-producing countries, like Japan, exported increasing numbers of cars into Britain and other European countries. As a result, car manufacturers were forced to compete more fiercely than ever before in both home and foreign markets. As output dropped and profits slumped, car manufacturers sought to cut production costs in numerous ways. The standardisation of products and techniques across car plants in different countries; the introduction of new technology and flexible working practices; and reductions in workforces were some of the strategies adopted by companies throughout the 1970s and, with increasing pace, in the recessionary period of the early 1980s.[6]

The changing fortunes of the car industry had important consequences for the employees of car-producing companies and the towns in which the factories were located. Between 1978 and 1983, for example, the workforce of the car industry in Britain declined by 40 per cent. In that period, Vauxhall reduced its total workforce by 36 per cent, from 33,000 to 21,000 employees (Marsden *et al*. 1985: 64). The company continued to streamline its workforce to 11,000 employees during the 1980s, leaving 6,000 employees at the Luton and Dunstable plants and 5,000 at Ellesmere Port in 1990 (*Vauxhall Annual Report*: 1990). While the interviews were being completed in 1986–7, for example, 1,700 redundancies were announced at the van plant in neighbouring Dunstable in May 1986 and a further 1,450 redundancies were made in September 1986 as the company decided to run down truck production in Luton and Dunstable altogether.[7] Heavily dependent on an ailing industry dramatically reducing the size of its workforce, Luton was a 'boom' town almost going 'bust'.

In the period of research in 1986–7, unemployment in the locality stood at over 15,000. This figure represented an unemployment rate of 14 per cent, making Luton a 'blackspot' in the prosperous South East. The impact of the redundancies from Vauxhall on Luton and Dunstable were fiercely debated by the local Council, the trade unions and others, and the political controversy was widely reported in the local press. There was considerable concern about the wider effect of the redundancies on other industries located in South Bedforshire which depended on Vauxhall for orders. Both the Council and the trade unions acknowledged their limited influence over General Motors when it made investment decisions which had far-reaching implications for the locality (The *Luton News*: 16 October 1986). In the less than favourable economic climate of the 1980s the implications of Luton's reliance on Vauxhall, a subsidiary of an American multinational company, as the major employer in the region were brought to the fore.

Throughout the 1980s the local Borough Council initiated a number of strategies to cope with the fall in manufacturing jobs in the car industry, and to develop new forms of employment in the locality. In 1988, for example, it established the Southern Bedfordshire Economic Development Council to increase job opportunities by cultivating small companies offering a range of job skills. In 1989 the Council inaugurated the Luton Initiative, an independent company financed by itself and private industry with the aim of encouraging the growth of indigenous companies and inward investment in the town (The *Guardian*: 10 November 1989). In other words, as the twenty-first century draws close, the Council has found itself trying to diversify Luton's industrial base and attract new industries just as it promoted Luton as an industrial centre at the turn of the twentieth century.

The car industry enjoyed a three-year boom between 1987 and 1989. In 1988, for example, Vauxhall announced record pre-tax profits of £152 million, enabling the company to make a profit share payment of approximately £300 for each employee for the first time in twenty years (The *Independent*: 10 April 1989). In the context of cutting costs and extensive investment, the company made more cars in 1989 than in any previous year in Luton. It did so, however, with a workforce a third of the size of the workforce in 1979. In 1979, 32,000 employees produced 230,000 cars, while in 1989, 11, 000 employees produced 240,000 cars (*Luton Gazette*: 3 January 1990). The high levels of productivity were achieved with approximately 500 new recruits in the three-year period. Despite its success, Vauxhall is not the source of new manufacturing employment in the town, although current plans to re-design the main Luton site, selling spare land for new business units and DIY superstores is expected to lead to the creation of 5,000 new jobs.

However, the boom in Vauxhall's fortunes, with limited benefits for the town, was short-lived and the company lost money, once again, in 1990. At the time of writing, Vauxhall remains one of the few car producers not to cut production or announce redundancies in the face of the steep downturn in UK car sales because it has stepped up exports to Europe. Production levels have been maintained as the plant continues to operate to full capacity (The *Guardian*: 18 July 1991). That said, the company has warned its workforce that international competitive pressure will increase, especially if European countries follow Britain into recession. Management insists that there must be a strong push to meet Japanese levels of efficiency. Despite company denials, however, there is considerable fear in Luton about the prospect of short-time working and redundancies, with rumours of over 1,500 jobs disappearing over the next five years. Fears of extensive job-cutting have returned to hang over the town and its workforce once again (The *Luton News*: 8 May 1991).

While Luton is still a major centre for manufacturing in South East England and Vauxhall remains the town's largest employer, the current official guide of the town claims 'there is an increasingly diversified and healthy look about the town's industry and commerce' (*Luton Offical Guide*: 1991). While the manufacturing sector of the local economy no longer generates new employment, the service sector continues to expand. Luton airport is the second major employer and the shopping centre and office work are important sources of local employment as well. There has been an expansion of professional, administrative and managerial jobs in health and education locally as well as a huge growth in commuting to London. Many of the employment opportunities for low-level white-collar work are for women, of course, rather than for men. In other words, Luton reflects some of the wider industrial and occupational shifts that began in the inter-war period and which were completed in the 1950s and 1960s. Luton's history also encompasses transformations away from those industries in the 1970s and 1980s. The locality also reflects the gendered and sectoral consequences of these shifts (Rose *et al.* 1984). As was recently noted:

> More recently Luton has mirrored many of the changes taking place across the country. The proportion of jobs taken by manufacturing industry has fallen from virtually half the workforce in 1950 to 37% in 1984 and 32% in 1988. And although this is still higher than the 25% for manufacturing across the entire south-east, it means that two in three jobs are provided by the service sector (The *Guardian*: 8 September 1989).

Nevertheless, while Luton still enjoys a prime location, it is Milton Keynes, further up the M1, which has been successful at attracting financial services and foreign companies into the town. While Luton struggles to overcome its low self-esteem and image as a boring, blue-collar manufacturing town with over 9,000 of its residents unemployed (The *Herald*: 22 August 1991), Milton Keynes has attracted more Japanese companies than any town outside London (Independent on Sunday: 17 March 91). Moreover, population estimates show that while Luton's population grew by 3.1 per cent, to 169,900, between 1981 and1989, the population of Milton Keynes expanded by 44.8 per cent, to 182,400 over the same period. Milton Keynes inherited the mantle of being a 'boom' town of the 1980s (*Regional Trends* 26, 1991).

National and international processes of economic restructuring, therefore, formed the background to 'revisiting' Luton. Indeed, revisiting Luton provided the opportunity to consider restructuring in the context of a local milieu as well as the central concern of exploring the nature of people's daily lives in general and the interconnections between geographical mobility, life-styles, consumer aspirations, industrial attitudes and socio-political proclivities in particular. It was in this milieu that the motives, the processes and the consequences of geographical mobility were discussed with members of the mature industrial working class in Britain in the mid-1980s.

NOTES

1. The distinction between issues of class formation and class action derives from Goldthorpe's (1987) empirical research on social mobility.
2. From here onwards, the authors of the *Affluent Worker* series – John H. Goldthorpe, David Lockwood, Frank Bechhofer and Jennifer Platt – will be referred to as the Luton team.
3. Hill (1990: 25), for example, argues that 'even the second time around embourgeoisement remains misconceived both empiri-

cally and theoretically', while Saunders (1990b: 112) asserts that the *Affluent Worker* 'effectively killed off academic concern with the issue of embourgeoisement for nearly twenty years'.

4. The secondary aims of the research and the details of the empirical research will be described more fully in Chapter 2.

5. The Luton team defined the emergence of home and family–centred life-styles as a process of 'privatisation' and described these life-styles as 'privatised'. However, since the term 'privatisation' is now associated with the de–nationalisation of state industries, another term is necessary to avoid confusion. For the purposes of this research, it is appropriate to use the concept of privatism to refer to the growth of home and family-centred life-styles and associated norms and values which, in turn, shape aspirations and socio–political proclivities. The concept of privatism will be defined and discussed more fully in Chapter 2.

6. Multinational companies like General Motors, of which Vauxhall was a part, adopted further strategies for survival in the increasingly competitive international market. The Vauxhall plants in Luton, Dunstable and Ellesmere Port were integrated into the world operations of the multinational company. Competition was increasingly internationalised as products and techniques were standardised so that a car could be assembled from parts made in different countries (Marsden *et al.* 1985: 4). General Motors invested in other plants in Europe so that the manufacture of components was undertaken in countries like Spain while cars were assembled in Luton. As a multinational, it could employ strategies for investment and growth which extended beyond its plants in Britain.

7. The redundancies arose, in part, from a national political controversy. At the beginning of 1986, General Motors became embroiled in a political debate when it was discovered that the company was having talks with the government and British Leyland on the take–over of the nationalised industry's bus and truck division. A political storm ensued and scuppered the sale. It was in this economic and political context that Vauxhall management decided to rationalise its commercial vehicle production and then to close it down altogether, leading to over three thousand redundancies in 1986.

2

PRIVATISM AND THE WORKING CLASS

In the post-war period of prosperity, numerous commentators argued that the working class had adopted middle-class norms and values as they enjoyed relatively high incomes and standards of living. Furthermore, affluence had undermined the cultural and socio-political distinctiveness of the working class. As a result of these changes, it was claimed, the class structure had changed. Goldthorpe and his colleagues set out to test this argument, which became known as the embourgeoisement thesis. This chapter examines the issues which the Luton team sought to address, the findings of their empirical research and criticisms of the study, before moving on to discuss subsequent research on the working class in modern Britain.

While members of the Luton team were fierce critics of the embourgeoisement thesis, it will be seen that their account of the demise of the 'traditional' working class and the rise of a 'new' working class, with its emphasis on changing values and aspirations, was remarkably similar to the thesis which they sought to challenge. Few commentators voiced this criticism when the series was published. It is only more recently, as commentators have re-evaluated accounts of changing working-class lifestyles, aspirations and socio-political perspectives from the vantage point of historical material on developments in the nineteenth century, that the the Luton teams' account of social change has been contested. That said, attempts to locate privatism among the nineteenth-century working class have effectively drawn attention away from the question of whether the concept of privatism adequately describes working-class life-styles and socio-political proclivities in the late twentieth century.

THE EMBOURGEOISEMENT THESIS

Accounts of the demise of the 'traditional' working-class occupational community took a variety of different forms in the late 1950s and early 1960s. As Marshall (1990: 103) has noted, 'some rooted their account in the sphere of production while others stressed changes in consumption'. The Luton team sought to refute both varieties of the embourgeoisement thesis, so it is necessary to explore each of these in turn.

In the field of industrial sociology, Goldthorpe *et al.* sought to address debates on the impact of technology on workers' industrial attitudes and behaviour. Woodward (1958) and Blauner (1964), for example, argued that the technological setting of work influenced the meaning and place of paid work in men's lives and their social relations with fellow workers, supervisors, unions and employers. The emergence of advanced automation, it was argued, fostered embourgeoisement by undermining work group solidarity and promoting greater integration and identification with employers. The decline of an occupational community at work also influenced worker's non-work lives. No longer socialising with a tightly-knit group of fellow men, workers led home-and family-centred life-styles directed towards individual material well-being. Technical developments at work and their impact on social relations had pushed men into the home. The debate on technology allowed the Luton team, in their own words, 'to incorporate into our research a full investigation of the industrial lives of the workers we studied' and to overcome 'a very one-sided emphasis on the worker as consumer rather than producer' in the discussion on embourgeoisement (Goldthorpe *et al.* 1968a: 3). These issues were, of course, discussed in Volume 1 of the *Affluent Worker* series.

More directly, the Luton team set out to address debates on affluence and the working class. A number of writers (Klein 1965; Mogey 1956; Young and Willmott 1957; Zweig 1961) argued that increased standards of living had fundamentally altered working-class life-styles, values and aspirations. Secure employment, relatively high wages, increased leisure, slum clearance and growing home ownership generated and sustained an existence which centred on the immediate family in the home rather than the 'traditional' occupational community. As a result of these favourable developments in consumption, men had been pulled into the home. Furthermore, affluence fuelled aspirations for individual family material well-being, which undermined solidarity with the working class and heralded the adoption of middle-class attitudes and behaviour instead. Finally, it was argued (Abrams *et al.* 1960; Butler and Rose 1960) that increased living standards had fundamentally altered 'traditional' working-class political attitudes. The 1959 General Election was taken to illustrate the decline of working-class radicalism and the rise of conservatism.[1] Developments in the economic and political sphere were, according to these commentators at least, clearly interconnected. Volume 2 of the *Affluent Worker* series focused on political attitudes and behaviour, while the third and final volume focused on life-styles, aspirations and social perspectives.

The original aim of the Luton study, therefore, was to consider the two varieties of the embourgeoisement thesis. Both heralded the demise of the occupational community, although one version emphasised that men were being pushed into a home-and family-centred existence while the other version described the processes by which men were being pulled into the arms of the immediate family in the home. As Platt (1984: 184) explained, it was Goldthorpe's interest in debates in industrial sociology which led him to draw out 'the possibilities of relating developments there to the idea of embourgeoisement in a way few others would have done'. In relating these somewhat distinct debates, the Luton team was able to examine several different aspects of people's work and non-work lives.

Both versions of the embourgeoisement thesis were 'benign perspective[s] on social change in the industrialised West', which were popular in the period of stability in the 1950s (Marshall 1990: 101). However, as Marshall has noted, the 1960s were, in contrast, a time of instability which saw the revival of Marxism both outside and inside the discipline of sociology. Goldthorpe and his colleagues sought to address these debates as well. Chapter 1 of Volume 3 explicitly addressed Marxist and non-marxist debates on the working class. Mallet's (1975) depiction of an increasingly alienated working class, for example, was considered alongside Blauner's optimistic view about the impact of technology on the workplace. Thus, in the monographs in particular, Goldthorpe *et al.* not only investigated liberal arguments about embourgeoisement but also considered radical theories of social change.

THE *AFFLUENT WORKER* SERIES

Before turning to the details and substantive findings of the series, it is worth noting that Goldthorpe and Lockwood undermined the embourgeoisement thesis in various papers almost before the empirical research in Luton had begun. In what is probably their most famous position paper, 'Affluence and the British Class Structure' (1963), they highlighted the conceptual problems of the thesis of embourgeoisement and the failure of its proponents to distinguish between the economic, normative and relational dimensions of class. In all three respects, they argued, the extent of change had been over-stated. Emphasising the importance of placing values, attitudes and aspirations in the context of 'the life histories and life situations of the individuals and groups concerned', they argued that the 'traditional' working class had adapted in the face of altered economic and physical conditions in the post-war period of prosperity (Goldthorpe and Lockwood 1963: 142). However, rather than assimilation, the two authors identified a process of 'normative convergence' at the 'class frontier' between the lower middle class and the upper working class (Goldthorpe and Lockwood 1963: 152). The distinctive socio-political identity of the working class was not being completely submerged into the middle class. There was no firm evidence of embourgeoisement.

The empirical study was conducted in Luton between 1961 and 1962. The town was chosen on the expectation that a group of people open to embourgeoisement could be contacted for the study. Luton had enjoyed economic growth since the late 1930s. It attracted large numbers of geographically mobile workers and their families into the locality in search of high wages in new industries, and offered relatively good living standards in new private housing. Luton was not an 'old' industrial town with well-established industries and long-standing industrial relations practices (Goldthorpe *et al.* 1968a: 2–3). It was to be a critical case study of the embourgeoisement thesis. If workers in the process of 'changing their class position' could not be found in Luton, they were unlikely to be found elsewhere (Goldthorpe *et al.* 1969: 31).

The Luton team interviewed a sample of men from three major employers in the town. The employers were Vauxhall, a car manufacturing plant and a subsidiary of the American multinational company, General Motors; Skefco, which produced ball and roller bearings, and was part of the international SKF Organisation; and Laporte, a chemical-producing company. The three establishments were chosen to include different types of production system – small batch, large batch and mass, and process production – in order to ascertain the impact of technology on the industrial attitudes and behaviour of assembly-line workers, machine operators, setters, craftsmen and process workers across different industrial settings (Goldthorpe *et al.* 1968a: 3–4) The tightly-defined sample consisted of men aged between 21and 46 who were married or living with their partners in or close to Luton, and who regularly earn £17 from their shop-floor jobs. The men were interviewed on their own at work about their jobs and related issues and at home with their wives/partners on their life-styles, aspirations and socio-political proclivities. Fifty-four clerical workers were interviewed as well, but the data from these interviews were used sparily. The main method of inquiry was structured interviews with two hundred and twenty-nine men.[2]

The Luton team rejected 'the view of Blauner and others who saw the more advanced forms of production technology as being generally conducive to more normatively integrated industrial enterprizes'. Nor did they give 'the same weight as these writers to the effects of technology in determining attitudes to work and the structure of class relationships' (Goldthorpe *et al.* 1968a: 175). On the contrary, they argued that an instrumental orientation to work accounted for the meanings which workers attached to largely boring and monotonous tasks:

> The primary meaning of work is a means to an end, or ends external to the work situation; that is, work is regarded as a means of acquiring the income necessary to support a valued way of life of which work itself is not an integral part. Work is therefore experienced as mere 'labour' in the sense of an expenditure which is made for extrinsic rather than for in trinsic rewards. Workers act as 'economic men', seeking to minimise effort and maximise economic returns; but the latter concern is the dominant one (Goldthorpe *et al.* 1968a: 38–9).

This instrumental orientation also explained the nature of relations between workers and their work group, the firm, the trade union and their
economic expectations. An occupational community was not in evidence
in Luton. The crux of this argument, on the sources of instrumentalism, is to be
found in the penultimate chapter of the first monograph. The Luton team
argued that an instrumental orientation to work derived from the men's
non-work aspirations to '*maintain* their relatively prosperous and rising
standard of living and for their *inclination* towards a family-centred style
of living' (Goldthorpe *et al.* 1968a: 150, emphasis in original). In turn,
these aspirations could be traced not only from their most demanding
stage in the family life-cycle. but also from their experiences of geographical and social mobility. The social cost of geographical mobility –
of being separated from kin and friends and their subsequent experiences of living in a town of migrants – both generated and sustained the
high level of motivation for material well-being among their respondents
(Goldthorpe *et al.* 1968a: 150–4). Similarily, with regard to social mobility,
they argued that feelings of 'relative deprivation' and 'status incon-
gruency' fuelled consumer aspirations as well, thereby reinforcing an
instrumental orientation to work (Goldthorpe *et al.* 1968a: 155–9). These
experiences were the social sources of instrumentalism.[3]

The interconnectedness between instrumentalism and privatism –
especially with reference to the experience of geographical mobility –
was subsequently explored in Volume 3 in the series. The search for
highly-paid work involved moving away from long-standing companions. Frequent and casual social contact with kin, neighbours,
fellow workers and other friends could no longer be enjoyed. Furthermore, demanding shift work and overtime to secure good wages militated against the development of new networks of friends (Goldthorpe
et al. 1969: 101–2). Rather, patterns of sociability and leisure were
restricted to the immediate family in the home. This privatised life-style
was com-patible with the search for a high 'economic pay-off' from work
and was, therefore, not 'entirely the unwanted and unwelcome consequence of their quest for affluence' (Goldthorpe *et al.* 1969: 104, emphasis
in original).

Finally, the Luton team established the links between instrumentalism, privatism and their respondents' individualistic socio-political
perspectives. Leaning heavily on Lockwood's (1966) article on the social
sources of working-class imagery, they argued that members of the
newly affluent working class did not share the same world view as the
'traditional' working class, but described the class structure and their
place within it in pecuniary terms. Rather than a solidaristic collectivism,
they found a 'pronounced 'instrumental' attitude to trade unionism and
to party politics', adherence to the Labour Party depending on evaluative
rather than cognitive support (Goldthorpe *et al.* 1968b: 79). Collective

support for the Labour Party was directed towards, and dependent upon, individual material gain.

Thus, while an occupational community was absent in Luton, it was not the result of developments in production as Blauner argued. The technological setting of the workplace did not explain the limited sociability between workers inside and outside the workplace. Men, in other words, were not being pushed reluctantly into a home- and family-centred existence. Rather, as British embourgeoisement theorists emphasised, the absence of an occupational community was the product of changes in the sphere of consumption. Consumer aspirations, external to the workplace, fuelled an instrumental orientation to work which, in turn, influenced the meaning of work in men's lives and their social relations with fellow workers and their employer. It also shaped their non-work lives, as the immediate family in the home became an attractive haven from the heartless world of work. In the pursuit of improving their material well-being still further, men were being pulled willingly into a home- and family-centred existence.

That said, the Luton team also criticised the British variety of the embourgeoisement thesis. Proponents of the thesis, they argued, had overstated the degree of change in working-class life-styles, aspirations and socio-political proclivities. The working class had not been assimilated into the middle class but a more complex process of convergence in working-class and middle-class norms and values was in evidence. The working class, for example, was not exclusively individualistic in the pursuit of consumer power. Unlike the middle class, they sought their individual material aspirations collectively through the trade unions and the Labour Party. It was from the vantage point of this measured account of social change that Goldthorpe and his colleagues concluded that their respondents, despite their distinctive economic motivations, were 'prototypical' – more representative of the future than the present working class.

REVIEWS AND DEBATES

Given the enormous theoretical and empirical scope of the *Affluent Worker* series, it is not surprising that the published findings of the study were widely reviewed and debated and became the source of numerous derivative studies (DeAngelis 1982; Kemeny 1972; MacKenzie 1974; MacKinnon 1980; Marshall 1990; Platt 1984; Whelan 1976). It attracted considerable, largely well-disposed, attention from newspaper commentators and columnists outside the discipline (Bulmer 1990: 130) and within it 'became a justifiably celebrated landmark in industrial sociology and, more generally social stratification' (Eldridge 1990: 167). The series became the most frequently cited example of 'good' sociology in that it addressed a wide range of theoretical debates in advance of the empirical research, and subsequently returned to those debates and amended them in the light of the empirical findings. If it had not been so before, the embourgeoisement thesis was finally laid to rest and the portrayal of the working class characterised by instrumentalism, privatism and individualism was, for the most part, endorsed.

While all the discussion surrounding the Luton study cannot be properly considered here, two themes, as Platt (1984) has noted, commanded significant attention and shaped subsequent research on the working class. First, numerous commentators debated the sources and the form of instrumental orientations to work. Secondly, and in a similar manner, interest centred on the sources and the nature of class imagery and class consciousness. As a result, the central arguments linking instru-mentalism, privatism and individualism were neither fundamentally confronted nor substantially challenged.

Even though Volume 1, on industrial attitudes and behaviour was a 'by-product' of the main research on embourgeoisement, the findings generated a number of controversies. A somewhat trenchant debate between Daniel (1969, 1971) and Goldthorpe (1970; 1972), for example, focused on the sources of an instrumental orientation to work. Daniel (1969: 366) rejected the voluntarism of the Luton team's arguments which attached importance to 'the actor's definition of the work situation', deriving from outside the workplace, in determining industrial attitudes and behaviour. Instead, he and others (Argyris 1972; Brown 1973; MacKinnon 1980; Whelan 1976) argued that experiences at work – and not just in terms of its technological setting – shaped the meaning of work in men's lives and the structure of relationships in the workplace. The daily experiences of boring and monotonous work tasks were a source of dissatisfaction which contributed to the significance of extrinsic rewards in men's lives. These work experiences could not simply be disregarded. Debate centred on the effect of work experiences inside the factory gate on the formation of industrial attitudes and behaviour. The key finding on instrumentalism was not undermined, and the role of economic motivations in shaping orientations to work did not attract a great deal of attention.

Subsequent research on orientations to work did not weaken the central finding on instrumentalism, or the importance of extrinsic rewards over the intrinsic rewards of work. Few researchers (Beynon and Blackburn 1972; Blackburn and Mann 1979; Brown 1973) could find a clearly and coherently expressed instrumentalism among other groups of workers. Blackburn and Mann (1979), for example, argued forcefully that workers are not as single-minded or as narrowly focused in the pursuit of economic rewards as the Luton team implied. Similarly, summarising the research on work orientations, Brown and his colleagues (1983) concluded that instrumentalism was the predominant attitude towards paid work, especially when searching for a job, but other intrinsic concerns were not prohibited by instrumental attitudes. Instrumentalism was dominant even if it were not as all-pervasive as Goldthorpe and his colleagues claimed.

The second controversial theme related to the Luton team's findings on class imagery and class consciousness.[4] Again, the discussion concentrated on the sources, and the form, of worker's world views. Criticism was voiced about the deterministic manner in which Lockwood (1966), in his highly-influential paper, 'read off' class imagery from an individual's immediate milieux of 'work and community relations'. Scase (1974: 151), for example, in his comparative study of English and Swedish workers with 'relatively similar institutional constraints', found divergent images of society. He attributed the optimism about the class structure and social mobility among Swedish workers to the success of the Social Democratic Party in government and the set of beliefs which it generated about Swedish society. He concluded that 'actors' conceptions of the class structure are shaped not only by "objective" patterns of structural relationships but also by interpretations generated by wider social proceses' (Scase 1974: 171). Gallie (1983), in his study of workers in France, showed that parties play an important role in the formation of class consciousness as well. A far wider range of variables than those identified by Lockwood individually, and by the Luton team collectively, shape people's class imagery or world views.

Similarly, commentators were highly critical of the notion that members of the working class hold clear and consistent images of the class structure and their place within it. All of the contributors to Bulmer's (1975) edited collection *Working-Class Images of Society*, which discussed Lockwood's (1966) paper on variations in working-class imagery, cast doubt on there being a neat fit between people's milieux and their sociopolitical proclivities given that circumstances varied so widely and were in a constant state of flux. This conclusion was reinforced by Roberts' and his colleagues' (1977) later empirical study on the fragmentary class structure. Somewhat ironically, while Goldthorpe was charged with voluntarism within industrial sociology, Lockwood was accused of determinism in class analysis.

For the most part, therefore, critics in both debates challenged the overly neat and tidy account of the interconnectedness between work, life-styles, aspirations and socio-political perspectives, but they did not detract from the main findings of the *Affluent Worker* series. The one critic who might be said seriously to have challenged the Luton team's arguments was Westergaard. Straddling the two controversies outlined above, Westergaard argued that the Luton team's findings on pecuniary instrumentalism were far from novel but, on the contrary, were a rediscovery of Marx and Engels's 'cash nexus'. Given the tenuous nature of the 'main residual binding force of capitalist society', Westergaard (1970: 120) viewed instrumentalism as a form of working-class radicalism not conservatism. Ultimately, however, as Marshall (1988) has argued, Westergaard did not challenge the central finding that workers were predominantly instrumental in their approach to work, but drew out different implications for class consciousness. Marshall asserted:

> Instead of deducing socio-political quiescence from instrument-
> alism (by postulating privatization), Westergaard paints a picture
> of a working class precariously balanced between attitudes of co-
> operation or resig nation, on the one hand, and a nascent class
> consciousness, for when the tenuous thread of the cash nexus is
> broken, on the other. Working-class instrumentalism is real
> enough. The dispute is about its implications for the timetabling of
> the revolution (1988: 104).

Even a Marxist such as Westergaard did not (and perhaps could not) challenge this aspect of Goldthorpe *et al.*'s neo-Weberian account of the changing form and nature of the working class in twentieth-century Britain.

The controversies and subsequent research on working-class instrumentalism and social imagery, therefore, did not generate substantially novel empirical findings over the 1970s. Even though many class analysts (Mann 1973a; Newby 1977; Parkin 1972) rejected the Luton team's implicit characterisation of the working class as conservative (given the lack of class consciousness) in preference to the notion of ambivalence, the debates as a whole were slowly 'grinding to a confused and untimely halt' during this period (Marshall 1988: 105). Writing about the impasse in debate on working-class consciousness in particular and the relationship between structure, consciousness and action in general in the early 1980s, Marshall concluded that social surveys were an inappropriate methodological tool for exploring 'the wants, preferences, feelings, interests and even the cynicism' (1988: 112) behind instrumentalism and, for that matter, privatism and individualism. His call for 'sociological enthnography' will be discussed further near the end of this chapter.

CRITICAL OMISSIONS

Furthermore, the central conclusions of Volume 3, on privatism in particular, did not warrant critical attention. Three crucial issues were, to a greater or lesser extent, neglected. First, did Goldthorpe and his colleagues provide an accurate portrayal of 'traditional' working-class life-styles? Secondly, did they offer a correct account of the processes of change from the demise of the 'traditional' working-class occupational community to the emergence of a newly-privatised working class? Thirdly, and finally, did they give a precise description of 'new' working-class life-styles?

Of course, numerous writers (Allcorn and Marsh 1975; Davis and Cousins 1975; Crewe 1973) cast doubt on the Luton team's distinction between the 'traditional' working class and the 'new' working class. Crewe (1973), for example, was highly sceptical of descriptions of the 'traditional' working class as unswervingly loyal supporters of the Labour Party in the early twentieth century at a time of great political change, as the Liberal Party was declining and Labour was only just emerging as a political force. The Luton team's portrayal of the 'traditional' working class relied on a small number of studies; most notably the community studies by Dennis and his colleagues (1956) and Stacey (1960). They never systematically evaluated the extent to which the 'traditional' working class led communal life-styles and whether communality was ever the bedrock of working-class solidaristic collectivism. The portrayal of the 'traditional' working class was taken for granted even though, as Kent (1981: 137) has argued, none of the cited research (Kerr 1958; Tunstall 1962; Walker 1950; Walker and Guest 1952) was representative of the 'traditional' working class of the first half of the twentieth century.[5] As Franklin (1989) has argued, the 'traditional' working class has rarely 'stood up to empirical scrutiny'.

On a related point, it should not be forgotten that community studies were later criticised for their focus on particular geographical entities and a tendency to emphasise the importance of the locale and the solidarity of groups. The debate on the value of community studies raged in the late 1960s (Bulmer 1985; Stacey 1969), yet the implications of the debate for accounts of changing working-class life-styles and socio-political perspectives were, with one notable exception (Bell and Newby 1971), wholly ignored. An exploration of connected issues raised in these somewhat distinct debates would have shown that the 'traditional' working class was not empirically soundly based or, at the very least, that working-class solidarity existed in specific conditions, like the dangerous and sometimes isolated workplaces in the primary and heavy manufacturing industries of mining, steel production and fishing.

If the bench-mark for change was somewhat unsteady, what of the processes of change? Again, the major processes of change – geographical mobility, physical separation and the demands of paid work – given prominence by the Luton team were never critically evaluated. Only Benson (1975) criticised the undue weight attached to geographical mobility to explain the demise of the 'traditional' working-class community and the rise of a newly privatised working class.

> Reading through the *Affluent Worker* volumes, it becomes increasingly obvious not only that the traditional worker is an extremely elusive figure, but that his 'demise' tends to be accounted for more or less with reference to the physical dispersal of workers from the traditional community (Benson 1978: 152).

Moreover, Benson (1978: 155) was alone in challenging the primacy given to 'new' economic motivations, fuelled by post-war prosperity, as the catalyst behind these processes of change. That is, few noticed that Goldthorpe *et al.*'s somewhat circular arguments about the sources of changing working-class norms, values and aspirations were merely a cautious version of the embourgeoisement thesis. The emphasis on normative convergence rather than assimilation, for example, was a dispute about the degree of change and not a serious challenge to the embourgeoisement theorists' account of social change since the Second World War.

Finally, the extent to which 'new' working-class life-styles could be accurately portrayed as privatised was not the subject-matter of subsequent ethnographies of the working class throughout the 1970s. Somewhat ironically, empirical studies of the working class (Beynon 1980; Beynon and Blackburn 1972; Blackburn and Mann 1979) continued to focus on paid work, even though the Luton team had emphasised the centrality of the home and family in people's non-work lives. Thus, Moorhouse observed that 'despite all the criticism and research that this study provoked: certain of its concepts and findings ... for example, that of a normative convergence or privatisation, remain almost uninvestigated' (1983: 423). For much of the 1970s and early 1980s privatism, describing a life-style compatible with instrumentalism and individualistic aspirations and socio-political proclivities, was never seriously contested within the field of social stratification research.

There is just one, almost accidental, exception to this neglect of privatism. The exception is to be found in the empirical research of Grieco mentioned in the Introduction. In her study of the role of family networks in shaping employment chances in the steel town of Corby, Grieco (1981, 1987) stumbled across people who had been recruited by Vauxhall and moved to Luton in the 1960s. It appeared that Vauxhall actively recruited workers from Scotland and the North East, where peripheral sectors of the economy were in decline and unemployment was far higher than the national average, to meet their own labour shortages. It was in these uncertain economic circumstances that families, with little experience of mass production methods, moved south. In other words, they were not typical workers. Nor had instrumental orientations for highly-paid work led them to move in search of employment. This finding, Grieco argued, raised some doubts about the Luton team's thesis regarding working-class instrumentalism.

More importantly, Grieco argued that Goldthorpe and his colleagues paid scant attention to the role of family networks in facilitating migration, especially over long distances, in search of jobs. The Luton team provided few details on extended kin living in Luton and gave little information on sociability between kin in the workplace. Drawing on her own study of chain migration, Grieco (1987) expressed grave doubts about the extent of privatism as well. She wondered whether the 'disrupted and attenuated kin and community ties' found in Luton were permanent, or were merely transitional changes as a result of recent migration. A later account of people's lives might find a regrouping of families in a new locale. As she noted: 'Relying solely on an early snapshot of a migrant stream may be seriously misleading, for organising the

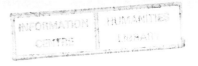
follow up migration, so frequently identified in the literature, might take time' (Grieco 1987: 197). In other words, as well as being highly sceptical of the notion of instrumentalism, Grieco cast serious doubt on the Luton' team's concept of privatism. The future working class, in other words, would not necessarily lead home- and family-centred life-styles.

ANOTHER WORKING CLASS?

In the 1980s and early 1990s there was a revival of interest in class life-styles, either as a direct aim of research or as an indirect by-product (Allan and Crow 1991; Crow and Allan 1990; Franklin 1989; Marshall *et al.* 1988; Pahl 1984; Proctor 1990; Saunders 1990a). Almost all of the studies have prefaced their empirical findings with a historical re-evaluation of working-class privatism, arguing that home- and family-centred life-styles emerged some time in the nineteenth century, if not before. In other words, these historical accounts no longer make reference to the 'traditional' working class of the early twentieth century which was so crucial yet so problematic in the *Affluent Worker* series. The catalyst and processes of change – with a greater emphasis on structural changes rather than changing values and aspirations – are also different. Yet, attempts to locate privatism among the nineteenth-century working class have effectively drawn attention away from the question of whether the concept of privatism adequately describes working-class life-styles and socio-political proclivities in the late twentieth century.

A wide-ranging historical review of the changing nature of the household and its central place in people's daily lives and in society as a whole, for example, prefaces Pahl's (1984) study of household work strategies on the Isle of Sheppey. He argues that a variety of material, political, religious and cultural influences led to the separation of the spheres of formal and informal work and, by association, men's and women's position outside and inside the home at the end of the eighteenth century and the beginning of the nineteenth century. Even so, Pahl stresses that the dominance of the male wage in sustaining the household emerged only gradually, as did men's separation from domestic tasks. Irregular male earnings meant that women, either formally or informally, played a significant role in maintaining the household as well. In other words, men's and women's daily lives have long been dominated by the work tasks and responsibilities associated with supporting the household, although the patterning of formal and informal work has varied according to contingent economic, social and political circumstances. Working-class life-styles, it is claimed, have long been home- and family-centred.

Against this historical background, and in the context of rising levels of male unemployment, Pahl found extensive self-provisioning and, by implication, privatised life-styles, among his working-class households. Echoing the Luton team's earlier arguments about the pressures of paid work on people's daily lives, it appears that household members are engaged in various forms of work and are extremely busy servicing their own needs (Pahl 1984: 100–1) Moreover, self-provisioning requires constant work, confining men and women to the home. A comfortable home- and family-centred existence was especially evident among those households with two or more incomes from the formal economy, while those dependent on low incomes – usually state benefit to relieve the hardship of unemployment – were less able to provide for themselves. Pahl and Wallace (1988) went on to conclude that there was a growing polarity between working-class households in the 1980s. While relatively affluent 'core' households were joining the comfortable middle mass, impoverished households were being marginalised.[6]

Finally, Pahl found that domesticity and familism – so central in people's everyday lives – shape their social and political consciousness. While paid work in the formal economy was viewed with fatalism and the government was perceived as remote and uninterested in local issues, Pahl found that 'People who want a better way of life for themselves and their families perceive that they can most readily achieve this through a distinctive mix of all forms of work by all members of the household' (1984: 327). That said, Pahl and Wallace (1988) rejected the thesis of growing privatised and personal politics. As history shows once again, domesticity and familism have long shaped working-class values and aspirations, and assumptions about the 'traditional' working class retreating from collective politics into the individual home and family should be refuted, once and for all.[7]

Likewise, the Essex team (Marshall et al. 1988; Newby et al. 1985) trace instrumentalism and privatism – which they define in terms of three levels of analysis: structural factors, cultural values and life-styles, and socio-political proclivities – back to the second half of the nineteenth century. The mid-Victorian boom saw wage increases, rising living standards, increased consumption and improved housing conditions, which, coupled with other changes, such as the shortening of the working week and the extension of educational provision, increased the significance of the home and family in men's and women's lives (Marshall et al. 1988: 203–4). In the first instance, these structural and cultural changes were enjoyed by the labour aristocracy of skilled workers and traditional artisans. Indeed, their lives of respectable domesticity separated them from the rest of the working class as well (Crossick 1978; Gray 1976). However, privatism did not prohibit solidaristic struggles: 'the emergence of a culture of domesticity centred on the home and on privatised life-styles co-existed with solidaristic and class-based political activity in the context of the trade union movement' (Marshall et al. 1988: 202). The labour aristocracy was the vanguard of the trade union movement and while many of their struggles were for increased wages for themselves, they were also active in securing a shorter working day which was subsequently enjoyed by the working class as a whole. Instrumentalism and privatism, it seems, did not prohibit collective action. Structural and cultural changes did not inevitably lead to a change in socio-political proclivities (Marshall *et al.* 1988: 206).

Even so, in their survey of class structure and class consciousness in Britain, Marshall *et al.* (1988: 207) found little evidence of a singular instrumentalism among their respondents as a whole. Members of the working class were more instrumental than were their middle-class counterparts because of the uneven distribution of intrinsic rewards across the occupational structure, but even they enjoyed some rewards from work like socialising with fellow workers and developing work skills (Marshall *et al.* 1988: 208–10).[8] Nor did they find firm evidence of privatism. While home and family life was important in people's lives, it was not a retreat from unfulfilling employment. Patterns of sociability hardly differed across the working class and the service class; the working class tending to be slightly more home-centred because of monetary constraints (Marshall *et al.* 1988: 214). Finally, although the working class was less likely to socialise with fellow workers outside work than the service class, none the less, there was 'a considerable overlap between the structure of spare-time association, and the friendships formed at work' (Marshall *et al.* 1988: 215). Unlike Pahl, the Essex team found plenty of communal sociability among members of the working class and, for that matter, the middle class as well.

However, the Essex team stressed that neither individual values and aspirations nor their structural sources can be used to explain people's socio-political proclivities. Class consciousness and class action is a product of collective organisation within an institutional framework, in Britain at least, of political democracy. The trade unions were successful in the 1890s in mobilising sectional and class struggles, but in the 1980s, the absence of collective struggle results from the failure of the two main vehicles of working-class support – namely the trade unions and the Labour Party – to offer a coherent industrial and political programme of policies which would benefit the working class as a whole. In other words, echoing the findings of Scase (1974) and Gallie's (1983) comparative research on the working class, they argued that political factors should not be neglected in the analysis of socio-political perspectives.

Finally, Saunders (1990a) cites the labour aristocracy and their status aspirations as a historical example of privatism in his examination of the impact of home ownership on working-class life-styles. Like Marshall and his colleagues, he argues that the desire for respectable domesticity did not foster individualism, since labour aristocrats were especially active in the solidaristic struggles of the trade union movement of the 1880s and 1890s and in the establishment of the Labour Party as a separate political force. That is, privatism is 'neither new, nor all pervasive' (Saunders 1990a: 286).

This conclusion is confirmed by data on privatism in the cultural sense from Saunders's survey of Slough, Derby and Burnley. He found that two-thirds of his respondents enjoyed social contact with people at work. Both work and the home and family had a significant place in their lives (Saunders 1990a: 283). Similarly, the respondents did not lead exclusively home-centred life-styles. Home owners and tenants alike went out frequently, although the latter were more home-centred than the former (50 per cent compared with 70 per cent) because of financial constraints (Saunders 1990a: 288). These findings concur with Marshall et al.'s nationwide survey, although, unlike them, Saunders (1990a: 289) concluded more forcefully that the 'privatism thesis is ... groundless'.

PROBLEMS OF REINTERPRETATION

There are, however, two major problems with these recent accounts of class life-styles and socio-political consciousness. The first criticism relates to the use of historical material to support the thesis that instrumentalism and privatism are not recent phenomena and the implications for our understanding of the working class over the nineteenth and twentieth centuries. The second and related criticism centres on the limitations of the empirical findings arising from the studies in question.

First, the step back into nineteenth-century history raises as many contentious issues as it attempts to solve. It is not altogether clear, especially in the work of the Essex team, as Proctor (1990) has noted, if they have merely backdated the historical 'moment' when working-class life-styles began to change from the post-war period of prosperity to the mid-to-late nineteenth century. Do they still hold to the thesis that a communal existence was gradually replaced with a home- and family centred life-style among the working class? Is the 'traditional' worker merely hidden in the deeper recesses of history than was previously thought, or did he never exist at all? Is privatised instrumentalism an accurate description of sections of, or all of, the working class since the late nineteenth century?

The changes to which the various writers refer, such as the impact of the mid-Victorian boom on standards of living, patterns of consumption, life-styles and so forth, and who enjoyed them – namely, the labour aristocracy – remain highly controversial in economic and social history. The existence of a labour aristocracy with its own distinct values and aspirations, to which both Marshall et al. and Saunders frequently refer, was and continues to be the source of an ongoing debate among historians (Davies 1992; Foster 1974; Joyce 1980; McLennan 1981; Moorhouse 1978, 1979, 1981, Reid 1978, 1986). Marshall and his colleagues (1988: 217) concede that their historical context 'is derived entirely from secondary sources relating to somewhat contentious developments during the mid nineteenth century'. They do not, however, detail what those controversies are nor their implications for our understanding of the working class since the period in question. Instead, and somewhat ironically, the neo-weberian Essex team found and isolated what they were looking for in the empirical studies of neo-Marxists Gray and Crossick. History, it seems, is used to resolve sociological disputes as if it were devoid of controversies itself.

Finally, these historical accounts of privatism lay great emphasis on structural changes, rather than changes in working-class norms and values in the cultural or socio-political sphere, to explain the emergence of home- and family-centred life-styles in the nineteenth century. However, it appears that almost every change associated with urbanisation and industrialisation over the last two centuries, including housing developments, transport developments and so forth, especially in the work of Pahl, have contributed to the seemingly unfettered and inevitable rise of privatised life-styles. It seems that there have been no processes at work which might act in the opposite direction. Somewhat surprisingly, therefore, rather than try to specify the possible sources and processes of privatism, current proponents of the thesis of working-class instrumentalism and privatism have become even more ambitious in their claims than earlier commentators.

This issue leads to the second criticism which may be levelled against the current writers in the field of class analysis. While they readily make reference to the current debates on privatism, their empirical evidence is somewhat partial in attempting to examine whether privatism is an apt description of working-class life-styles in the late twentieth century. Pahl's interest in household work strategies, for example, prohibits him, as Proctor (1990: 172–3) has also noted, from examining patterns of sociability and leisure beyond the individual household. Instead, the impression is formed of preoccupied households existing in splendid isolation. Similarly, Saunders's primary focus on home ownership prevented him from exploring patterns of sociability and leisure in greater depth as well.

More importantly, the survey data from which the Essex team, Saunders and Proctor draw their findings have their shortcomings. As Marshall and his colleagues concede, conducting a survey using somewhat 'insensitive' questions on the place of work and home and family in people's lives, constrained them in what they could say about 'privatism as a process' and the 'complex structure of social relationships in local communities' (Marshall *et al.* 1988: 217). Similarly, Proctor's preliminary findings on communal sociability from a survey of Ivybridge, a post – war suburb of Coventry, provide few insights into 'privatism in a cultural sense' as he freely admits. Proctor found a

> people with a relatively long residence in the city and neighbour-hood and an attachment to the local areas, in regular and frequent contact with relatives, knowing a large number of their neigh-bours, having local relatives and friends to help with problems,

joining in organisational activity and spending some leisure time outside the home with associates from outside the household (1990: 171).

Yet, his quantitative data on patterns of sociability and leisure say very little about what people enjoyed doing in their spare time and why they enjoyed it; whose company they enjoyed and why they enjoyed their company. Like the respondents of the Essex study and Saunders's three towns survey, we know almost nothing about the people who were interviewed on their biographical histories.

In other words, the existing empirical data cannot tell us about the meanings and feelings which people attach to different aspects of their daily lives and how they might prefer things to be different. Once again, social surveys appear to be an inappropriate methodological tool, as Marshall (1988) noted in his review of research on working-class consciousness, for exploring privatism, especially as a cultural and socipolitical experience, in depth. A more sophisticated and complex account of the content and meaning of people's hopes and plans, fears and misgivings in the context of their individual lives is needed. The in-depth study of working-class life-styles and socio-political perspectives, on which this book is based, seeks to rectify this omission within the field of class anlysis.

CONCLUSION

While publication of the *Affluent Worker* series in the late 1960s generated a number of debates on the working class throughout the 1970s, the central findings on privatism – as a style of life compatible with instrumentalism and one of the main sources of individualistic socipolitical proclivities – remained largely uncontested in the field of social stratification. A renewed interest in class life-styles in the 1980s initiated debate on whether the concept of privatism aptly describes working-class life-styles in the late twentieth century and the ways in which a person's style of life may or may not generate and sustain their consumer aspirations and social and political consciousness. To date, though, people's feelings about the place of work, home and family in their daily lives, and how their life interests shape and inform their norms, values, aspirations, attitudes and behaviour remain unexplored. In seeking to overcome this shortcoming, the way in which an in-depth study of these issues was conducted is described in the following chapter, with special reference to the biographical histories of the interviewees.

NOTES

1. As Giddens suggests, the popularity of the embourgeoisement thesis in Britain can be attributed to a specific political context in need of explanation:

The electoral defeats of the Labour Party in the 1950s seemed to many observers to both signify, and result from, a transformation of the affluent sections of the working class. If the belief that the high income manual worker has become an 'Orpington man' seems rather whimsical today, it was certainly advanced not long ago as a profound significant indicator of the erosion of the existing class structure (1973: 216). See also Laing (1986).

2. While the Luton team drew heavily upon community studies for their portrayal of the 'traditional' working class, their own research was not a community study. The main method of inquiry was a survey of men employed in three factories in Luton. The limitations of their social survey – especially the lack of any information on the respondents' work histories – will be discussed in subsequent chapters.

3. The causes of the demise of the 'traditional' working class and the emergence of home- and family-centred life-styles are quite difficult to discern in the *Affluent Worker* series. The Luton team argued that the sources of an instrumental orientation to work, for example, were to be found in a worker's non-work life yet, at the time, they argued that a home- and family-centred existence was itself the product of an instrumental search for high wages and a better standard of living. Ultimately, it was 'new' economic motivations and consumer aspirations, fuelled by the post-war period of prosperity, which propelled workers out of the occupational community.

4. Lockwood has been highly critical of the way in which commentators have conflated discussion of communal sociability or class imagery with class consciousness. He argued 'It would be nonsensical to try to explain the formation of a societal and political ideology of this kind exclusively from the vantage point of work and community relations' (1975: 241).

5. Madeline Kerr's *The People of Ship Street* (1958), for example, was a study of the psychological effects of poverty and deprivation based on research in a Liverpool slum.

6. The implication of this argument is that the class structure has changed, in that the lower middle class and affluent working class enjoy similar material conditions. The Luton team, of course, argued that a process of normative convergence had occurred but the market and work situations of the two groups remained distinct.

7. Pahl and Wallace (1988) were highly critical of some of the assumptions about the 'traditional' working class underlying an early position paper by the Essex team (Newby *et al.* 1985). From a reading of this paper, it seemed as if the Essex team were going to develop the familiar arguments about instrumentalism, privatism and the retreat from the public world of work and politics into the private sphere of home and family. However, as Proctor (1990) has also noted, the paper is reproduced as Chapter 8 of *Social Class in Modern Britain*, where primacy is given to the failure of the trade unions and the Labour Party to mobilise the working class beyond sectional concerns. The link between life-styles and socio-political consciousness, therefore, is broken.

8. In other words, the structural properties of a person's work situation (Newby 1977: 119), and not solely instrumentalism originating outside the workplace, shape industrial attitudes and behaviour.

3

GEOGRAPHICAL MOBILITY

The *Affluent Worker* study has become the *locus classicus* of class analysis in Britain. The theoretical underpinnings and empirical findings of the research in Luton were widely reviewed and debated at the time of publication, and went on to shape the subsequent research agenda on the working class in the 1970s and 1980s (Newby 1982). However, the central finding on privatism – on the growing importance of the home and family in people's daily lives – was largely ignored until the late 1980s and early 1990s. Yet recent attempts to locate privatism among the nineteenth-century working class have effectively drawn attention away from the question of whether the concept of privatism adequately describes working-class life-styles and socio-political proclivities in the late twentieth century. Are people's lives home- and family-centred even in a period characterised by economic stagflation rather than growth and prosperity? Do the lives of working-class families living in Luton centre on the immediate family in the home? In other words, do some of the main findings of the *Affluent Worker* study still stand today?

This chapter describes a study of the life-styles, aspirations and socio-political perspectives of a sample of Vauxhall workers and their wives living in Luton in the 1980s. By way of an introduction to the interviewees, the circumstances in which they came to live and work in Luton are considered at length. It will be seen that half of the interviewees, like the respondents of the *Affluent Worker* study, had moved to the town from other parts of the country as well as from abroad. However, rather than being lured to Luton in search of highly-paid manual work, many of the interviewees were forced to move in search of employment and affordable housing *per se*. They were not singularly instrumental. Similarly, many of the interviewees followed or were followed by kin, 'regrouping' in Luton rather than adopting exclusively home- and family-centred life-styles. They were not necessarily privatised. These biographical details sit somewhat uneasily alongside the Luton team's findings on instrumentalism and privatism, and go some way to confirming Grieco's (1981, 1987) picture of migration and employment in Luton.

METHODOLOGY

In-depth interviews were conducted with sixty-two Luton residents, all either Vauxhall workers or their wives since only Vauxhall had remained a major manufacturing employer in the town between the 1960s and the 1980s.[1] While the company employed six thousand workers in Luton and Dunstable, establishing a sample, as others have noted (Burgess 1982, 1984), was far from easy. The company was approached for help in generating a random sample of employees, but the request was turned down. Against the background of redundancies and complex negotiations with the trade unions over the introduction of a new shift system in the factory, the board did not want to whip up unwarranted fears and expectations among its workforce, nor to see the company presented in a bad light.[2] As a consequence, a number of different people and organisations played a part in the construction of the final sample. A list of Vauxhall workers and their families was drawn up with the help of the regional organiser of the Workers' Educational Association and a trade union official. In addition, the director of one of the two community centres in the town allowed me to approach people using the centre, and an official of a local church provided a list of Vauxhall workers belonging to his parish.

The interviewees, therefore, did not constitute a randomly selected sample. The trade union official, for example, provided a list of willing recruits from employees he met at work. People approached at the community centre were drawn from one residential area of Luton, while the names of Vauxhall workers and their families from the church official came from a small, albeit different, part of the town as well. Even so, various means of talking to a wide variety of people were employed. Only a small number of names from the three sources were randomly selected for interview, while the others were approached and asked to provide further names. The overwhelming majority of them, along with the interviewees themselves, were more than willing to provide additional contacts. Indeed, many of the interviewees wanted other members of their family – parents, siblings and extended kin – to be interviewed, but to have done so would have limited the sample to a network of interconnected families. Instead, contact was confined to fellow workers at either the husbands' or wives' workplaces. The process of 'snowballing', therefore, confirmed Grieco's (1981, 1987) finding that family members often work alongside each other, and people's work and non-work lives are invariably intertwined.

The final sample comprised a diverse range of people in terms of their ages, stages in the family life-cycle and standards of living, work histories and geographical histories. Five shop stewards from Vauxhall, however, appeared in the sample. Only two of them – Peter Ibbotson and Roy Mayes – knew each other, one mentioning the other as a potential interviewee. Both of them were enthusiastic supporters of Luton Town Football Club and acted as stewards at the ground when Luton Town were playing at home. They had two young daughters each and the two families occasionally went on a picnic or a day out in the summer. While Peter Ibbotson was a long-standing Conservative Party supporter, Roy Mayes was an equally long-standing, if somewhat critical, supporter of the Labour Party. Like the other shop stewards – Brian Richards, Simon Sawyer and Richard Graves – their socio-political proclivities were quite different. They did not form a distinct grouping within the sample.

THE INTERVIEWS

Sixty-two qualitative interviews were completed between July 1986 and May 1987. Sixty of those interviewees constituted thirty couples. Two additional women were included in the sample for, although their husbands were unwilling to be interviewed, their interviews were still interesting and the data relevant to the research.[3] The interviews were conducted in the interviewees' homes, and each interview lasted approximately two hours. Husbands and wives were interviewed separately and on different occasions so that each interviewee could speak as freely as possible. Equal weight was attached to the interviews with the husbands and wives, since it was their individual and family life-styles which were the main focus of the study. Their confidentiality assured, all of the interviewees agreed to the conversations being tape-recorded and transcribed later.

A wide range of topics was discussed over the course of the interview, including the interviewees' geographical and residential mobility, their work histories, sociability with kin, neighbours and colleagues from work, conjugal roles, leisure activities, consumer aspirations and social, industrial and political perspectives. The topics of conversation were broadly similar to those themes considered by Goldthorpe and his colleagues. However, rather than use a structured questionnaire like the Luton team, an *aide-mémoire* was employed to conduct semi-structured interviews.[4] It acted as a check-list of topics for discussion to allow for as free-flowing a conversation as possible. In this way, the interviewees could develop their own ideas and concepts, and present their own arguments rather than being forced to think in unfamiliar ways. Issues could be discussed and connected to other topics raised without it being necessary to infer links and consistencies as is often the case with highly-structured questionnaires (Burgess 1982, 1984; Rose 1982; Silverman 1985). In other words, qualitative interviews were undertaken to facilitate an understanding of people's feelings about their daily lives, aspirations and socio-political perspectives. These were the advantages of conducting in-depth interviews with Vauxhall workers and their wives.

THE SAMPLE

The final sample included a group of people whose ages ranged from 21 to 67 (Table 3.1). They came from different generations, with experiences of both pre- and post- Second World War Britain. Some of the older

TABLE 3.1 Age of Interviewees[1]

Interviewees	Age of Wife	Age of Husband
Kim and Anthony Dodd[2]	21	23
Bridget and Stephen Underwood	29	31
Rita and Malik Aziz	29	29
Uma and Anhok Kasim	27	28
Lisa and Matthew Smith	28	23
Jane and Andrew Bennett	28	27
Delia and Colin Burgess	29	35
Alison and Michael Clark	28	27
Sheila and Peter Ibbotson	34	36
Sandra and Trevor Davis	38	47
Teresa and Gerald Mills	35	39
Elisabeth Adams	33	
Angela and George Stone	36	39
Marion and Bruce Capel	42	40
Irene and Edward Cass	42	37
Anita and Neil Palmer	43	40
Catherine and Roy Mayes	46	45
Rachel and Robert Edwards	43	39
Julia and Martin Farrell	40	48
Judith and Geoffrey Hayward	48	56
Christine and Timothy Merrick	46	46
Brenda and Brian Richards	41	43
Heather and Kevin Jackson	47	48
Margaret and Leslie Kent	49	48
Karen and David Osborne	58	64
Maria and Daniel Knight	52	54
Carol and Simon Sawyer	50	54
Barbara Wright	51	
Pauline and Richard Graves	53	57
Frances and John Hills	57	59
Dorothy and Lawrence Atkinson	63	56
Daphne and Jack Foulds	67	62

[1] In this and subsequent tables, fictitious names have been adopted to protect the confidentiality of the interviewees.
[2] The interviewees are listed according to their stage in the family life-cycle.

interviewees, for example, had experienced unemployment and economic uncertainty in the 1930s as well as the 1940s and 1950s (though others had escaped unemployment altogether), while some of the younger members of the sample had been unemployed in the early 1980s. Between them, their experiences encapsulated Britain's economic

TABLE 3.2 Number of Dependent and Independent Children[1]

Interviewees	Dependent children	Independent children
Kim and Anthony Dodd	–	–
Bridget and Stephen Underwood	–	–
Rita and Malik Aziz	1	–
Uma and Anhok Kasim	1	–
Lisa and Matthew Smith	1	–
Jane and Andrew Bennett	1	–
Delia and Colin Burgess	2	–
Alison and Michael Clark	1	–
Sheila and Peter Ibbotson	2	–
Sandra and Trevor Davis	2	–
Teresa and Gerald Mills	2	–
Elisabeth Adams	1	–
Angela and George Stone	1	2
Marion and Bruce Capel	–	–
Irene and Edward Cass	–	–
Anita and Neil Palmer	1	–
Catherine and Roy Mayes	4	–
Rachel and Robert Edwards	2	–
Julia and Martin Farrell	2	–
Judith and Geoffrey Hayward	–	2
Christine and Timothy Merrick	–	5
Brenda and Brian Richards	–	1
Heather and Kevin Jackson	–	2
Margaret and Leslie Kent	–	3
Karen and David Osborne	1	3
Maria and Daniel Knight	1	1
Carol and Simon Sawyer	–	5
Barbara Wright	–	2
Pauline and Richard Graves	–	1
Frances and John Hills	–	3
Dorothy and Lawrence Atkinson	–	2
Daphne and Jack Foulds	–	2

[1] Dependent children are defined as children under 16 and children 16 or over still in full-time education. The Luton team defined dependent children as children under 15 and children over 15 still in full-time education since 15 was the school leaving age at the time of their study.

and social history since the 1930s. The age profile is, of course, somewhat different from the relatively young men who had begun their working lives in the post-war period of prosperity who were interviewed by the Luton team.

The interviewees also occupied a diverse range of positions in the family life-cycle. The number of dependent and independent children in each family can be seen in Table 3.2. Two couples – Kim and Anthony Dodd, and Bridget and Stephen Underwood – were newly married and had no children. Six couples had young children under 5 and two of them – Lisa and Matthew Smith, and Jane and Andrew Bennett – were expecting another child at the time of the interview. A further two couples – Marion and Bruce Capel, and Irene and Edward Cass – had no children, although both couples were in their early forties and had been married for over ten years. At the other end of the family life-cycle, the three oldest couples in the sample who were in their late fifties and early sixties – Frances and John Hills, Dorothy and Lawrence Atkinson and Daphne and Jack Foulds – lived alone, since their children were in established households of their own. Therefore, over half of the sample (nineteen couples) had at least one dependent child living at home. Again, the life-cycle profile of the interviewees is somewhat different from the Luton team's sample. Given the strictly-defined age range of the sample, a large majority (83per cent) of their sample had one or more dependent children (Goldthorpe *et al.* 1968a: 147).[5] More often than not, each household's position in the family life-cycle, including the number of dependent and independent children, the age of the youngest child and whether the wife worked or not, accounted for the interviewees' different standards of living. The homes of the younger interviewees with dependent children being cared for full-time, for example, were less well-equipped than those of the older interviewees. In other words, some of the households could be described as affluent working-class while others were relatively poor and money was tight.[6] These findings are in line with Pahl's (1984) study of families on the Isle of Sheppey, where he found very different standards of living among members of the working class. As we shall see, the interviewees frequently referred to their stage in the family life-cycle when discussing their past, present and anticipated future standards of living and class location. Their stage in the family life-cycle was an important social identity.

These brief comments on the interviewees' standards of living derive from observations, albeit impressionistic ones, of the interviewees' homes. The interviewees were asked if they owned their homes. The majority (twenty seven) of the families owned their own homes and only five families lived in properties rented from the council. These included Mr and Mrs Aziz and Mr and Mrs Burgess, who were young members of the sample; Mr and Mrs Mills and Mr and Mrs Farrell, both of whom had teenage children; and Mrs and Mrs Knight, an older couple who had relied on one income for most of their married life. A further five couples had occupied council property in the past. Again, these five couples were spread across the age range and family life-cycle. Mr and Mrs Smith and Mr and Mrs Bennett were young members of the sample who had lived

TABLE 3.3 Husbands' Jobs and Length of Service at Vauxhall

Men interviewees	Job title	Length of service (years)
Anthony Dodd	Production Operator	4
Stephen Underwood	Production Operator	10
Malik Aziz	Production Operator	10
Anhok Kasim	Quality Controller	11
Matthew Smith	Sprayer	3
Andrew Bennett	Fitter	9
Colin Burgess	Fitter	14
Michael Clark	Production Operator	9
Peter Ibbotson	Fitter	9
Trevor Davis	Sprayer	15
Gerald Mills	Mechanic	17
George Stone	Production Operator	7
Bruce Capel	Driver	18
Edward Cass	Production Operator	15
Neil Palmer	Production Operator	16
Roy Mayes	Production Operator	23
Robert Edwards	Chaser	20
Martin Farrell	Sprayer	8
Geoffrey Hayward	Setter	34
Timothy Merrick	Welder	25
Brian Richards	Quality Controller	13
Kevin Jackson	Cutter	10
Leslie Kent	Cutter	28
David Osborne	Paint Rectifier	34
Daniel Knight	Fork Lift Driver	10
Simon Sawyer	Production Operator	16
Richard Graves	Quality Controller	36
John Hills	Production Operator	32
Lawrence Atkinson	Trim Rectifier	23
Jack Foulds	Mechanic	34

in their own homes for less than two years. Mr and Mrs Stone, in their late thirties, had bought their council house when the opportunity first arose in the early 1980s and they had subsequently sold that home and moved to another privately owned home.[7] Finally, Mr and Mrs Hills and Mr and Mrs Foulds moved from their council houses into privately owned houses in Luton in the 1950s when relatively cheap housing was being built. The data confirm wider national trends which have shown that home ownership has increased significantly among the working class over this century (Saunders 1990a).

EMPLOYMENT

All of the men worked on the shop-floor in a variety of departments in the car and van sections of the Vauxhall plant. Some of them were production operators working on the track, while others worked in smaller groups or alone. Some of them were skilled workers, while others were unskilled. Three of them had worked at Vauxhall for over thirty years – much of their working lives – while the younger men had spent less time with the company. The different jobs and lengths of service with Vauxhall can be seen in Table 3.3. As waged workers, of course, all of the men could be classified as working-class according to Goldthorpe's (1987) threefold class schema.

In contrast, not all of the women, for a variety of different reasons, were in gainful employment. Four women – Rita Aziz, Uma Kasim, Lisa Smith and Jane Bennett – were raising young children full-time, while one women – Maria Knight – had not worked since the birth of her two children, the youngest of whom was 17. Another woman – Rachel Edwards – had been made redundant from her job and was looking for work. Finally, two women – Dorothy Atkinson and Daphne Foulds – were retired. For a variety of reasons, eight of the thirty-two women in the sample were not in gainful employment.

The remaining twenty-four women divided equally between part-time and full-time hours of work. Of the full-time workers, Teresa Mills worked long shifts as a cashier at a bingo hall over the weekend while her husband or mother-in-law looked after her 10-year-old daughter and 15-year-old son. She was free to look after them during the week. Alison Clark was a self-employed teacher who taught at a number of schools and privately at home. While she usually worked Monday to Friday, her hours of work varied in any one day. Finally, Irene Cass, a machinist, and Frances Hills worked slightly less than a thirty-seven-hour week, both of them finishing work in mid-afternoon.[8] Among the part-time workers, Sheila Ibbotson's hours, as a self-employed caterer, varied according to demand. She also worked a small number of hours as a school helper. Two of the part-timers – Delia Burgess and Margaret Kent – worked at home and their hours of work varied as well.[9] For the most part, however, the women's hours of work were related to the age of the youngest child and stage in the family life-cycle. This finding, of course, is in line with survey data on women's patterns of employment (Dex 1984; Martin and Roberts 1984).

The women's jobs, as Table 3.4 shows, were more varied than their husband's jobs, although five women – Bridget Underwood, Elisabeth Adams, Anita Palmer, Julia Farrell and Carol Sawyer – worked as production operators for Vauxhall.[10] Sandra Davies also worked for Vauxhall as a part-time cleaner. Even so, given the gender segregation of the labour market (Hakim 1979), all of them worked in 'typical' female jobs such as semi-skilled or unskilled manual work, personal services and

TABLE 3.4 Wives' Jobs and Hours of Work

Women Interviewees	Jobs	Hours of Work[1]
Kim Dodd	Cashier	Full-time
Bridget Underwood	Production Operator	Full-time
Delia Burgess	Packer	Part-time
Alison Clark	Teacher	Full-time
Sheila Ibbotson	Caterer	Part-time
Sandra Davis	Cleaner	Part-time
Teresa Mills	Cashier	Full-time
Elisabeth Adams	Production Operator	Full-time
Angela Stone	Nursing Auxiliary	Part-time
Marion Capel	Computer Office Manager	Full-time
Irene Cass	Machinist	Full-time
Anita Palmer	Production Operator	Full-time
Catherine Mayes	Home Help	Part-time
Julia Farrell	Production Operator	Full-time
Judith Hayward	School Helper	Part-time
Christine Merrick	Nursing Auxiliary	Part-time
Brenda Richards	Secretary	Full-time
Heather Jackson	Clerical Assistant	Part-time
Margaret Kent	Machinist	Part-time
Karen Osborne	School Helper	Part-time
Carol Sawyer	Production Operator	Full-time
Barbara Wright	Clerk/Typist	Part-time
Pauline Graves	Cleaner	Part-time
Frances Hills	Cook	Full-time

[1] Part-time work is defined as less than a thirty-hour week.

routine non-manual work. The occupational and employment data suggest that the majority (nineteen) of these women were members of the working class if placed in class locations according to their individual work and market situations. Using Goldthorpe's amended sevenfold and threefold class schema (Goldthorpe and Payne 1986), these women were in working-class jobs such as assistants and cashiers with 'straightforward wage labour' employment relations and conditions – and in semi-skilled and unskilled jobs (Goldthorpe 1987: 280).

A further three women – Brenda Richards, who worked full-time as a secretary to a security firm; Heather Jackson, who worked part-time as a clerical assistant for the local authority; and Barbara Wright, who also worked part-time as a clerk/typist for the local authority – fell into class IIIa and are, therefore, members of the intermediate class according to Goldthorpe's class schema. They occupied different class positions from their husbands, thereby constituting cross-class families. However, these are widely defined (McRae 1986) cross-class families, and Goldthorpe (1987: 297) would probably prefer to include Heather Jackson and Barbara Wright in class IIIb and in the working class according to his amended class schema (Goldthorpe and Payne 1986). All three women had working-class origins, and only Barbara Wright had attended college on a one-year commercial course after leaving school. None of the women was on a recognisable career path leading to occupational mobility in the future. [11]

Finally, two women – Alison Clark, a music teacher and Marion Capel, a computer office manager – fell into Class II (semi-professional workers) according to Goldthorpe's sevenfold schema, and into the service class according to his threefold schema. Again, both of these women are in different classes from their husbands, constituting cross-class families in the strictly-defined sense. However, Alison Clark's employment situation was not particularly secure in that she had no formal teaching qualifications beyond her specialist subject of music and she worked a small number of hours in various schools and at home. She was not following an easily recognisable career path. Marion Capel's parents were farmers in Ireland. On leaving school at 16, she came to Luton and started work in an office. Occupational mobility had been facilitated by on-the-job training and a continuous work history since she did not have any children.

The varied occupational and class profiles of the women interviewees have been discussed in some detail. Unfortunately, the Luton team provided only a few details on the wives' patterns of employment in their published monographs. The Luton team asked about their previous work histories, their jobs, what hours they worked and how they combined paid work and family commitments (Goldthorpe *et al.* 1969: 217). Almost all of the women who did not have dependent children were in paid work, as were a small number of women raising young children. A third (32 per cent) of the women in their sample worked, 17 per cent of them worked full-time while the others worked part-time (Goldthorpe *et al.* 1969: 98).[12] We do not know in which jobs they were employed, and without data on their work and market situations we do not know about the individual class positions of the wives as opposed to their adopted class positions from their husbands. There was little interest in women's employment and their individual class positions in the early 1960s when the *Affluent Worker* study was undertaken. This may have been the result of less discernible trends in the participation of married women in the labour market at that time. In retrospect, the Luton team certainly neglected these issues, not only in themselves but also in relation to their own central interest in changing life-styles and social and political perspectives among the working class. By attaching equal weight to the interviews with the husbands and wives of the sample, this study seeks to overcome this oversight.

GEOGRAPHICAL MOBILITY

The Luton team, of course, attached considerable importance to geographical mobility in the search for a good standard of living. They stressed the positive 'choice' involved in moving away from family and friends in search of well-paid work. In Luton they found a highly mobile sample who had been attracted to the town by the high wages offered by such companies as Vauxhall, Laporte and Skefco. Less than a third (30 per cent) of their sample had grown up in Luton, while a further 24 per cent of the sample had spent their childhood in London and the South East, and just under a half (44 per cent) had grown up outside the region altogether. Only half (50 per cent) of their sample had held a previous job in Luton (Goldthorpe et al. 1968a: 150–1).[13] The Luton team also emphasised the way in which families became separated from kin as a result of geographical mobility. Only a third of the sample (36 per cent) 'had a majority of their closer kin (parents, siblings and in-laws) living in the town' (Goldthorpe et al. 1969: 38). Families who moved in search of higher standards of living, therefore, lost the close proximity of the main body of their kin in their daily lives.

Yet recent work by Grieco (1981, 1987) on the recruitment practices of the Vauxhall company in North-East England, Scotland and Ireland has cast some doubt on this central argument. She contests the evidence that the workers interviewed by the Luton team exercised unfettered choice in moving to Luton for highly-paid work. Despite the full employment of the post-war period, pockets of regional unemployment existed in the late 1950s and early 1960s. It was in these areas of high unemployment that she found that Vauxhall had instigated recruitment drives. This implies that many of the men who moved to Luton were escaping from unemployment or the 'atmosphere of economic insecurity' (Grieco 1987: 127). A particularly acute instrumentalism did not prompt them to leave family and friends in search of higher wages and a better standard of living. Many of the families who moved from the North did so in order to secure a reasonable standard of living for themselves. In so doing, they often provided information about job prospects to kin at home, initiating a process of chain migration of networks of people to a new locale. Employers like Vauxhall were keen to promote such migration as a way of exercising control over the 'green' workforce with the help of other members of a family (Grieco 1987: 130–4).[14]

The discrepancy betweeen the findings of the Luton team and the subsequent research by Grieco can be assessed by looking at the geographical history of the interviewees of this study and the circumstances in which they moved to Luton. The geographical origins of the *Affluent Worker* sample and the sample of this research are remarkably similar. The Luton team interviewed a highly mobile sample. Under a third of the sample had spent most of their lives in Luton before employment, although they comprised the largest grouping in the sample. Families from

TABLE 3.5 Interviewees' region of upbringing

Region of origin[1]	Interviewees
Luton area[2]	32
London and the South East	11
Northern Ireland and Eire	9
Abroad	5
Other parts of Britain	5
Total	62

[1] In keeping with the Luton team's definition of upbringing, the term refers to the locale in which the interviewees grew up.
[2] The Luton area is defined as the town and all land within a 10 mile radius of the town's boundaries.

London and the South East and Northern Ireland and Ireland made up the next two categories in the sample (24 per cent and 14 per cent) (Goldthorpe *et al.* 1968a: 150). Many of the interviewees in this research shared the same regions of origin. As Table 3.5 indicates, just over half of this sample (thirty-two interviewees) spent the majority of their childhood in Luton and the surrounding area. The most significant groups of geographically mobile interviewees came from London and the South East and Northern Ireland and Eire. A sizeable minority of the sample came from abroad or from other parts of Britain.

Despite these similarities, the parents of many second-generation Lutonians and the geographically mobile members of the sample moved in search of employment *per se* and/or affordable housing. They did not move to Luton as freely as Goldthorpe and his colleagues described but took the opportunities which were open to them to improve their standard of living in the post-war period of prosperity.[15] The move in search of jobs and housing did not amount to a single-minded instrumentalism nor, as we shall see, necessarily privatism. A full appreciation of the opportunities and constraints which shaped the interviewees' actions and motives for action can be fully understood only by looking at each of the categories in turn, distinguishing the interviewees according to their region of origin.

The Lutonians

Just over half of the predominantly younger members of the sample (thirty-two interviewees) had spent almost all of their childhood in Luton and the surrounding area. However, few were born in the town itself because their parents came from elsewhere. Only eight interviewees could claim that both parents came from Luton. The young interviewees were the second generation of geographically mobile families who had moved to Luton. Their parents came from a variety of regions, most

TABLE 3.6 Lutonians and their parents' geographical origins

Lutonians	Parents' Geographical Origins	
	Father	Mother
Kim Dodd	North	Surrey
Anthony Dodd	North	North
Bridget Underwood	Eire	Eire
Stephen Underwood	Poland	London
Rita Aziz	India	India
Uma Kasim	India	India
Ashok Kasim	India	India
Lisa Smith	London	Luton
Matthew Smith	Wales	Wales
Jane Bennett	Luton	Luton
Andrew Bennett	London	London
Colin Burgess	West Indies	West Indies
Alison Clark	North	North
Michael Clark	Scotland	Scotland
Teresa Mills	Luton	Luton
Gerald Mills	Wales	Wales
Angela Stone	Lincolnshire	Luton
George Stone	Lancashire	Suffolk
Irene Cass	Eire	Eire
Edward Cass	Wales	Wales
Anita Palmer	Luton	Luton
Roy Mayes	Eire	Eire
Robert Edwards	Wales	Cambridgeshire
Judith Hayward	London	London
Geoffrey Hayward	Hampshire	London
Christine Merrick	Eire	Eire
Heather Jackson	North	Luton
Kevin Jackson	Luton	Luton
Pauline Graves	Luton	Luton
Richard Graves	Luton	Luton
Dorothy Atkinson	Luton	Luton
Jack Foulds	Luton	Luton

notably from London, the North, Wales, Scotland and Ireland. The Lutonians and their parents' geographical origins can be found in Table 3.6.

Many of the interviewees' parents had moved to Luton for jobs. Employment opportunities in their own regions in the 1930s and 1940s were limited. Some of the fathers of the interviewees had worked at the Vauxhall car plant as well. As Edward Cass explained: 'My parents were from South Wales. They came to Luton to find work as there was none in South

Wales. My father also worked at Vauxhall.' This is not to say that all of the interviewees' parents had experienced unemployment. Many of them were escaping from the prospect of insecure and low-paid employment and low standards of living for most of their lives. Within these constraints, they chose to move to Luton. It was not a case of entirely restricted choice but neither were their choices completely free. The interviewees actively sought to improve their lot, but whether they were more single-minded than members of the 'traditional' working class is open to question. It is probably more appropriate to remember that the opportunities to improve their standard of living were greater in the post-war period of prosperity than they had been in the past. There is no reason to assume that the 'traditional' working class would not have taken these opportunities as well if they had been given the chance.

For a number of interviewees, their parents had followed kin to Luton. Michael Clark described the migration of his family from Scotland to Luton in the early 1960s, when he was aged 4:

> I was born in Glasgow in Scotland. I used to visit Luton because I had an uncle living there who worked at Vauxhall. He moved to Luton because there were no jobs in Glasgow. My grandmother then moved down because she was by herself. My uncle told her to come down as he was getting a good wage and he could look after her in Luton. I came down with my grandmother when I was four because she looked after me at the time. Later my mother came down with the rest of the kids.

Chain migration was evident among families who moved to Luton in search of jobs. Indeed, Michael Clark's comments suggest that high wages facilitated his grandmother's move to Luton. Affluence was shared with kin beyond the immediate family. Families did not necessarily move away from wider kin networks and friends in search of highly-paid jobs.

Six of the native Lutonians – Jane Bennett, Robert Edwards, Judith and Geoffrey Hayward and Pauline and Richard Graves – were born and spent their childhood in the villages surrounding Luton. Given their close proximity to the town and visits to family and friends in Luton, they knew that Vauxhall paid high wages. As Geoffrey Hayward explained:

> I just got fed up with my other job. I was bored. I was twenty-one and I had just come out of the RAF. I had come back home to work. I had worked there previously but I lasted a year. A friend of mine went into Vauxhall and he told me about the good wages.

Vauxhall was a large employer which offered high wages, a measure of security and a wide variety of benefits which the smaller employers of the region could not match.

Housing was also an important attraction to people who lived on the outskirts of Luton. The opportunity for young couples to have a home of

TABLE 3.7 Interviewees from London and the South East

Interviewees	Region of origin
Sheila Ibbotson	London
Peter Ibbotson	London
Sandra Davis	London
Trevor Davis	London
Timothy Merrick	London
Brenda Richards	London
Brian Richards	London
Maria Knight	London
Daniel Knight	London
Frances Hills	St Albans
John Hills	St Albans

their own in the surrounding villages was limited. Returning to Geoffrey Hayward, he described how he moved to Luton with his wife in the mid-1960s:

> There was no chance of getting a council house. The village was in a green belt area and there was no building being done. I also got a mortgage on a fixed rate with the council which you could get at the time.

Luton drew in many young families in the late 1950s and 1960s from the local area. The town offered employment which was highly paid and cheap housing for young families wishing to establish themselves for the first time. As we shall see in Chapter 4, the move to Luton did not hinder sociability with parents and other kin who remained in the villages.

Clearly, Luton in the 1960s was 'a town of migrants', as the Luton team suggested (Goldthorpe *et al.* 1968a: 151). From the 1930s onwards Vauxhall, with its mass production of cars, was a thriving company which attracted workers from all over the country. Many of these workers faced unemployment in their own regions or, at the very least, insecure and ill-paid jobs for most of their working lives. Vauxhall offered good wages and security at that time. Thus, it appears that workers and their families travelling from long distances were escaping the prospect of unemployment, while local families moved to Luton for the high wages and attractive housing. The reasons for moving to Luton, therefore, were varied.[16]

Interviewees from London and the South East

Eleven interviewees had grown up and worked in London and the South East. They are listed in Table 3.7. They moved to Luton in search of housing. This confirms the Luton team's finding that Londoners, in particular, sought better housing in Luton (Goldthorpe *et al.* 1968a: 153).

TABLE 3.8 Irish Members of the Sample

Irish interviewees	Region of origin
Marion Capel	Eire
Catherine Mayes	Eire
Rachel Edwards	Eire
Julia Farrell	Eire
Martin Farrell	Northern Ireland
Margaret Kent	Eire
Leslie Kent	Eire
Karen Osborne	Eire
David Osborne	Eire

However, the interviewees stressed the importance of finding affordable housing in Luton. They wanted to buy a house but were unable to do so in London because property prices were too high. Their geographical mobility must be seen in the light of this constraint. As Sheila Ibbotson suggested:

> We moved to Luton as we wanted to buy our own place. We couldn't afford any in London. At first we only looked at Watford and St Albans. Then we looked in the local paper for the Luton and Dunstable areas. We hadn't intended coming quite this far. Luton was convenient with the motorway as my husband was still travelling to work there initially.

The interviewees did not move anywhere in search of their own home. They searched for a house within a certain distance of where they lived. The close proximity of Luton to London was a bonus to those who were mobile from the capital. With a car and a good motorway to London, kin, neighbours, workmates and friends were not too far away. Maintaining contact would not be difficult. As Brian Richards noted: 'I didn't particularly like Luton. Having a house and carrying on working was the main thing. It was only half an hour to see our parents in London anyway.'

The interviewees had come to Luton to buy houses which they could not afford to do in London. They may well not have moved if they had enjoyed some choice in London. Luton offered the opportunity to buy their own homes and they took this opportunity. As we shall see in the next chapter, many of their kin followed them to Luton.

The Irish

Like the parents of the native Lutonians, the majority of the Irish interviewees had come to Luton in search of work which Eire could not offer them in the post-war period. The nine interviewees are listed in Table 3.8. As Catherine Mayes: said 'I came to Luton when I was 20 since there were no jobs in Eire.' They migrated to Luton because their kin already

TABLE 3.9 Interviewees from abroad

Interviewees	Country of origin
Malik Aziz	Kenya
Delia Burgess	West Indies
Neil Palmer	West Indies
Simon Sawyer	Jamaica
Carol Sawyer	Jamaica

lived in the town or they knew friends who had moved to Luton to find work as well. Established kin or friends could provide accommodation and information about jobs. They were also an important source of sociable contact. As Leslie Kent described: I came to Luton when I was 18 because my aunt and uncle were here and it was the only place I knew. They put me up and I stayed with them until I got married. I've been here ever since.'

Emphasising this same point, David Osborne also described how he migrated to Luton in 1937:

There was little work in Eire. My brother was working in Luton, and Luton was the place where jobs were known to be. I stayed with my brother originally. My sister and one brother came to Luton as well so the others followed over. Another brother settled in Luton after serving in the army in the war. One sort of followed the other.

As single people, these interviewees had moved to Luton where they knew other people who could offer them accommodation and where jobs were available. Kin and friends were important in facilitating migration over a long distance. They were particularly important, as Grieco also found (1987: 54), when regular contact with parents and others could not be sustained. In the next chapter, we shall see how these families regrouped in Luton. They were keen to live in close proximity to their kin so they could enjoy their company.

Migrants from Abroad

Five interviewees, who can be found in Table 3.9, came to Luton from abroad, although the circumstances and reasons why they were mobile varied. Two interviewees, Malik Aziz from Kenya and Neil Palmer from the West Indies, moved with their families to Luton in their teens. Simon Sawyer moved to Luton from Jamaica in the late 1950s and his wife Carol followed him later. Delia Burgess came to Luton to marry her husband, Colin, whom she had met when he was on holiday in the West Indies to visit his extended kin.

The search for jobs, and not necessarily highly-paid jobs, precipitated the men's mobility. Mr Aziz, who was born in Kenya of Indian parents, explained how he had come to settle in Luton:

TABLE 3.10 Migrants from other parts of Britain

Interviewees	Region of origin
Elisabeth Adams	Tyne and Wear
Bruce Capel	Yorkshire
Barbara Wright	East Anglia
Lawrence Atkinson	Cambridgeshire
Daphne Foulds	West Midlands

> My family moved to England when I was 18 mainly for us, the children. My eldest brother had already settled in England and he was studying law. My father decided to move to Luton to do something about the future for the rest of his children. There were no chances of a job in Kenya. My father had reached the age of fifty and he had to retire out there so he decided to start a fresh life.

Simon Sawyer came to Britain to search for work, too, going ahead of his wife and two children who were born in Jamaica. They followed him when he had settled in Luton and three further children were born in the town.

> I would have liked to stay in Jamaica but it was a matter of looking at where the opportunities were for work. I had heard about England so I wanted to come here. I had friends from home here, people who had moved to Luton and I asked them if they would see me over. I came over on my own and my family followed me later.

Again, geographical mobility was not the result of unfettered choice and friends were an important source of help to the interviewees in an unfamiliar locale.

Migrants from other parts of Britain

Finally, five interviewees, listed in Table 3.10, came from various parts of Britain. Yet again, the search for jobs and housing were important for these interviewees. The interviewees from the North of England mentioned Vauxhall's recruitment practice referred to by Grieco (1981, 1987). Elisabeth Adams's parents and siblings moved to Luton when she was 18. She had not moved with them since she was married and living in an independent household of her own. She recalled how her parents moved to Luton:

> My parents moved to Luton for work in 1971. Jobs were advertised in the North East as there was a recruitment drive. People wouldn't normally move 200 miles for a job but for the recruitment drive.

When her husband lost his job they moved to Luton as well:

> We came down to Luton for the work. My husband lost his job and he was unemployed for a number of months. He went to Vauxhall

and they were prepared to take him on. I suppose we've gone to where the work is.

In this instance, family members followed each other into the Vauxhall plant.

The recruitment drive also brought Luton to Bruce Capel's attention, although he was not employed by Vauxhall as a direct result of its recruitment policies. The recruitment drive certainly brought Luton to the attention of people who might not of known of its job potential given that they lived so far away from the town. As Mr Capel explained: 'Vauxhall was recruiting in the North as well as Ireland and Scotland so I knew Luton was the place where work was.' On this basis, he travelled to Luton to get some impression of the town before applying for a job at the Vauxhall plant.[17]

The interviewees' geographical histories and their reasons for moving to Luton have been described at length. How did the interviewees feel about moving to Luton? What did they perceive to be the advantages and disadvantages of moving? In retropect, were they glad they had moved to Luton? Did they have any regrets? Were the interviewees as single-mindedly instrumental as the Luton team argued of their own geographically mobile sample? These questions required the interviewees to reflect and weigh up their feelings towards mobility which had occured many years ago. Unlike the relative newcomers of the *Affluent Worker* study, the interviewees of this study were established migrants of longstanding. The most recent migrants had lived in Luton for eight years, while some of the older migrants had lived in the town for over thirty years. Their comments revealed some interesting evaluations of their move to Luton and privatism as a process.

ADVANTAGES AND DISADVANTAGES

Not surprisingly, Goldthorpe and his colleagues highlighted their respondents' positive attitudes to moving in search of higher standards of living. While noting that over a third of the couples had missed kin and friends, they emphasised the advantages of moving. Their respondents were encouraged to weigh up the relative advantages and disadvantages of moving, and the Luton team concluded that

It is clear that it was overwhelmingly the attraction of better living conditions and higher incomes which brought these couples to Luton, and further, that almost invariably they felt that they had achieved advantages in these respects (1968: 152–3).

The interviewees of this research gave a more complicated picture of their feelings about moving to Luton. Sheila Ibbotson and her husband Peter had moved to Luton from London in search of an affordable house. Sheila recalled the enthusiasm with which she had moved to Luton. It was only after moving that she experienced the loss of kin and friends.

I hated Luton at first. I just wanted to move back to London. I was very lonely. I missed my parents and I had some very good friends, school friends, there. They were a good circle of friends to see. Originally I was excited at moving but I regretted it once it was done.

Barbara Wright moved from East Anglia to Luton when she married and bought a house which she and her husband greatly desired. Like many of the interviewees, owning their own home was very important to them. Barbara's husband worked away from home for two years before they were married to save for a house. They wanted to save up enough money for a deposit rather than rent. The search for work had taken him to Luton and it was here that they looked for their first house. Whether she would like her life in a new town away from kin was not considered:

It came to me gradually. My mother wasn't too keen on the idea but I didn't have any doubts about it. My husband suggested it and I thought it was a good idea. I didn't think about whether I would like it or not.

As we shall see in subsequent chapters, the sense of loss was experienced only after the move, and, for some, it took a long time to meet new friends. Many of the interviewees, especially the women, felt isolated, as Young and Willmott (1957) found. However, they had to adapt to the new circumstances in which they found themselves. This issue of privatism as a process will be explored in subsequent chapters as well.

Rather than describe the varied circumstances in which each of the thirty-two families came to live and work in Luton, this information has been presented in tables throughout the chapter. By way of a conclusion, the context in which one couple - Sheila and Peter Ibbotson – moved to Luton and the subsequent life-style which they adopted is described at length. The 'case study' serves to show the nature of their daily lives as fully as possible. It goes without saying that although Mr and Mrs Ibbotson were not typical of all of the families in the sample, neither were they atypical.

Mr and Mrs Ibbotson

Sheila and Peter Ibbotson, aged thirty-four and thirty-six, had lived in Luton for ten years. Both were born and brought up in London. They had been married for sixteen years, and they had two daughters: Helen, aged 12, and Chloe, aged 9. Both of them were born in London as well. After the birth of their second child, Mr and Mrs Ibbotson decided to move from their rented flat in search of an affordable house. They looked for a property in Watford and St Albans before buying a small terraced house in the old part of Luton. The quest for an affordable house had taken them a little further afield than they had originally anticipated but Luton, situated close to the M1 motorway, was still convenient. This was important since Peter Ibbotson initially travelled to work in London. They could visit both sets of parents every weekend as well.

Two years later, they moved into their present home. It is a well-maintained, semi-detached, three-bedroomed house in a residential area of privately-owned properties built in the 1930s. It is situated close to both the town centre and the Vauxhall plant. They could afford the house because it was in need of renovation. They had wanted a larger house so that the children could each have a bedroom of their own. While they had felt very isolated when they moved to Luton initially, they had made friends with people locally when they moved into their present home in the town. Many of these people were ex-Londoners like themselves.

Sheila's parents now live in Luton, although on the other side of town. As council tenants, they had moved to Luton under a mobility scheme when her mother retired from work. Mrs Ibbotson had suggested to her parents that they move to Luton since her father had suffered ill-health for most of his life and she did not want her mother to live alone when he died. She visited her parents once or twice a week, with her children and/or husband at the weekend and sometimes on her own during the week. Peter's parents still live in London and they try to visit them every other weekend.

Sheila has one married brother, who lives on the south coast. They meet only two or three times a year, although they speak to each other regularly on the telephone. Peter has one brother and he and his wife live around the corner from them. They had followed the Ibbotsons to Luton five years previously. Peter visits his brother at least twice a week, usually after work, and Sheila and her sister-in-law have become close friends who see each other at least twice a week but usually during the day. The four of them often go out together for a meal or to a dance.

Mrs Ibbotson's sister-in-law was part of a network of five other women friends from the locality. Sheila had met the others when taking her children to the local nursery and school. They met once or twice a week for coffee or keep-fit. She had worked with one of these friends in a local pub and they worked together on a new catering venture. She was a particularly close friend who was an ex-Londoner, too. Otherwise, Mrs Ibbotson met her immediate neighbours only 'to say hello to', although she knew a lot of the older people in the area having worked in the local pub for four years. Peter was less familiar with people in the surrounding streets, being at work all day and seeing his brother rather than anyone else in the evening.

Sheila had recently started work as a school helper and worked two hours a day during the school term. She combined this work with a catering business with her close friend. She had always worked a small number of hours for some extra money since the children were born. The numerous jobs had always 'fitted around' the children. Her husband had looked after the children in the evenings when she worked at the pub, and her present job left her free in the school holidays to be with them. She particularly valued part-time work because her mother had been

forced to work full-time due to her father's ill-health. She would probably get a 'proper' job in the future when the children had left school, but
she was unsure about what to do. Before the children were born, she had
worked in the post office, rising to sales supervisor. She had never liked
office work but had been pushed into it for financial reasons when she
left school at 16. She would have liked to have been a nursery nurse
instead and might eventually become a teaching assistant.

Peter Ibbotson had worked as a fitter in Vauxhall for nine years. He
had completed an apprenticeship and had taken City and Guilds exami-
nations on block release at the local college. He had worked for the Gas
Board in London and had intended to work for them in Luton. However,
he decided to work for Vauxhall as the family needed the money to pay
the mortgage on their first home. He had not intended to stay there but
the good wages had stopped him from looking for another job. He would
stay there now because he had 'his family to support' and other employers could not offer the same level of wages. He had one or two friends
from the plant whom he saw when he went to watch Luton Town play at
home every other Saturday. One of them had young daughters the same
age as his own children and the two families often went out together in
the summer. Although Peter and his wife were life-long Conservatives,
he was a shop steward at Vauxhall and felt that without unions 'working
men and women would not lead the lives they led today'.

Sheila and Peter did not got out very often in the evenings during the
week. Peter worked shifts, while Sheila invariably ferried the children to
and from Brownies and other activities. They often stayed at home and
watched television. At weekends, she and the children saw her parents
while Peter watched football or they travelled to London to see his
parents. They did not mind 'not doing much' because they liked to save
their money for holidays abroad. They were 'mad keen' on holidays and
tried to have one holiday abroad every year. They also enjoyed a 'comfortable life' because they saved all of Sheila's money from her jobs to go
towards the upkeep of a well-decorated house, a car, a wide array of
consumer durables and fashionable clothes for themselves and the children. While the threat of redundancies at Vauxhall was a worry, they
expected life to continue unchanged. In the future, and once the children
were settled, they hoped to live in a more attractive place than Luton,
either a small village in the countryside or on the south coast like Sheila's
brother.

CONCLUSION

By way of an introduction to the empirical material, this chapter focused
on the biographical details of the interviewees. Special·attention was
devoted to the circumstances in which half of the sample came to live and
work in Luton from other parts of the country and abroad. Contrary to
the Luton team's findings, the interviewees did not choose to migrate to

Luton in search of highly-paid work. On the contrary, many of them were forced to move in search of employment and affordable housing *per se*. They were not singularly instrumental. Moreover, many of the interviewees followed, or were followed by, kin and friends, 'regrouping' in Luton rather than adopting privatised life-styles. In subsequent chapters, it will be seen that their daily lives were neither exclusively family-centred, nor entirely home-centred.

NOTES

1. Laporte and Skefco were no longer major employers in the town, both having substantially reduced their workforces since the 1960s.
2. The introduction of a new shift system was a source of dispute while the research was being conducted. The company proposed to end the night shift and to introduce a 'double-day' shift system. The unions and employees were concerned about the loss of payments for the night shift and the unsociable aspect of the 'double-day' system. At the beginning of 1988 the company was still in 'difficulty' over its plans to introduce the 'double-day' shift system (IDS Report 513/January 1988).
3. The two women, of course, discussed their husband's jobs, life-styles and socio-political attitudes so they shall be referred to as families as well. The final sample comprised thirty-two families.
4. The *aide-memoire* can be found in Appendix 1.
5. Goldthorpe and his colleagues discussed whether men in the most demanding stage of the family life-cycle are more likely to be instrumental in their attitudes to work than men in less demanding stages of the family life-cycle. They argued that position in the family life-cycle could only partly explain an instrumental orientation to work. They suggest that

    the question of the extent to which the economic and social implications of having a young family will lead to an instrumental view of work must become ultimately one of values; specifically, that is, one of the value which is set on a steadily rising standard of domestic living and on devoting one's non-work life to one's wife and children (1968a: 149).

    Franklin (1989: 111) has noted that the evidence of privatism invariably derives from interviews with people in the most demanding stage of the life-cycle.
6. Unfortunately, when information on income was requested, some of the interviewees referred to their gross income, others referred to their net income; some included overtime earnings in the figures they quoted, while others did not. Many of the interviewees were unsure how much they earnt, while others were unwilling to provide information on their wages. Thus, the income data collected were unreliable and certainly did not reflect household income as a whole.
7. As we shall see, Mr and Mrs Stone were life-long Conservative Party supporters. In this instance, electoral support for the Conservative Party preceded their decision to buy their council house at the earliest opportunity. Mr Stone also held what might be described as the most racist views towards the black and Asian residents of the town.

8. Kim Dodd and Brenda Richards finished work early on a Friday afternoon, 'conveniently' allowing them to do the week's shopping and other domestic duties.

9. While an industry shift at the turn of the century had seen the demise of the hat industry and other garment industries which had been an important source of female employment in Luton (Mark-Lawson 1988), numerous small clothing companies still required sewing machinists. The industry, though much reduced, continued to offer employment opportunies to women to work at home or on site.

10. In line with findings on the gender segregation of the workplace (Martin and Roberts 1984), it was clear from the interviews that the women who worked at Vauxhall invariably worked with other women. However, only two of the four women who worked at the Vauxhall plant in Luton – Julia Farrell and Anita Palmer – worked alongside each other. Sandra Davis, who worked part-time in the evenings as a cleaner at the Luton plant, was unconnected to any of the full-time women workers at Vauxhall in the sample.
    A further six women had worked for Vauxhall and its subsidiaries in the past. Uma Kasim had worked on the production line at A.C. Delco on a temporary contract for eight months. She had worked part-time in the evenings, when her husband or her mother took care of her young son. Before the birth of her first child, Jane Bennett had worked as a production operator at the Vauxhall plant in Luton for over five years. Marion Capel had worked as a computer operator in an office at Vauxhall for sixteen years before moving to another company. Christine Merrick and Karen Osborne had worked at Vauxhall for a short period in their youth. Finally, Daphne Foulds had worked as a clerk in an office at the Luton site for eleven years before her retirement.

11. As we shall see, Heather Jackson and Barbara Wright were Labour Party supporters. If they are categorised as working class, their own class origins, occupations and class destinations rather than their husband's class position accounted for their political perspectives. These two instances are at odds with Marshall *et al.*'s (1988: 72) finding that the political affiliations of women in the intermediate class are influenced by their husband's class more than by their own individual class location.

12. The wives of men in the Luton team's white-collar sample were more likely to work than the wives of men in the blue-collar sample. Nearly a quarter (24 per cent) of them worked full-time while just over a quarter (26 per cent) of them worked part-time (Goldthorpe *et al.* 1969: 98 fn 3).

13. The majority of the percentages quoted from the main body of the text of the *Affluent Worker* study refer to their male respondents only. Less detailed information on the wives' geographical mobility was provided in a footnote (Goldthorpe et al 1968a: 151 fn 3).

14. By a 'green' workforce, Grieco was refering to workers who had little or no experience of mass production methods.

15. Grieco's research does not necessarily undermine the central findings of the *Affluent Worker* series, although she views her findings in this light. Since a diverse group of people moved to

Luton for a variety of reasons, it is possible that the Luton team and Grieco are both correct.

16. It could be argued, therefore, that the local families were more instrumental than families travelling from further afield. They left jobs in the locality for the highly-paid work at Vauxhall. Whether this amounts to instrumentalism or making the best of available opportunities is, of course, a moot point.

17. This example suggests that Vauxhall did not have as much control, as Grieco (1987: 119) alleges, over whom it employed as a result of its recruitment practices. Grieco's argument is rather conspiratorial, implying that employers have clear and coherent recruitment strategies by which they can control the workforce. While Vauxhall deliberately recruited in areas of high unemployment in search of 'green labour', it does not necessarily follow that they had absolute control over the workforce. There is no reason to suppose that a workforce consisting of 'green' recruits would remain eternally grateful to the company for their jobs either. Mass production work could be a more gruelling and unpleasant experience for a 'green' workforce than would be the case for experienced workers, generating an instrumental orientation to paid work among the former group in particular.

4

SOCIALIBILITY WITH KIN

Goldthorpe and his colleagues argued that families were prepared to move away from a locale where the majority of their kin resided and to forgo the extensive sociability facilitated by close proximity in return for relatively high standards of living and domestic comfort. The form and content of the interviewees' patterns of sociability with kin are explored in this chapter. Do the interviewees' life-styles centre on the immediate family or do they take a more communal form embracing wider kin? Whose company do they enjoy? In what context do they enjoy the company of kin? What is the meaning of sociability with kin for the interviewees?

It will be seen that the three-generation family continues to be an important source of companionship and mutual support. Sociable contact between parents and children, for example, is usually sustained throughout a lifetime, although it is particularly important when care is needed, be it child-care or care of ageing parents. Siblings remain a significant source of company and support in adult life as well, although to a lesser degree than that between parents and children. Geographical mobility obviously curtails frequent and casual, unplanned contact with kin, but the intimacy of relations is not necessarily undermined by physical distance. There is no simple relationship between levels of contact and the degree to which wider kin are an important source of companionship and support. Contrary to the assessment put forward by the Luton team, these findings suggest that the interviewees were far from isolated from wider kin, whether they resided in Luton or not. Neither did they have any desire to lead privatised life-styles.

More importantly, the interviewees did not hold a set of distinctly working-class values about acceptable levels of sociability with kin. Rather, they stressed the opportunities and constraints which shaped their daily lives. Both paid work (formal employment) and unpaid work (domestic and child-care tasks), for example, were perceived as the major constraints on extensive sociability with kin. These opportunities and constraints varied, not surprisingly, between the men and women of the sample and across the family life-cycle. The interviewees' material existence – of sustaining the household – prohibited extensive contact with kin, whether they liked it or not. It certainly militated against the kind of extensive sociability found in studies of the 'traditional' working class (Dennis *et al.* 1956; Kerr 1958; Young and Willmott 1957; Zweig 1952). This finding suggests that additional structural changes, such as the increasing participation of married women in the labour market since the Second World War, may have changed the form of sociability with kin although not necessarily its content. Contrary to the findings of the Luton team, there is little evidence to suggest that changing working-class norms and values account for family-centred life-styles in the late twentieth century.

THE CONSEQUENCES OF MOBILITY

Goldthorpe and his colleagues (1969: 97) argued that the desire for high standards of living led members of the working class to move in search of well-paid manual work. They were prepared to move to a new locale even though kin were absent.[1] As a result of physical separation, they could not enjoy frequent, unplanned contact with them but were forced, instead, to lead a home- and family-centred existence. Yet the Luton team (1969: 89) were struck by the 'quite large part that parents, siblings and in-laws still play in our respondent's lives'. Those in reasonably close proximity within Luton were of greater importance than those who lived outside the town. Thus, 41per cent of those couples whose kin lived in Luton enjoyed their company in their free time compared with 22 per cent of those couples whose kin lived elsewhere. Kin were visiting partners in the case of 52 per cent of wives if they lived nearby in comparison with 22 per cent of wives if they did not. Finally, 58 per cent of the respondents entertained their kin at home irrespective of whether they lived in Luton or not. The Luton team argued:

> What these findings suggest, therefore, is that for our affluent workers and their wives those of their kin who were *reasonably* available represented a major source of friends and companions, despite the fact that these kin rarely lived in such close proximity that contact could be maintained with them in a largely casual and unplanned way (Goldthorpe *et al.* 1969: 89, emphasis in original).

However, they emphasised that nearly half (46 per cent) of their respondents had grown up outside either London or the South East so that the majority of kin were not readily available for sociable contact. The significance of kin was limited by physical separation.[2]

Returning to the subject of geographical mobility, the Luton team went on to argue:

> Couples had no doubt often approached the move with misgivings about its effects upon their social lives, and from our interviews we know that some remained much aware of what they had lost in this respect. But generally, one may infer, staying near their kin had not appeared to these migrants as being compatible with achieving the material standards to which they aspired. To break away from

their existing pattern of sociability had been, in other words, a prerequisite of their becoming affluent; and this, despite the possibility of social isolation, was the course of action that they had chosen to follow (Goldthorpe *et al.* 1969: 97).

Moreover, the Luton team noted that highly-paid manual work often entailed long and unsocial hours of work. The desire for high standards of domestic comfort led men at the bottom rungs of the occupational ladder to work overtime and unsociable shifts for a high wage. As a result, long hours of paid work militated against extensive sociability with kin. This was also true for wives who went out to work to raise the family income. It left little free time outside the domestic routine to spend time with kin (Goldthorpe *et al.* 1969: 101–2).

Finally, Goldthorpe and his colleagues argued that a home- and family-centred life-style was not unwanted. Their affluent workers did not always maintain close contact with kin who were available in the locality. While close relationships were usually sustained with parents, the respondents were selective about maintaining sociable relations with their siblings. Close ties did not exist between husbands and two-thirds of their siblings living in Luton, nor did they exist between wives and half of their siblings living in the town. It led the Luton team to conclude that

> The possibility has therefore to be recognised that for some proportion of the couples we studied, being separated from the body of their kin or living in a community in which kinship ties were of slight importance was actually experienced as an advantage in that it made it easier to restrict or to discontinue kinship relations that were found not to be rewarding (Goldthorpe *et al.* 1969: 104).

Rather, respondents emphasised the importance of the immediate family in their lives.[3]

As we have already seen, half (thirty) of the interviewees in this research had moved to Luton from elsewhere. However, geographical mobility did not necessarily entail physical separation from kin since families frequently followed, or were followed by, kin into the new locale. They were an important source of information on jobs and accommodation. Thus, of the geographically mobile members of the sample, nearly half of them (twelve) had kin (parents and/or siblings) living in Luton at the time of the interview. The majority of the interviewees, therefore, were not physically separated from kin.[4] In this context, it was interesting to explore whether the interviewees led a home- and family-centred existence despite the close proximity of kin, or whether companionship and mutual aid was widely enjoyed. Moreover, it was possible to examine whether the interviewees were selective in their relationships with kin and especially with siblings. Finally, the extent to which they preferred to lead a home- and family-centred rather than a more communal existence could be explored as well. As we shall see, patterns of sociability varied according to gender and position in the life-cycle and the work roles associated with them. These two factors shaped the opportunities for, and constraints on, sociability with parents and siblings.

PRACTICAL HELP AND CHILD-CARE

All of the interviewees had maintained contact, to a greater or lesser degree, with their parents throughout their lives. Most notably, the two newly-married couples in the sample – Kim and Anthony Dodd, and Bridget and Stephen Underwood – maintained extensive contact with their parents and siblings. Without child-care and related domestic chores, they made frequent visits for a chat and coffee with their parents on their way to and from work, shopping, visiting others or any activities which found them close to the 'kinship home'.[5] Of course, they were able to 'pop in and out' because they had the time available to do so, but their parents' companionship and practical help, at a time when then were establishing independent households of their own, was very important.

However, the value of parents' and especially a mother's companionship and mutual aid was greater still among those young women who had temporarily withdrawn from the labour market to raise young children. While the four women concerned – Rita Aziz, Uma Kasim, Lisa Smith and Jane Bennett – had new, more demanding child-care and domestic responsibilities than before, they were able within these bounds to structure their day's activities. Thus, time was spent with mothers, sisters and sisters-in-law when they were available. Their companionship was significant at a time when the women felt somewhat isolated from 'the rest of the world' during the day and when everyone seemed to be at work. Furthermore, female kin were important for support at a time when child-care tasks were new and daunting. Jane Bennett, for example, recalled the arrival of her first child and the times when:

> I used to panic about doing things right and was forever on the 'phone to her asking her advice. Me and Mum have always been close, there's not much difference there. I don't always like the advice but I know I would get an honest answer. If she thinks you've done something wrong she'll tell you. She wouldn't say anything behind your back and I can say anything to her. She's not worried about upsetting anybody. I do mind sometimes but then she's my Mum, she must know best.

There was, then, a strong sense of solidarity between these interviewees and their female kin which arose from their common experiences of motherhood and the attendant duties. These findings confirm Oakley and Rajan's (1991) recent study of support between women and their female kin, although they also found that working-class women are not more closely involved with kin than their middle-class counterparts.

The daily lives of these young women, therefore, were far from privatised, even though they did not necessarily live in close proximity to female kin. While the form of contact with their female kin had changed in some instances, the content of their relationship had not. Indeed, the findings appear to substantiate the picture of female solidarity found by Roberts in her study of Lancashire in the early twentienth century:

> Working-class women did not live extensively within the confines of a nuclear family but were members of neighbourhood groups and extended families. These groups were of great importance in working-class lives, giving social and material support, and providing a strict system for establishing and maintaining social mores (1984: 169).

These types of 'small-scale practical support' illustrate

> the continuing importance for women to be able to call upon relatives to assist them with childcare and that this still is a key element in women's organisation of their daily lives, as it has been in the past (Finch 1989a: 31–2).

As Bell (1968, 1990) found among middle-class families, the extended family continues to play an important role in modern, industrial societies.

That said, these interviewees also made it clear that there were boundaries to the extent of contact with female kin. Like the other women of the sample, they attached considerable importance to their work roles – child-care and domestic responsibilities – in the household. Only when domestic tasks like washing, ironing, cooking and cleaning had been completed could they spend time with kin. Likewise, casual contact could be enjoyed as they went about their daily tasks like shopping or taking the children to school. Jane Bennett asked her husband to act as a go-between and curtail contact between herself and her sister-in-law because it interfered with the completion of domestic duties. While Jane still looked after her nephew when her sister-in-law went to work, she explained that

> I like to be left alone to get on with what I have to do. It got to the stage where Andrew was coming in from work and with a tiny baby as well it made it awkward. In the end he told her to stay away because he got fed up of coming home to do the housework. She was upset at the time but she stayed away. I don't get to see that much of her now even though she just lives round the corner. She lives her life and I live mine. I just see her twice a week when she brings her son round and picks him up.

Thus, while the physical harshness and time-consuming nature of domestic chores may no longer dominate women's lives as it did in the first half of the twentieth century (Slater and Woodside 1951; Spring Rice 1981), women's child-care and domestic responsibilities continue to structure their day-to-day existence. It dictates the opportunities for, and constraints on, seeking the company or assistance of female kin. Unromantic portrayals of female solidarity (Cornwell 1984; Roberts 1984; Yeandle 1984) also suggest that women's daily lives have been and continue to be shaped by their child-care and domestic roles in the family. As Roberts has argued:

> Working-class women had learned when young that their place was in the home: they might work outside it for greater or lesser periods; they could leave it freely for social or charitable excursions; their husbands and children might well help in its care and maintenance; but it was accepted by all that the ultimate responsibility for the home was theirs (1984: 125).

The influence of child-care and domestic demands on people's (especially women's) patterns of sociability with kin was evident throughout their lives.

COMPANIONSHIP

So far, attention has focused on the relationship between parents and adult children. All of the interviewees regarded their relationship with their parents, after their spouses, as the most intimate tie in their lives. Who they were – their personal identities – had been shaped by their parents. Intimacy and solidarity with their parents was born out of the ties of blood and their shared experiences of childhood and parenthood.[6] As Kim Dodd explained: 'My parents are my friends. With my parents I can just let myself go and be myself. I am a lot more relaxed with them.'

In this sense, their relationships with their kin, and especially their parents, were considered 'special'. This quality, as Finch suggests, derives from irrevocable membership of a family and the long history of the relationship and its emotional ties. They are 'special' because

> the fact that your family of origin (although not of course the family into which you may marry) are people with whom you have interacted over your whole lifetime builds into these relationships a dynamic which can significantly reinforce the social definition of kin as people you treat differently. In a sense, that applies even when the history of the relationship has been stormy – it remains a relationship with a long history and has distinctly strong emotions associated with it (Finch 1989a: 235).

The geographically mobile members of the sample also placed a 'special' premium on the companionship and support of siblings who lived in Luton. Their siblings, whom they had followed to Luton or who had followed them, appeared to replace absent parents. The migrants into the town often lived in close proximity to their siblings, passing on their knowledge of available jobs and housing from the area in which they themselves lived. Close proximity certainly facilitated sociability, allowing for fortuitous meetings when they used local facilities. Catherine Mayes, who lived within a few minutes' walk of her two sisters, said:

> My family is very important to me. We are very close. With my sisters and brother in Luton, we go out together for most activities: picnics, barbecues, shopping. If I go shopping I don't go out without some other family member.

Aziz Malik also described the process by which he came to live close to his brother, and the ways in which residential proximity enhanced communication with his parents in London:

> The reason why we bought this house in particular was that we wanted a house in this area as my brother just lives around the corner. So whenever my parents come it is nearer for them to visit us both. That's the whole idea.

This picture confirms the role of kin as carriers of information about jobs and accommodation (Anderson 1975; Grieco 1981, 1987; Hareven 1982; Mann 1973b). Moreover, it highlights the ways in which the geographically mobile may 'regroup', at least initially, in a new locale, especially where they do not have other companions (Willmott 1963). Finally, it throws light on the ways in which kin relations are sustained over physical distances. For these reasons, as Harris suggests: 'the individuals who inhabit a given geographical area are likely to be more connected by ties of kinship within the area than they are to people outside it' (1969: 136).

RESIDENTIAL PROXIMITY

At this juncture, the issue of residential proximity between kin should be considered further since physical closeness was a key characteristic of 'traditional' working-class communal living. As has just been suggested, some of the geographically mobile into Luton lived near to their kin and wanted to live close by. This was not necessarily the case with the residentially stable members of Luton and the surrounding countryside, although, on the whole, they liked to live within a reasonable distance so that contact was relatively easy to sustain.

There was no desire among the residentially stable interviewees to live close to their parents or siblings within Luton. Thoughts were turned instead towards the search for affordable housing, a home which was large enough for a particular family, one that was in good condition, in a respectable area and within a reasonable distance of kin, work and the main facilities of the town. Anyway, living in a different side of the town was not a constraint on sociability. Modern transport – cars and buses – made it easy to pop in and see kin and modern communication – the telephone – allowed them to talk as often as they wanted as well. While they might not share the same local supermarket or school, Luton was still small enough for fortuitous contact, especially in the town centre on a Saturday morning. John Farnham described how his life was interwoven with kin, even though they did not live in the surrounding streets. He recalled the time when both he and his father worked at the Vauxhall plant and he used to have lunch with his parents every day, and how a similar arrangement now existed with his daughter:

> She works round the corner and she often has lunch here. When I take Daphne to the hairdressers on a Saturday morning I often go

down to my daughter's home and wait for her there or I may call
on my brother and sister-in-law.

Referring to a time when his two daughters would no longer be living at
home, Peter Ibbotson echoed these sentiments:

As they get older I would like them to be within a reasonable
distance so we could keep in contact with them. So long as you can
see them, places are so easy to get to these days.

Once again, structural changes in terms of modern transport and communication appear to have altered the form of sociability with kin but not
necessarily the content of those relationships.

A little physical separation was seen in a positive light by many of the
interviewees. It allowed them to 'get on with their lives' as they saw fit.
Lisa Smith, at home with her young daughter during the day, enjoyed the
companionship of her mother and sister, but she also felt

If you live too near your parents, they expect to see you every day.
If you don't they want to know what's wrong. I wouldn't have
minded living on the estate but not too close. My sister lives very
close to my mother and she can't do anything without Mum knowing what she's doing. I like to have time to myself.

Distance gave her some freedom from her family and some degree of
choice about when she would see them rather than being forced, by close
residential proximity, to see them every day. She was less than keen to
embrace the closeness and solidarity associated with the 'traditional'
working class, or perhaps more appropriately, with ideal-types of the
working class at the turn of this century. These findings raise the question of whether the 'traditional' working class was solidaristic through
force of circumstance or by choice. At the very least, the data suggest that
neither studies of the 'traditional' working class nor the *Affluent Worker*
series fully revealed the diversity of patterns of sociability and norms and
values to be found among members of the working class.

SOCIABILITY AND EMPLOYMENT

Not surprisingly, the women's return to formal employment reduced the
time available to spend with female kin. While those women who
worked part-time could still meet female kin during the day (although to
a lesser extent than before), those who worked full-time could not. A
degree of regularity had to be introduced into sociable contact with kin.
Nevertheless, even though fortuitous contact might decline, they would
still see parents when they had some tangible free time. In other words,
the extent to which the women could socialise with their kin took a
similar form to their husbands' patterns of sociability.

It has long been assumed that men were largely isolated from the
main body of their kin until the post-war period, when they became more
home- and family-centred (Dennis *et al.* 1956; Goldthorpe *et al.* 1968a,
1969; Mogey 1956; Young and Willmott 1957; Zweig 1952, 1961). How-

ever, the men interviewees also remarked upon the intimate relations which they enjoyed with their parents and, to a lesser degree, siblings. The importance of sustaining regular contact with parents was emphasised by the men as well as the women interviewees. The ability to enjoy their companionship and help, however, was curtailed by the fact that they worked all day. Tiredness at the end of the working day also prohibited them from casually visiting kin, except occasionally. Thus, the men and women workers made a point of seeing their parents when they had some tangible free time away from paid work, which usually meant at the weekend or on another free day. Robert Edwards, whose parents lived in a small Bedfordshire village, disclosed, 'I think an awful lot of my mother and father. I see them every other weekend, usually on Sunday but depending on when I'm working.'

Like their wives, and by way of legitimating their life-styles, the men were largely content with the amount of time they spent with parents and siblings. They also emphasised the advantages of not seeing too much of kin – of being able to get on with their own lives as they saw fit – and the disadvantages of excessive sociability. As Colin Burgess indicated:

> I see my brothers and sisters and mother mostly at weekends as everyone is working. Everyone goes to my mother for dinner on Sundays and we 'phone my brothers and sisters in other places. I'm quite happy with the level of contact. You can see too much of them. Otherwise it gets on your nerves. The contact you do have is more friendly while if they're around all the time, it wears down the friendship. When we do see each other, we have a laugh.

Paid work, therefore, shaped the men's patterns of sociability with kin and increasingly their wives' social relations with kin as well.

Of course, physical separation influenced the form of sociability among those interviewees whose parents did not live within reasonable travelling distance of Luton. That is, resources such as the availability of money, transport and free time away from the daily routine of family life dictated the extent of contact with kin. Nevertheless, the interviewees who found themselves in these circumstances emphasised the importance of visiting their parents and of sustaining that contact over the years. For those with parents living reasonably close to Luton, weekly or monthly contact was feasible. Judith and Geoffrey Hayward's parents, for example, had both lived in a village outside Luton. Judith Hayward recalled the time when both of her parents were alive: 'We used to see them every Saturday. We often left the children with them and shopped locally. We did keep in close contact.' The twenty or so miles which they had to travel in their car was not perceived as a major constraint in fulfilling their obligation to their parents. The companionship and mutual support between parents and children remained strong irrespective of the physical distance between them.

For the Irish interviewees, obviously, such regular contact could not be sustained. Instead, contact was confined to yearly family holidays in Ireland, although they spoke to their parents more regularly on the telephone. Indeed, the intimacy of parental relationships over the years was sorely missed and the personal consequences of geographical mobility, especially long-range mobility in search of jobs and housing, was discussed with a tinge of regret. Their relationships with parents and siblings were particularly valued because the opportunities to see each other were constrained. There was no great desire to limit contact with kin voluntarily and to embrace a home- and family-centred existence.

Finally, three interviewees – Delia Burgess and Simon and Carol Sawyer – experienced almost complete isolation from parents. All three of them had moved to Luton from abroad. The sheer distance between kin militated against almost any contact. The money needed for such long-distance travel was the major constraint on contact, coupled with the time to make such travel and cost worth while. The interviewees were not more concerned with the material well-being of the conjugal family over and above contact with wider kin. They genuinely could not afford to travel such considerable distances. Not surprisingly, such isolation from parents and siblings was unwanted and their companionship was greatly missed. Delia Burgess had moved to Luton from the West Indies to marry after meeting her future husband while he visited his parents' home country. As she described: 'I don't get to see anyone at all. I've not seen them for six years. I would like more contact, obviously, but it's not possible with the money and distance involved.' Isolation from all of her kin was compounded by the difficulties of meeting new friends as she looked after two children during the day and tried to do most of her packing job in the evenings to pay the bills. Her great loneliness had placed a considerable strain on her marriage and more than once she had considered going home. Only her children kept her in Britain.

To a greater or lesser degree, therefore, sociable contact with parents was sustained throughout their lifetime, irrespective of physical separation and the associated resources of time and money necessary to travel. For most of the mobile interviewees, geographical mobility did not lead to the separation of the conjugal family from wider kin to the extent suggested by the Luton team.[7] As both Allan (1979) and Finch (1989a) have noted, there is no simple relationship between the form of a relationship – the extent of frequent sociability – and the nature – the companionship and mutual support – of a relationship. As Bell (1968, 1990: 20) also found, the extended family was alive and well among the most geographically mobile members of his middle-class sample even though rates of contact tended to be lower among them compared to the residentially stable respondents. The effect of geographical mobility on patterns of sociability is far from straightforward.

DECLINING SOCIABILITY

While the interviewees maintained contact with their parents, there was evidence of declining sociability with siblings over the family life-cycle. It was easy for largely unplanned contact to become increasingly sporadic. For the native Lutonians, for example, fortuitous sociability with siblings was still enjoyed, but the number of occasions when they visited each other's homes declined. Contact, therefore, could be highly irregular, with siblings not meeting each other for as long as three or four months.

The interviewees emphasised the constraints of paid and unpaid work on socialising with brothers and sisters. This begs the question of why contact with siblings declines over time but is maintained with parents. The answer lies in their shared position in the family life-cycle. Siblings who are close in age are usually constrained by a similar range of domestic and child-care responsibilities. Parents of adult children, on the other hand, have passed through the most demanding stage of the family life-cycle and have greater opportunities for sociability than have siblings. Unlike siblings, especially if both members of the household are working full-time, they are available for social contact. Anita Palmer, for example, worked the opposite shift to her husband at the Vauxhall plant. Their 4-year-old son attended a nursery in the day and one of them looked after him in the evenings. Anita saw little of her brother, contact being confined to 'the children's birthdays, Christmas and the holidays, because we work the same hours'. Julia Farrell reiterated these sentiments when she described the impact of paid and unpaid work on her daily life: 'With working full-time I feel tired. I just want to get on and do the domestic work and I have to look after the children.'

The interviewees could recall times when they had more contact with their siblings and especially when their children were young. Heather Jackson's sister lived in Luton, but she noted: 'I frequently see her in town where she works or when she is visiting my mother but not otherwise, I don't know why. We used to see more of each other when the children were younger and we all went out together.' In this instance, fortuitous contact was still enjoyed but the joint entertaining of children had declined. Their children had grown up and had friends of their own, while they themselves had returned to paid work.

As Allan (1979: 104) also found, sociability with siblings declines when parents are no longer alive. Parents play an important role as intermediaries in sustaining contact between siblings. Irene Cass recalled a time when her parents' house had acted as a 'meeting place' but since their death the situation had changed:

> We have grown further and further apart. I don't feel that I could just pop in on my sisters. I feel I would be intruding on them even though they would make me welcome. I don't feel I can just go up to their houses without prior notice. I just can't impose on them.

Even where they had been absent from the 'kinship home' for a number of years, the interviewees still perceived it as their home which they could visit at almost any time. It was the family home where they had all grown up and it was still open to all of its members. Casual visits to parents at the 'kinship home' were deemed acceptable, especially if they were keeping a watchful eye over ageing parents. It was not always acceptable, however, to 'pop in and out' of their siblings' family homes. They were independent households, whose members had busy lives to lead and into which they should not intrude too often.

Obviously, the interviewees expressed personal preference for particular siblings. Nevertheless, the decline in sociability with siblings was more evident among the men than the women in the family, who were able to see sisters, especially if they worked part-time. Those women who worked full-time expressed regret at not seeing more of their brothers and especially sisters. Their husbands, on the other hand, emphasised the positive side to declining sociability. They had less desire than their wives to socialise with siblings. Casual contact could still be enjoyed but only very occasionally. As Trevor Davis suggested: 'When you're married and settled down and you have your own family, you feel that you don't want to go over that much. You have your own life to lead.' For the men within this specific stage of the family life-cycle, there was evidence of a voluntary withdrawal from certain kin relationships. The husbands clearly saw their relationships with siblings in a different light from their wives. They wanted to be more self-contained as a household than did their wives. Finch (1989b: 98–9) found that gender differences in family relationships of this kind are especially noticeable in Britain, Australia and the USA compared with European countries like Germany, Austria, Hungary and Italy. In Britain it seems that maintaining contacts with relatives is the 'woman's business rather than the man's' (Finch 1989b: 99). Men and women play different roles in relation to kin.

Nevertheless, all of the interviewees felt that they could and would turn to their siblings in times of need. As family, they could be called upon without ill-feeling. They would not feel 'beholden' to siblings in a way that they might have done to neighbours or friends. After all, they might be called upon to help their siblings in the future as well. Judith Hayward described how she felt about going to siblings for help:

> If I need them, I could contact them. If I wanted my family for anything, we are close enough to go to each other. When my husband was ill my sister was there. They are there when you want them.

That said, the interviewees also stressed the importance of not requesting too much help from kin, be it siblings or parents. Yet again, they placed considerable importance on the independent working of the household. They disliked dependency intensely. Explaining the ways in which independence was preserved, Daphne Foulds recalled the support which she and her husband, Jack, had received in the past from his parents:

> My husband's parents were very good. They clothed our children when we were young, knowing we were struggling. We didn't have to ask for help but they gave it to us in a roundabout way so that we didn't have to ask for it. We do the same for the children without them having to ask for it.

The extent to which kin look to each other for assistance in an instrumental way has, of course, been a source of much sociological and historical debate (Anderson 1971: Roberts 1984; White 1986). It is now widely agreed that aid networks were prompted both by a willingness to help others in genuine need and an acute awareness that help might be needed in the future. Kinship assistance, in other words, operated as a form of mutual insurance. The interviewees themselves did not discuss mutual aid instrumentally. Rather, as Finch (1989) has rightly argued, reciprocity was and is an important dimension of kinship assistance, leaving no one feeling indebted or unequal to another. Independence, therefore, can be retained. The form and content of mutual aid between kin can be properly understood only in the context of kin relations and what those relations mean.

Overall, these findings suggest that siblings are an important source of companionship and support in adult life, although to a lesser extent than that between parents and their adult children. As with parents, the form and nature of the relationships between siblings varied betwen the men and women of the sample and across the family life-cycle. In other words, the data do not concur with Goldthorpe *et al.*'s (1969: 104) description of increasing selectivity among siblings or the reasons for that selectivity. Their survey data were unable to tap the process of privatism. Except for a small number of men, the interviewees did not consciously think of excluding siblings from their lives in pursuit of a life-style compatible with individual family well-being. Declining sociability was an unintended consequence of the changing opportunities and constraints which they faced as they passed through the family life-cycle interacting with their personal preferences for particular brothers and sisters. These structural factors shaped the interviewees' norms and values regarding sociability with kin. The pursuit of individual family well-being above everything else did not account for selectivity among siblings. Privatism, on this basis, was not in evidence.

Only indirect mention has been made so far of wider kin such as grandparents, aunts, uncles, cousins and so forth. It appeared that sociability with these relations had declined as well as the interviewees established independent homes of their own and their lives had become embroiled in the work needed to sustain the household. The importance of the three-generation family suggests, of course, that contact beween grandparents and grandchildren should be maintained. Many of the interviewees could recall regular contact with grandparents and with aunts, uncles and cousins (especially if they were close in age) to a lesser extent in their youth. Parents were important intermediaries, but as they had married and had their own families contact had declined. Bridget Underwood found that she did not see her aunt and uncle now that she was married:

> I used to visit them every weekend and just pop round for an hour. I haven't got the time, things just seem hectic. I come home and cook our dinner and weekends I mostly spend catching up with housework. I don't mind. Now that I'm married I'm more settled. I have my own home I suppose.

At the other end of the family life-cycle, Jack Foulds reflected on the fact that relatives had not been seen over the years: 'We were building a nest and bringing the fledglings up. We did not have time for cousins and that sort of thing especially if they lived out of town.' These findings confirm Morgan's 'picture of the kinship universe' as: 'one of increasing fuzziness at the edges and more definite, but still flexible notions of duty, reciprocity and closeness (with the possibilities of conflict) nearer the centre' (1975: 206-7). Sustaining the household, irrespective of standards of domestic comfort, structured the opportunities for, and constraints on, sociability with distant relatives.

RETURNING TO CARE

Finally, three interviewees – Heather Jackson, Angela Stone and Gerald Mills – were caring for elderly parents or a parent who lived alone. Angela Stone, for example, described the ways in which she catered for her elderly father:

> I do his washing and see him once or twice a week. Otherwise he does everything for himself. Then he comes round for dinner every Sunday… I don't have to worry about him. It will come to a point where I will have to look after him more but at the moment he is all right.

Similarly, Gerald Mills, as an only son, liked 'to see my Mum a lot, especially in the cold weather. I pop round to check she's alright, see how she is although she's not an invalid. She's quite independent. Mr Mills saw his mother every day and he and his two children regularly spent Saturday at her house while his wife was at work. His mother enjoyed the children's company and he pottered around the house doing odd jobs, maintaining the property much as he did at home. Like Mrs Stone, however, he emphasised his mother's independence in the same breath that he talked about the practical help he provided. Neither wanted to breach that independence until the time came for more substantial care.

Indeed, all of the interviewees expressed strong feelings of obligation and responsibility towards their parents as they aged. Even the youngest interviewees, still only in their early twenties, spoke on the subject with passion as they envisaged caring for their parents in the future. By supporting their parents, they were reciprocating the help which they had received from their parents in the past. It was a pattern of care which travelled both ways across the generations. In time, they hoped that their children would care for them. Of course, the ways in which a sense of duty translates into practice varies according to how strongly a person feels their responsibilities and the resources at hand to meet those obligations. For the three interviewees in this study, helping their parents to live in a reasonable degree of comfort meant they visited their parents numerous times in the week, if not every day. This help was particularly important as their parents grew frail, although companionship was obviously important, especially for a parent who lived alone. It also meant that they saw more of any siblings who shared, to a greater or lesser degree, the responsibilities of care.

The data confirm the wealth of literature on the 'new' role of kin, and especially female kin, in caring for elderly relatives (Allan 1985; Finch and Groves 1983; Ungerson 1987). It is a 'new' role in that demographic changes mean that people now live longer than previous generations. Moreover, to take the Griffiths Report (1988) as but one example, the responsibility of adult children to care for their elderly parents underpins much current social policy. These factors, along with numerous others, have shaped the emotions and feelings which the interviewees held on caring for their ageing parents. In other words, as Finch (1989a: 84) suggests, rather than families supporting each other less than in the past, the evidence implies that the feelings which people have for their family remain strong. Individual families have not become more self-reliant in the post-war period of prosperity than they were in the past. Contrary to the Luton team's findings, the daily lives of the interviewees of this study were closely bound up with the lives of kin.

CONCLUSION

The three-generation family remains an important source of intimacy and support which generates and sustains family solidarity. Geographical mobility and physical separation have changed patterns of sociability but modern forms of transport and communication provide different ways of remaining close to kin. Similarly, factors other than geographical mobility, like married women's increasing participation in the labour market, have altered patterns of sociability, but even then, going out to work often depends on the support of female kin (Yeandle 1984). Numerous structural factors shape the opportunities for, and constraints on, patterns of sociability with kin. Nevertheless, the evidence suggests that, on balance, the content of kin relationships and the meanings which people attach to them remain strong.

These findings weaken the central argument of the *Affluent Worker* series: that geographical mobility entails physical separation from kin and inevitably leads to a home- and family-centred style of life. Given that geographical mobility, as we saw in Chapter 3, often depended on the help of kin, it was not surprising to find that sociable contact between kin was, by and large, sustained over the life-cycle. Similarly, since separation from kin was not necessarily desired, neither was it surprising to find that the interviewees valued the intimacy and support of parents and, to a lesser extent, siblings.

Moreover, there was little evidence to suggest that the interviewees' daily lives were guided by a coherent set of working-class norms and values regarding patterns of sociability with kin. The men and women in the sample emphasised, instead, the opportunities and constraints which structured their day-to-day living. More specifically, they cited the impact of both paid work (employment in the formal economy) and unpaid work (child-care and domestic responsibilities) on their time. As we have seen throughout the chapter, patterns of sociability with kin did indeed vary according to the different work demands of men and women, as well as across the family life-cycle. The interviewees tended to justify and legitimise their daily lives against the background of this structural context, sometimes irrespective of any discontents or satisfactions which they felt about their lives. The work involved in sustaining the household dictated their life-styles and this was an inescapable fact of life.

In his subsequent work on social mobility, Goldthorpe (1980) emphasised the ways in which structural factors shape and pattern people's lifestyles and their norms and values and, in turn, are shaped by them. He found that where kin are in close proximity levels of contact are not significantly different between the middle class and the working class. While the working class is more likely to socialise with kin in their leisure time than is the middle (or service) class, this finding derives 'primarily from differences in the ready availability of kin rather than in normative orientations to kinship ties' (Goldthorpe 1980: 156). Class differences in the organisation of sociability are small and are due to 'class linked constraints on kinship relations of a physical kind, associated chiefly with differences in the degree of dispersal of kin, rather than in sharply divergent class norms' (Goldthorpe 1980: 156). 'Normative orientations' alone could not explain the different patterns of sociability between the middle class and the working class.

This is not to suggest that the interviewees had no normative guidelines whatsoever, or that these were completely unimportant. Two broadly defined normative guidelines can be identified. First, the interviewees were concerned for the well-being, emotional, economic or otherwise, of their parents and siblings. Thus, the family was an important source of intimacy, companionship and mutual support. Secondly, the interviewees greatly valued the independence of their own individual household and the households of their kin. They felt that they should not undermine the day-to-day workings of the household. Hence, the interviewees did not seek extensive sociability with kin, and support was given in such a way as not to undermine household independence.

Whether this fierce adherence to household independence is evidence of a 'new' form of working-class individualism as Goldthorpe and his colleagues argued is, of course, a moot point. The historical evidence suggests that independence and respectability have been part of working-class culture since the end of the nineteenth century, if not before. As Robert Roberts (1974) argued so forcefully in *The Classic Slum*, the independence and respectability of the individual family household was of paramount importance, especially to working-class women at the turn of the century. He also insisted that independence and respectability were by no means the exclusive property of labour aristocrats.[8] Once again, it seems that the ideal-type construction of the 'traditional' working class is, as Proctor (1990: 175) suggests, 'a millstone around our understanding of working-class history'. Working-class independence has a long history. In other words, working-class norms and values have not changed over the course of this century as much as Goldthorpe and his colleagues argued. Despite structural changes, continuities persist.

NOTES

1. According to portrayals of the 'traditional' working-class community (Dennis *et al.* 1956; Hoggart 1958; Young and Willmott 1957) sociability with kin and long-standing friends was the 'stuff of life', for companionship was one of the few pleasures of a harsh life. The weighty decision to move away from kin and friends in search of high standards of living, according to the Luton team, must be placed in this context. Whether the companionship of the community was as important as commentators including the Luton team, presumed or whether it was an artefact of the romanticism surrounding the solidaristic working class will be considered in the course of this book.

2. As will be seen in the course of the chapter, the Luton team placed great emphasis on the impact of physical separation on 'traditional' working-class life-styles.

3. The Luton team's arguments regarding geographical mobility and physical separation from kin actually sit rather uneasily with their empirical findings on kin as a continued source of companionship and support.

4. A further two interviewees, both originally from Eire, had had kin living in Luton in the past. Marion Capel had followed her sisters from Eire to Luton but they subsequently moved to other parts of Britain. Leslie Kent lived with his aunt and uncle in Luton when he first moved to Luton but they had died some years ago.

5. The term 'kinship homes' is taken from the Luton team (1969: 89), who, in turn, derived the term from Hubert (1965).

6. This is not, of course, to suggest that conflict between kin never occurs.

7. The Luton team (1969: 101–2) acknowledged the impact of paid and unpaid work on people's daily lives but placed greater

emphasis on the 'new' consumer aspirations of the 'new' working class.

8. This argument also implies that some members of the so-called
labour aristocracy drank heavily and gambled away the family
income. See, for example, Davies's (1992) oral history of issues
of poverty, leisure and gender in Salford in the early part of the
twentieth century.

5

SOCIALIBILITY WITH NEIGHBOURS

While geographical mobility has changed patterns of sociability with kin, the three-generation family remains an important source of intimacy and mutual support. Companionship and aid are given and taken, however, without undermining the independence of the individual household. This chapter explores the form and content of the interviewees' patterns of sociability with neighbours. Are neighbours, by dint of their close residential proximity, significant companions? Is extensive sociability with neighbours the bedrock of working-class communality? What is the role of neighbours in people's daily lives?

Contrary to the Luton team's findings, it will be argued that neighbours are a significant source of companionship and mutual support in themselves. They are not merely substitutes for absent kin. Women neighbours, for example, are often important friends, especially if they are looking after their children at home all day. Patterns of sociability with neighbours varied between the men and women in the sample as well as across the family life-cycle according to the demands of paid and unpaid work which they faced. These structural factors shaped the opportunities and constraints for sociability with neighbours and the form it took. They explained why there was little evidence of extensive sociability with neighbours often associated with the 'traditional' working-class community as well.

The interviewees' normative guidelines reinforced and legitimised the structuring factors patterning sociable contact with neighbours. The interviewees viewed most of their neighbours as acquaintances who just happened to live in close proximity. They expected and preferred their neighbours to be friendly rather than friends. They wanted some distance so that they could get on with their own lives without unwarranted interference. Yet again, therefore, the interviewees attached considerable importance to the autonomous working of the household and the paid and unpaid work required to uphold its independence. Their daily lives centred on the household. In this sense, the households of this research occupied their own time and space.[1] Against this background, the interviewees did not share a strong sense of solidarity with their neighbours. A weak sense of familiarity and similarity – of working for a living, being 'respectable' rather than 'rough' and sharing geographical origins – was in evidence. Race, however, was the basis of schism. Neither extensive sociability with neighbours nor working-class communality could be found.

THE DEMISE OF COMMUNITY

The Luton team argued that geographical mobility led to the dispersal of people who might otherwise have spent much of their lives in close proximity. Many of their respondents, for example, had lived in their present accommodation for only a short period of time. A fifth of the total sample (21 per cent) had lived in their accommodation for not more than two years, while just under half (44 per cent) had not done so for more than five years (Goldthorpe et al. 1968a: 151).[2] Against the background of a growing population and an extensive house building programme, the Luton team found 'considerable residential mobility among 'natives' and migrants alike' (Goldthorpe et al. 1968a: 151). There was little evidence to suggest that a stable working-class community, based on relative stability and social homogeneity, or the communal solidarity it engendered, existed in Luton at that time.

Even so, the Luton team found that sociable contact with neighbours was still enjoyed. In terms of the respondents' 'associational patterns', neighbours were as significant a source of friendship as were kin. Indeed, for some migrants, they acted as substitute attachments for absent kin. They were certainly more important as a source of companionship and support than their colleagues from work. Unlike the white-collar couples, their working-class respondents, therefore, confined their friendships to kin or neighbours (Goldthorpe et al. 1969: 89). The Luton team argued that their respondents' 'friendship relations' were 'for the most part neither guided by middle-class norms nor aided by middle-class social skills' (Goldthorpe et al. 1969: 91). They went on to argue:

> To the extent that kinship could not provide the foundation of their social life, these couples turned most readily for support and companionship to those persons who, as it were, formed the next circle of acquaintances – that is, to persons living in the same neighbourhood. Thus, in much the same way as working-class people in traditional contexts,they would appear to build up their friendship relations largely on the basis of social contacts that are in the first instance 'given'. Actually *making* friends – through personal choice and initiative – from among persons with whom no structural relationships already exist could not be regarded as at all a typical feature of their way of life (Goldthorpe et al. 1969: 91, emphasis in original).

They also noted that husbands and wives had quite separate and not joint friends. Women sought the company of family and neighbours while men had a few local friends as well as workmates. They argued:

> that among our manual sample there is still maintained, although in some obviously attenuated form, the traditional working-class

pattern of wives having important sets of friendship relations based essentially on family and neighbourhood and largely segregated from their husbands' networks; while in turn, the latter, unlike the white-collar workers, still sometimes find it possible to have a number of 'mates' recruited from the locality, as well as from work, with whom they typically associate independently of their wives (Goldthorpe *et al*. 1969: 92).

On the other hand, the white-collar husbands interviewed by the Luton team had no regular friends which they did not share with their wives. On this basis, they concluded that there was little evidence of an assimilation into middle-class patterns of sociability but a process of privatisation instead. Thus, despite geographical mobility, the Luton team stressed the continuing importance of neighbours in their working-class respondents' lives. Indeed, they suggested that neighbours grew in significance if kin were not readily available.

While the Luton team did not provide very full details on the length of time which the geographically mobile members of their sample had lived in Luton, the evidence suggests that they were relatively recent migrants to the town. On the other hand, while half (thirty two) of my sample had been geographically mobile into Luton, they were, on the whole, an established group of residents. The length of residence in the town ranged from six to forty-nine years. Looking more closely at the geographical history of the interviewees, thirty of the 'migrants' had lived in Luton for ten years or more, while twenty-five of them had lived in the town for fifteen or more years. Indeed, many of the 'migrants' had spent the majority of their lives in Luton. They had moved to Luton as young people in search of employment and affordable housing. Moreover, they were an established group of people within the town as well. While the length of residence in present accommodation ranged from five months to thirty-two years, the majority of the interviewees had lived in their present homes for a considerable period of time. Eighteen couples (thirty-five interviewees), for example, had lived in their homes for ten years or more. Thus, many of them may have lived alongside neighbours for a considerable time.

Against this background, what was the nature of the interviewees' patterns of sociability with neighbours? Did they enjoy companionship with neighbours who, although they were not necessarily long-standing friends, were in immediate proximity? Did the women and men enjoy distinct groups of friends in the neighbourhood? Were neighbours more important to the migrants than to the native Lutonians? Were there any norms and values which governed their patterns of sociability? Again, the findings will be discussed in terms of the women's and men's patterns of sociability across the family life-cycle, since work roles associated with gender and position in the family life-cycle structured the opportunities and constraints for sociable contact with neighbours. The interviewees' normative guidelines – keeping neighbours at a distance to retain the independence of the household – can be understood only in the context of these limiting factors.

SOCIABLE WOMEN

The two young, newly-married couples at the beginning of the family life-cycle – Kim and Anthony Dodd, and Bridget and Stephen Underwood – had lived in their new privately-owned homes for a relatively short period of time. Since all four of them worked full-time, they had not developed friendships with their neighbours to any great extent. They were not a source of companionship and mutual support. As native Lutonians, this did not concern them because they had friends – previous school friends or other young people with whom they had grown up – in reasonably close proximity.[3] They could easily ring them up or drive around to their houses if they needed anything, unless it was terribly urgent and immediate help was necessary. Kim Dodd, for example, had come to know two of her husband's school friends and their wives very well. They were joint friends and she explained their greater importance than neighbours:

> I suppose it is nice to be friendly but I'm not worried about having friends round here. I have a couple of friends in the next estate. I borrow things from them and they borrow things from me.

In these instances, neighbours were largely insignificant. Joint friends in reasonably close proximity were important sources of companionship and mutual aid instead.[4]

However, as the Luton team found, the majority of women in the sample valued (or had valued) the company and support of women neighbours. The women who for various reasons were at home for most of the day and those women who worked only a small number of hours enjoyed frequent casual contact with some of their neighbours. Invariably, they socialised with other women in similar circumstances to themselves. They had met when using the local facilities like the corner shop or supermarket or, through their children, as they used the local clinics and schools. Friendships had developed within this structural context. In this sense, they were 'given', although personal preferences dictated if the relationships developed into friendships.

The company of other women in reasonably close proximity and in similar circumstances to themselves was highly valued by the women who were responsible for young children and who found their activities were confined by child-care and domestic commitments. Jane Bennett, who looked after her young daughter on a full-time basis, lived next door to a woman who also looked after her children at home all day. She explained how 'She pops in here if she's bored and I pop in there if I'm bored. We drink coffee, smoke fags and not a lot else.' It's terrible really.

Women neighbours were also an important source of support if it was needed. Help was often needed with child-rearing responsibilities. Lisa Smith had met her friend Marion as she struggled onto the bus with her pram and they had 'got talking'. Now, as a firm friend who shared similar problems, she did not feel uncomfortable about turning to her for help.

> I was very ill when I had the last baby and Marion came in every day to see that I was O.K. When I am more pregnant, Linda and Marion will come in every day to help me look after the baby.

This picture of sociability between women is not unlike the findings of Young and Willmott's (1957) study of the 'traditional' working-class community in Bethnal Green. The women's kinship and neighbourly relations were inextricably bound up, irrespective of whether they were migrants to the town or native Lutonians. Neighbours were not more important to the migrants than to the Lutonian women. However, the women of this study relied on the companionship and support of only two or three friends living in the streets around them. They did not have extensive networks of women neighbours in immediate proximity with whom they spent their time. Of course, the small group of women neighbours derives from the fact that many married women are engaged in formal employment outside the home for part if not all of the day. There are fewer women available in the locality with whom women may share their time. Indeed, although they had kin and neighbours as companions, the young women conceded that they were very lonely (and looked forward to a time when they could return to work). As Abrams also found in his study of neighbours:

> For the women, especially those tied to the home by young children, neighbours who were also friends made up a major part of their social network. It might be argued, too, that for many of them the neighbours were a vital source of friendship and that their helping function was often secondary (Bulmer 1986: 63).

Furthermore, there was little evidence of extensive sociability between the women friends which Young and Willmott (1957) described at length. As with kin, sociable contact with neighbours could be enjoyed only after domestic and child-care tasks had been completed. The efficient functioning of the household was all-important. Returning to Jane Bennett, she stressed: 'In the morning, I like to get the housework done so the rest of the day is my own. Janice often knocks on my door and asks if I've finished. If I have we might sit in each other's houses for a couple of hours.' Echoing these sentiments, Karen Osborne, who worked for two hours at the local school every lunchtime, suggested:

> I'm not really one for going into people's houses and I never was. Well, in the daytime, I like to get on with my work and get the house clean. I don't mind who comes into me in the afternoons or at night-time. I like to get everything done before one o'clock and then I go out to work.

The perceived demands of both paid and unpaid work left little time for extensive sociable contact with neighbours. Sociability was not unfettered. This picture falls far short of the portrayal of the working-class community in Bethnal Green in the 1950s, but then Young and Willmott's account has been subject to sharp criticism. Cornwell's (1984) re-study of Bethnal Green, for example, also emphasised the ways in which domestic and child-care responsibilities were limiting factors on sociability. In other words, the picture of eternal 'cups of tea and women gossiping together at the doorstep' was largely a 'myth' (Cornwell 1984: 24).

For the most part, it was these same women who supported elderly neighbours. Being in the locality for all or part of the day, they had come to know elderly neighbours who lived alone and/or those in poor health. They were happy to assist by shopping for them or by picking up a prescription as they completed their own household chores. The interviewees stressed that giving practical help was the basis of their contact. They were friendly acquaintances rather than friends. Much closer attachments were formed with women of their own age and in the same stage of the family life-cycle in the vicinity. Marion Capel spoke of an elderly neighbour who 'is a single lady who pops in and out and we chat across the fence in the summer more. She is more dependent on us for company and help than we are on her.'

Examples of informal care, therefore, were found among many of the women and their neighbours. However, practical help was not provided by the women exclusively, since husbands were often subsequently involved in the maintenance of a neighbour's property and other DIY tasks. Husbands, then, might also come to know elderly neighbours in the locality as their wives enlisted their help with large, sometimes physically demanding, tasks. The kind of support each partner provided, therefore, reflected the 'gendered' division of domestic responsibilities elsewhere. These instances of practical help and informal care between both women and men neighbours concur with other research into neighbourly relations and assistance (Bulmer 1986; Willmott 1986).[5]

SOCIABILITY AND EMPLOYMENT

However, as women pass through the family life-cycle, previously close attachments in the vicinity tend to dwindle. As children grow up and lead increasingly independent lives of their own, women's lives are less bound up with those of other women neighbours. This is especially the case if they return to formal employment. Paid employment, coupled with domestic and child-care responsibilities, is a constraint on sociable contact with intimate neighbours. While the distinction between patterns of sociability of women in and out of paid work should not be overstated because many women work part-time for a small number of hours, previously close attachments can be difficult to sustain. Moreover, returning to formal employment provides women with the opportunity to meet new friends. Angela Stone worked part-time as a nursing auxiliary but her hours and the time spent travelling to work meant she was away from home for most of the day. She described the process of declining sociability as her children grew up and she returned to paid work:

> When you have young children, you make friends easier with being up at the school but you don't when they're older. When the children were younger, I got to know friends around the district through the play groups and school. I did get to know them well but we seem to have lost contact as the children have grown up. We all have jobs and we have tended to drift apart.

Of one 'old' friend in particular she felt:

> We know where each other is. The problem is time since I'm out working all day. I work with people now so obviously I'm meeting more people every day. I don't miss her because I've made a new set of friends at work.

Circumstances, therefore, changed and many of the women found themselves unable to maintain sociable contact with other women in the vicinity. They were less involved in each other's daily lives and the intimacy of the previous closeness was lost.

These constraints were reiterated by a number of the women workers in the sample, although they stressed the different ways – both negative and positive – in which employment was a limiting force on sociability with neighbours. Irene Cass, with no children, had always worked full-time and she noted the restrictions on her time. Even when she was free, it was not always the case that others were available as well. It was easy to miss neighbours, despite close residential proximity, if they started and finished work at different times of the day. As she explained:

> I go out in the dark and come home in the dark sometimes. Everybody goes home, gets dinner and settles down for the evening. People don't knock and go and see each other in the evenings.

In other words, irrespective of close proximity, households occupy their own time and space which do not always coincide with those of other households. This finding concurs with Abrams's study of neighbourly relations, where he found:

> One group for whom neighbouring ties were notably weaker were married couples both of whom were working, where the wife did not have time to foster contacts with those living nearby (Bulmer 1986: 84).

Domestic work further constrained the opportunity to meet and come to know the neighbours for the women who worked full-time in particular. As Bridget Underwood reflected:

> I suppose I should see more of the neighbours and relax and find the time but I haven't got the time. On Saturdays and Sundays, I want to catch up with all the work. If I had neighbours coming in, I wouldn't be able to do anything.

She stressed the ways in which domestic work structured her time but she also preferred to complete her household tasks rather than spend time with her neighbours. The smooth running of the household came first. Similarly, other interviewees had little desire for sociable contact with neighbours when they returned home from work. The home was a 'haven' from the outside world, where they could relax and enjoy 'peace and quiet'. Kim Dodd described how her work as a cashier in a betting office involved 'socialising all day. When I get home, I don't really want to go round to someone's house and start chatting again. By the time I get home from work I've had enough. I just want to relax.' As we shall see in Chapter 8, leisure activities included watching television, reading newspapers and knitting. They were home-centred activities which did not usually involve sociable contact with others outside the household. For many women, the home was a 'haven' after a 'hectic' day (Devine 1989). This was the preferred option.[6] Once again, structural factors and the interviewees' normative guidelines were closely intertwined.

Of course, the impact of paid work on men's patterns of sociability with neighbours has long been noted (Dennis et al. 1956; Young and Willmott 1957; Zweig 1952). For the men interviewees, being way from home for most of the day meant there were not many opportunities to get to know people well in the locality. They might see neighbours at the weekend or in the summer evenings but not much beyond that. As Matthew Smith explained: 'I just don't see them. Even in the summer I come in from work and I have my dinner. I might work in the garden and then I go to bed. I don't see much of the neighbours.'

He had lived in his house for a relatively short period of time. Other men, however, met and chatted to their male neighbours as they went about their daily lives such as cleaning and fixing the car or maintaining the outside of their homes. They borrowed tools, gave advice and practical help. As Malik Aziz suggested: 'I might see one or two of the men at weekends or sometimes in the evening when I'm in the garden. I popped in to Terry to help him fix a burglar alarm or I might help him with the car. I'm always glad to help.' In this context, the men had come to know each other and 'chatted about life'. Richard Graves spoke of one particular neighbour in these terms: 'Brian across the road is a very chatty bloke. We borrow things from each other, chat about allotments, decorating, all the normal things. He is a friend. I could rely on him for help.'

Unlike the women who were based at home, these men enjoyed more casual and non-committal patterns of sociability. To a large extent, they were less dependent than were their wives on the companionship and help of neighbours. Comparing neighbourly relations between himself and his wife, Andrew Bennett reflected upon this point:

> They talk about things already that you wouldn't talk about with other people until you had known them for two or three years. The

wife is at home all day and they go in and out of each other's houses. That might be the reason, I don't know, but they seem to get down to the nitty, gritty things. Maybe that's the way women do things. Women find it easier to talk to other women. Blokes get on with general things; sports, cars and that's it, but women get to talk about everything. They really have got to know each other.

The men interviewees, therefore, had come to know one or two men who lived in close proximity to themselves. Like their wives, they met when they spent time in and around the home and when they used the local facilities. Socialising with neighbours, however, was casual and non-committal because most of their day was spent in work beyond the home and they wanted to relax quietly at home after a hard day's work. There was neither the time nor the inclination to socialise extensively with other men in the locality. The acquaintance of one or two men locally was satisfactory in these circumstances.

Many of the interviewees' neighbours were fellow workers, although they did not usually work alongside each other in the plant. Recognising a face from Vauxhall acted as a starting point for conversation between neighbours which might lead to greater familiarity. Gerald Mills suggested he knew a Vauxhall worker to a greater extent than other neighbours along the road precisely because they had their employer in common:

> I know a few blokes to say hello to and to have a chat. I don't know them more than that. I know one bloke a bit better who is a convenor at Vauxhall. We often have quite long chats.

Michael Clark also knew those neighbours who were Vauxhall workers better than other men in the locality:

> It helped when we moved in that there were a couple of people from Vauxhall living around here. It not so much broke the ice but it made a path for us to get started.

Sharing the same employer and living in the same street increased the likelihood of these men knowing each other. In this structural sense, they were 'given' rather than chosen acquaintances. On the whole, however, relations with other men in the locality did not go beyond general friendliness and practical help. They were not simply ready-made friends. The evidence also suggests that people's work and non-work lives are not distinct from each other as the Luton team suggested. This issue will be taken up further in the following chapter on sociability between colleagues from work.

NORMS ON NEIGHBOURS

So far, the opportunities and constraints on patterns of sociability with neighbours have been emphasised. At this juncture, it is interesting to explore the interviewees' attitudes and feelings towards neighbours. In this context, it is possible to see why long-standing friendships were not found among those interviewees and their neighbours who had lived alongside each other for a considerable number of years.

Despite the various patterns of sociability which were found among the interviewees, the similarity in the perceived role of neighbours was striking. The interviewees were in agreement about acceptable levels of sociability with neighbours. Particular stress was placed on the fact that neighbours are people who just happen to live in close proximity. Neighbours are not automatically intimate friends simply because they live close by. As Dhooge (1982: 117) also stressed, people do not become 'close friends merely because they live next door or in the same street'. Again, they might be 'given' attachments in the structural sense but the interviewees still exercised choice as to whether or not they became more than acquaintances.

Given physical proximity, it was important to live in relative harmony with each other. The interviewees did not want fraught relations with people who lived nearby. As Brenda Richards explained: 'it is important to be friendly to the neighbours. You get a better atmosphere if you just say "hello". The right note was struck if neighbours were considerate and there was some 'give and take'. Robert Edwards felt this was especially true with children, when a little extra understanding was needed:

> If a ball breaks a window, that's a child for you. You just have to accept these things. A good neighbour is someone who has a bit of give and take in them If you wanted, you could pick fault with everything all day.

In other words, the interviewees recognised that close physical proximity could lead to conflict as much as communality. It was for this reason that it was important to keep a reasonable distance from neighbours while, at the same time, remaining on good terms. Robert Roberts (1974) also found this fear in Salford in the early twentieth century, although he portrayed denser neighbourhood relations than was evident from this study.

Good neighbourly relations were sustained if people were 'friendly'. As others have found (Bulmer 1986; Keller 1968; Wallman 1982, 1984; Willmott 1963), 'friendliness' rather than 'friendship' is an important dimension of neighbourly relations. Abrams defines 'friendliness' as 'a medium of casual sociability and routine interaction; stylised, superficial, at once outgoing and restrained: it corrects by presuming separation' (Bulmer 1986: 29). This general friendliness allows people to lead their own lives. Excessive friendliness only leads to unwanted interruptions in the smooth running of the household. As Richard Graves noted: 'Good neighbours keep to themselves. They go about their own business and don't worry about what you are doing.' Cautious and restrained relations with neighbours, therefore, allow people to lead their own lives as they see fit. In this way, the independence of the household, to which the interviewees aspired, could be maintained.

FRIENDLINESS

The majority of the interviewees, therefore, enjoyed a general friendliness with neighbours. They 'passed the time of day' with neighbours but their relations did not extend beyond this routine interaction. They could not name any particular neighbours who were close friends. This type of neighbourly relationship was especially evident among those interviewees who had passed the most demanding stages of the family life-cycle. The women may have had closer attachments with other women locally when the children were young and played together but their children no longer generated these wide contacts in the locality.

Thus, even though many of them had lived in their present accommodation for a considerable number of years, their relations with neighbours were not intimate. Relations with neighbours were good but there were clearly defined boundaries to sociable contact. Timothy Merrick suggested:

> I know lots of people in the area and along the road who I might stop and chat to. I can't walk from one end of the road to the other without being stopped. It's very friendly and a good area to live in. Everybody has their own family and does their own thing and we don't discuss things with everyone. It is only occasionally that we might pop in and out. I don't believe in being too friendly and living in each other's houses. That causes trouble and I would get fed up with it. We don't overdo it.

Over the years, Daniel Knight had come to know of lots of people:

> Everybody nods to you although I don't know them. I see them every morning when I walk up the road to get the paper. I don't know who they are but we just pass the time of day and all that.

Residential stability generated a sense of familiarity in the sense of coming across the same faces over the years. As Keller (1968: 115) also argued, length of residence does strengthen attachment to an area – both to people and place – but given the nature of neighbourly relations, the strength of that attachment should not be over-stated. Familiarity did not amount to the binding communal solidarity associated with the 'traditional' working class.[7]

However, the areas in which they lived were fluid. Just as they were familiar with faces in their immediate locality, they also came across people whom they did not know at all. People had married, moved and died, and there were many new faces. As Pauline Graves stated: 'people that I knew all my life have either died or moved away and then new people come and you don't get to know them'. It took time to get to know newcomers to the area, especially if they were young couples out at work all day. Again, the interviewees spoke of having very little free time which overlapped with the spare time of neighbours. Carol Sawyer reflected:

> Most of the neighbours I considered friends have left now. I got to know one woman when I moved in and she was already living

there. We knew each other for a long time before the children were born. We used to pop in and out but she lives too far now for us to see each other but we speak on the 'phone. I don't know so many now with people moving and new ones coming in who I don't know.

Barbara Wright found:

I haven't got to know some of the new people since I've been working. I mainly know the people that I got to know over the years and they have lived here most of the time. Those are the ones I have anything to do with now.

Getting to know new neighbours well was difficult if they did not share the same stage in the family life-cycle. Both of these women had passed through the most demanding stage of the family life-cycle and they had had close neighbours as friends in the past. Back in paid work, however, they were not available and, anyway, they had friends at work or their old neighbours to turn to for companionship and support if they wanted it. The interviewees, then, had a sense of both change and continuity.

There was some sense of regret that more familiar neighbours had moved away and new neighbours had moved into the area. Not surprisingly, the women rather than the men expressed these feelings of loss. Recalling a neighbour who had become a close friend, Teresa Mills described how she felt when she moved to a new council property:

She was great and I was ever so sorry to see her go. If ever I had a problem, she'd always help. She knew if anything was worrying me. She was that sort of person and would say 'come in and talk'. It's funny her not being there, out in the garden. I had a little cry at the time. Sometimes, I can't beleive she's gone although she has. Sometimes, I feel like knocking on the door and I realise she's not there.

Despite this attachment to people and place, the attachment was not as binding as to exclude any thoughts of moving. The housing aspirations of the interviewees – for bigger houses, for more bedrooms for their children, for a garden and so forth – to be discussed in Chapter 9, certainly led the interviewees to think about moving. The interviewees also strongly asserted that they would move out of Luton altogether, leaving family and friends behind, if the livelihood of the family were threatened by unemployment. If tangible opportunities existed elsewhere, Andrew Bennett, who was a native Lutonian, felt:

It's hard to start all over again once you've known so many people. I still see people about from my school days. It's harder to make friends when you're older. When you're at school, you are always going to meet new kids but you're not going to meet new blokes when you're working.

None the less:

If there was a job or something like that I would move. I've got my wife and children to think of. If it meant that Vauxhall shut down and I had to move I would.

The well-being of the household was paramount, even if the social costs were harsh.

Finally, the interviewees were asked to describe the area in which they lived and the people who lived alongside them. The purpose of the discussion was to ascertain the extent to which the interviewees experienced a sense of homogeneity or heterogeneity from the locale in which they lived. Did the interviewees live in a community in which people were perceived as similar to each other? Did they feel a sense of solidarity with their neighbours?

Unlike the Luton team's respondents, the interviewees were not asked for detailed information on their neighbours' precise occupations. The interviewees gave the impression that they lived alongside other manual workers with their reference to Vauxhall workers as neighbours. However, rather than describe them in explicitly class terms, they referred to themselves and to their neighbours as 'ordinary working people'. No distinction was made, for example, between working-class and middle-class occupations or manual or non-manual employment. People around them were considered 'ordinary' in the sense that, irrespective of their occupations, they were in paid work outside the home for much of the day. They worked to secure a reasonable standard of living for the household. Most men's and women's lives were devoted to this end. The interviewees identified similarities between themselves and their neighbours but only in a very broadly defined way.

Nor were the locales in which the interviewees lived described in explicitly class terms. Areas were divided into 'rough' and 'respectable' (or 'ordinary') areas. This distinction has, of course, been noted elsewhere (Kuper 1953; Roberts 1974). A 'respectable' area was defined by the interviewees as one where, it could be said, people enjoyed some degree of material comfort. Most importantly, people strove to achieve that comfort. Thus, houses were invariably owned by the occupiers, well maintained, clean and tidy. The people were also 'respectable' in their manners and dress, and children were 'properly' looked after rather than allowed to 'roam the streets' for long periods of time. They were able to live in relative tranquility with their neighbours. Speaking of good neighbours, Sheila Ibbotson suggested that 'they keep the houses tidy and nice, which you want'.

'Rough' areas were associated particularly with houses and facilities which were not well maintained by the residents. The reputation of 'rough' districts was also bound up with the reputation of specific families within them, where men were violent husbands, noted fighters, football hooligans for example. The interviewees quickly equated 'rough' areas with the council estates of the town. This view was shared by the home owners and council tenants of the sample alike. Council estates suffered from petty crime such as theft and vandalism, which only added to the squalor of the area. They were 'unsafe' areas in which to live. Indeed, Luton suffered from a high rate of crime while this study was being conducted.[8] Describing the council estate in which she grew up and where she had no desire to live, Lisa Smith described the area as 'rough', adding: 'There are a lot of fights in the pub and drunkenness. There are a lot of burglaries and it's not safe any more.' Similarly, Andrew Bennett had lived in what he considered to be a rough area, on the edge of a council estate, for a year:

> I lived over there because it was the only house we could afford but I didn't want to go over there. It was a nice house but I didn't like the area. I never liked the area because of what I had heard in the newspapers. I didn't know what I was dealing with and I was wary of who was there. Luckily, we were at the back end where the private housing was. The centre, where the council houses are and the shops, that's where all the trouble is.

Both interviewees, along with other members of the sample, were keen to live in what they defined as 'respectable' rather than 'rough' areas. This aspiration for domestic respectability was, of course, also found by Gray (1976) and Crossick (1978) among the labour aristocracy at the turn of the century. Other evidence (Roberts 1974; White 1986) also suggests that such aspirations were not confined to a particular section of the working class – the labour aristocracy – whose boundaries have always been heavily contested anyway, but were to be found among other working-class families as well.[9] Such aspirations, therefore, are far from new. The evidence suggests, then, that aspirations for material well-being, respectability and independence are not especially novel characteristics of the working class as a whole in the post-war period.

RESPECTABILITY AND RACISM

The interviewees also described Luton and its residential areas in terms of the different groups of migrants who had settled there. They were able to identify the regrouping of people of the same geographical origins and, employing popular stereotypes, the subcultural differences between them. This was not surprising since, as has been suggested, the geographically mobile members of the sample lived in relatively close proximity to kin where possible. Thus, the interviewees easily described how Luton, once a 'boom' town with plenty of employment opportunities, had attracted people from a variety of parts of Britain, Ireland and other countries. They explained how the Welsh – miners from South Wales in search of jobs – had been one of the first waves of immigrants into the town in the 1930s, although their distinct identity was declining as the original migrants died and the next generation were native Lutonians. They were followed in the 1940s and 1950s by the Scots and Irish, and eventually in the 1970s by migrants from India, Pakistan and other parts

of the New Commonwealth. Like Stacey's (1960) Banbury, districts in Luton were easily equated with different waves of migrants from particular places.

The way in which the interviewees saw themselves and others – either as natives or migrants – in Luton was influenced by this significant identity which they readily used (Devine 1992a). Being a native Lutonian, for example, was an important identity and a status to which many of the interviewees referred. The older native Lutonians of the sample identified themselves as a small and dwindling group – 'we're pretty hard to find, you know, there's not many of us left' – with deep roots in the town. They fondly recalled Luton before it had expanded to cater for the large influx of people. As Anita Palmer suggested:

> Luton has changed a lot. If I went down the road I was out in the country. All these new estates didn't exist but they were built for all the people coming into the town. I find that people who move to different towns tend to find their own people. They mix with lots of people but they still stay very close to their own.

In this instance, finding 'their own' people referred to a social group with a shared sense of place.

In their discussion about the 'demographic characteristics of Luton *as a community*', Goldthorpe and his colleagues (1968a: 151–2, emphasis in original) noted that native Lutonians were often outnumbered by migrant families whose 'subcultural differences' gave them 'a certain distinctiveness'. The interviews, and the debate in the *Luton News* about natives versus migrants, led them to argue that 'it was apparent that in Luton consciousness of such differences was quite a definite influence on individuals' attitudes and behaviour towards each other' (Goldthorpe *et al*. 1968a: 152). Despite the intervening period since the Luton team conducted their interviews, this 'consciousness' was apparent among the interviewees in this research. Against the background of their geographical origins and histories, this social identity – a regional identity – influenced the way in which they defined themselves, how they viewed others and interacted with them.

However, in one important respect, Luton and its residents were different from the town which the Luton team, and Zweig (1961) before them, visited in the early 1960s. In the late 1960s and 1970s, a fresh influx of people from the New Commonwealth – Indian East Africa, Pakistan, Bangladesh and the Caribbean Islands – moved to Luton. It is estimated that these ethnic minorities amounted to approximately 14,000, or 8.8 per cent of Luton's population in 1986, rising to 21,000, or 13 per cent if children born in Britain and belonging to these households are included *(Report of the County Secretary: Luton Law Centre)*. Like the migrants from other parts of Britain and Ireland, they invariably moved to Luton in search of a livelihood – a job and a home – although the circumstances in which they moved were far less favourable than those of earlier migrants to the town. Like them, they relied on kin and friends to find them jobs, temporary and then permanent accommodation and, as a consequence, regrouped in Bury Park near the centre of the town as well. Again, kin and friends were an important source of companionship and support as the small number of interviewees from abroad in the sample explained.

Discussion on the influx of people of different origins into the town, and of the Indian or Pakistani communities in particular, led almost all of the British/Irish interviewees to assert their British/Irish identity, their Christianity and, of course, their whiteness. While the distinctions between people of different geographical origins within Britain and Ireland had been drawn light-heartedly, the divisions between them and 'coloured immigrants' were discussed in distinctly pejorative terms. Racist beliefs were prevalent. They spoke of the decline of the residential areas in which they lived with the proliferation of families living together in the same house. The 'immigrants'' poor housing and the way in which they stayed so closely to their family and friends indicated their failure to assimilate themselves into the town in particular, and into Britain in general, and to adopt the respectable life-styles of the British. As one native Lutonian explained:

> Luton has changed and not for the better. I don't like the coloured element that has come in. It has been overdone. I'm not against them. I've worked with many of them and some of them are very nice but there are too many here for the size of the town. Then again, they've done what others have done and come for the work in the town. I just don't like it.

In a similiar vein, George Stone suggested:

> Too many overseas people have congregated in the area. Of all the towns with jobs, they have congregated in small patches, spreading out taking over all the shops and ruining the area. Bury Park used to be a different area with nice houses, gardens and trees but now it looks as if a bomb's been dropped. If we went to their country, we would have to abide by their rules. They have bought in their own rules, their own culture.

Similarly, the interviewees from abroad closely identified with their country, its people and culture. Of course, being non-white was a particularly important dimension of this identity, heightened by racial conflict in the town. As Anhok Kasim, from Kenya but of Indian origin, who had moved to Luton with his parents in the 1970s, recalled:

> When we first came here, there were a lot of racial attacks on people. There were a lot of National Front people, a lot of problems. Basically, we never used to go out of the house after 7 p.m. It was better to stay at home.

He now felt that Luton had changed for the better, one reason being that 'a mosque has been built which is good for us being Muslims. It is somewhere for us to go and pray.' He also identified himself as British, referring to India, his parents' country of origin, as an ex-colony, and still closely linked to Britain as a Commonwealth country. Thus, in a town of migrants, a national/regional and ethnic identity rather than class identity was uppermost in the interviewees' minds when asked to describe the place and the people alongside them.

CONCLUSION

In opposition to the Luton team's findings, the findings of this study suggest that neighbours are often an important source of intimate relations and mutual support, especially for women in the most demanding stage of the family life-cycle. That said, neighbours are not as significant a source of companionship and support as kin. There was no evidence to suggest that neighbours act as a substitute for absent kin among the geographically mobile because few of the interviewees moved without kin in one way or another. If anything, neighbours are less significant to the mobile than the immobile, as families regroup in a new locale.

The interviewees, however, were not engaged in extensive socialising with their neighbours as is often associated with the 'traditional' working class. Rather, the interviewees' work roles in sustaining the household structured the opportunities and constraints on sociable contact with neighbours. The different work roles of the husbands and wives and changes across the family life-cycle explained the variations in sociability which were found among the interviewees. Thus, women confined to the home and the immediate vicinity while they were caring for young children invariably met other women who shared these circumstances. They often became close companions. On the other hand, men away from the home for the majority of the day did not have substantial contact with neighbours. Only one or two neighbours became friends, while others remained casual acquaintances. Structural factors, therefore, played an important part in shaping and re-shaping the men's and women's relations with neighbours during their lives.

Structural factors alone, however, cannot explain the interviewees' patterns of sociability. They held normative guidelines which defined acceptable and unacceptable levels of sociability with neighbours. They viewed neighbours as acquaintances but not necessarily as friends. Given physical proximity, it was important to be on good terms, but distance was important as well if people were to be allowed to live their own lives independently and without unwanted interruption from others. Once again, the interviewees attached great significance to the autonomy of the individual household. These normative factors appeared to legitimise the structural opportunities and constraints on the interviewees' daily lives and to be shaped by them. Clearly, however, a more complex process of interaction was in operation, as their normative guidelines in turn shaped the impact of structural factors on their lives as well. Indeed, the interaction both of structural factors and normative guidelines explained why length of residence had only a limited impact on patterns of sociability with neighbours, facilitating familiarity rather than communal solidarity.

Finally, it was found that the interviewees had a sense of similarity (although not necessarily solidarity) with their immediate neighbours and others in the locality. However, the interviewees did not define the people around them and the place where they lived in explicitly class terms. More broadly speaking, they defined themselves and those around them as 'ordinary working people' living, for the most part, in 'respectable' residential areas of the town. National, regional or ethnic identity were more powerful than class identity. These expressions of both solidarity and schism were, perhaps not surprisingly, particularly powerful in a town with an economic and social history of rapid population growth facilitated by migrants from other parts of Britain as well as abroad.

These findings sit somewhat uneasily alongside the Luton team's portrayal of a privatised working class, but they do not fit comfortably with descriptions of the 'traditional' working class either. It appears that stability and homogeneity do not necessarily lead to the kind of all-embracing communal solidarity envisaged by numerous writers (Dennis *et al.* 1956; Hoggart 1957; Young and Willmott 1957; Zweig 1952) and uncritically accepted by the Luton team. The instances of the combination of circumstances and factors which might have engendered the 'traditional' working class were probably few and far between, being confined to heavy primary and manufacturing industries around which isolated communities existed. In turn, the findings raise some awkward questions about the Luton team's account of the demise of the 'traditional' working-class community, and the emergence of home- and family-centred life-styles and individualistic socio-political proclivities. How is solidarity socially constructed? Did working-class solidarity ever simply emerge from the communal sociability of the 'traditional' working-class community? Social historians (Kirk 1991) and sociologists (Pahl 1984) are agreed in arguing that 'traditional' working-class sociability should not be automatically equated with social and political solidarism. In his conclusion to his study of working-class households in the 1980s, for example, Pahl states:

> The argument that a certain section of the social structure has some privileged access to affective solidarity, which determines its consciousness in a distinctive way, has as much validity as dividing up the population into classes based on those who sing choral works and those who do not (1984: 232).

The following chapter will explore the form and content of sociability with colleagues from work which, for commentators on the 'traditional' working class, was the bedrock of solidarity.

NOTES

1. As Giddens (1984: xxii) also notes, social interaction is located in time and space.
2. Despite the importance which they attached to mobility, the Luton team did not specify the length of time which the migrants had lived in Luton in any detail.
3. Originally, the *aide-memoire* included a section on sociability with friends. However, it was dropped from the list of topics to be discussed because the majority of interviewees could not think of friends who were not kin, neighbours or colleagues from work. Only the younger members of the sample made reference to a distinct category of friends who were invariably old school friends or friends from the locality of the 'kinship home'.
4. Once again, this example shows the ways in which modern forms of transport and communication have made it easier to contact people than was the case in the past.
5. Men's and women's lives, therefore, are not as distinct as the Luton team suggested but are inextricably bound up with each other.
6. There has been some debate as to whether the home is a 'prison' for women while it is a 'haven' for men (Robertson Elliott 1986; Saunders 1990a). The young women of the sample felt their lives were restricted while they were at home looking after their children full-time. However, for those women in formal employment, the home was a 'haven' after a hectic day. Thus, as has been noted elsewhere (Devine 1989), the meaning of the home varies during a woman' life, depending especially if she is economically active or inactive.
7. Yet familiarity was not limited to the immediate area in which the interviewees lived. Some of the native Lutonians still knew neighbours close to the 'kinship home'. They, of course, enjoyed fortuitous contact with kin, old and new neighbours and colleagues from work when they went shopping in the town centre. They might not know these people well but they knew their faces. There was, then, a sense of belonging to Luton based on this familiarity of faces and the place itself.
8. Bedfordshire was ranked sixth of the thirty-five metropolitan forces for reported crime in 1985, with 16 per cent of that crime occurring in Luton town centre (The *Herald*: 30 October 1986; The *Citizen*: 27 November 1986). The problem of crime in Luton was frequently discussed in the local newspapers and the interviewees were particularly concerned with the high rates of burglaries in the town.
9. Similarly, looking at the issue the other way around, social historians (Roberts 1974; Davies 1992) have found plenty of evidence of skilled labour aristocrats who were 'rough' in the sense of drinking heavily and gambling, thereby denying other members of the household a reasonable standard of living.

6

SOCIALIBILITY WITH FELLOW WORKERS

Kin and neighbours are important sources of companionship and mutual support. Neighbours, for example, play an important role in women's lives during the most demanding stages of the family life-cycle, although attachments are not always sustained like relations with female kin. Yet, sociability between the interviewees and their neighbours was not extensive. The demands of paid and unpaid work were limiting factors on sociability which in turn shaped and reinforced the interviewees' normative guidelines regarding sociability and the independence of the household. This chapter explores the interviewees' experiences, attitudes and feelings about socialising with colleagues from formal employment beyond the workplace. Before doing so, however, the interviewees' orientations are examined briefly. Is instrumentalism an accurate description of their orientations to paid work? What are the sources of instrumentalism? Do people shun sociable contact with fellow workers in preference for a materially comfortable home- and family-centred lifestyle?

The findings indicate that the interviewees socialised with their fellow workers in their free time. They enjoyed occasional excursions with their work group and regularly enjoyed the intimacy of one or two colleagues from work who had become friends. These friends invariably shared the same stage in the family life-cycle. Once again, the evidence suggests that paid and unpaid work structured the men and women's patterns of sociability differently, and the way in which it shaped the opportunities for and constraints on sociable contact was constantly changing across the family life-cycle. Thus, contrary to the Luton team's findings, the interviewees' daily lives were not entirely family-centred to the point of excluding all sociable contact with colleagues from work. Nor did an instrumental orientation to work account for the interviewees' patterns of sociability. Indeed, an instrumental orientation to their jobs was found to be a source of solidarity rather than schism among the interviewees.

That said, the interviewees were not engaged in the kind of extensive socialising with fellow workers in the free time associated with the 'traditional' working class. To repeat: paid and unpaid work militated against extensive sociability with colleagues from work for the men and women interviewees alike. Moreover, the interviewees, for the most part, were not unhappy with the level of contact with their friends and acquaintances at work. They valued their independent lives instead. The interviewees' normative guidelines, it seemed, legitimised the structural forces shaping their patterns of sociability. In other words, the interviewees' lives were neither family centred nor communal.

FROM SOLIDARISM TO INSTRUMENTALISM

As was suggested in Chapter 2, the Luton team addressed two rival accounts of the demise of the occupational community, characterised by the declining significance of work as a central life interest and the concomitant decline in extensive sociability and solidarity with fellow workers, as embourgeoisement took hold. In industrial sociology, Blauner (1964) argued that technology undermined work group solidarity and fostered greater integration and identification with employers than had existed previously. The decline of an occupational community had consequences for workers' non-work lives as well. No longer socialising with a tightly-knit group of fellow men, workers led home- and family-centred life-styles directed towards individual material well-being instead. Technical developments at the workplace, therefore, pushed men into a privatised existence.

While Blauner emphasised changes in the sphere of production, proponents of the decline of the occupational community and embourgeoisement in Britain dwelt on the pull of consumption. In other words, increased standards of living in the post-war period of prosperity easily lured men away from the company of fellow workers into a home and family-centred existence (Zweig 1961: 27). Increased consumption generated an instrumental attitude to work in that workers were interested only in their wages to meet their ever-spiralling material aspirations (Zweig 1961: 12).[1] Again, the consequences of these processes was a decline of the solidaristic occupational community and extensive sociability with fellow workers in and outside the workplace (Zweig 1961: 82). As work was no longer a central life interest, men's work lives and home lives were quite separate. Paid work was discussed at home between partners only 'as a way to get money and so as a way of purchasing the standard of living they would attain' (Mogey 1956: 132).

Goldthorpe and his colleagues found that their respondents' experiences of work were unrewarding, unsatisfactory and lacking in intrinsic value. Men viewed their jobs in purely instrumental terms, as a means of securing a wage rather than as a site for fulfilling 'expressive and affective needs' (Goldthorpe *et al.* 1968a: 41). However, the Luton team stressed that instrumentalism was an orientation to work which originated from men's non-work lives and not from their experiences of paid work. It was fuelled by the economic boom and the consumption aspirations which it engendered, leading men to forgo the intrinsic rewards of work in search of material well-being instead. As we know, of course, the

Luton team argued that workers were prepared to move away from kin and long-standing friends in search of highly-paid manual work to meet their new consumer desires. Like British embourgeoisement theorists, the Luton team underlined changes in the domain of consumption rather than production in their account of instrumentalism.[2]

The Luton team also noted the impact of an instrumental orientation to paid work for men's non-work lives. Given that work was no longer valued for its own sake, it was not the site of significant social relationships. The Luton team found little evidence to suggest that workers were members of work groups with a strong sense of solidarity. Few workmates were considered friends. Relations with fellow workers in paid work were restrained, taking the form of a 'camaraderie' which provided 'diversion and possibilities of tension release within an often highly taxing work situation' (Goldthorpe et al. 1968a: 60). As a result, low levels of sociability were found among their respondents and their fellow workers beyond the factory gates. Even those workmates who were considered friends were seen outside work in 'semi-casual or purely casual ways or not at all' (Goldthorpe et al. 1968a: 56). They preferred to keep their work and non-work lives quite separate. Paid work, therefore, was 'insulated' from other parts of a man's life (Goldthorpe et al. 1968a: 61).

Overall, the Luton team emphasised the conscious choices which men exercised in search of satisfactions in their non-work lives. Men and their families embarked on definite careers which led them to look for highly-paid work in a calculating fashion. (Goldthorpe et al. 1968a: 116). They did not look for intrinsic work satisfactions or rewarding relationships with others in the work situation. They did not want the company of workmates in their leisure time. Rather, they adopted a home and family-centred life-style. The Luton team concluded:

> Work, that is to say, tended to be devalued in other than its economic aspects; the family rather than work was for these men their central life interest...To the extent that his non-working life is committed to his immediate family, the individual is the less able, and the less motivated, to enter into involvements which might interfere with his family life through placing seriously competing claims upon his time and energy. And, further still, it is also the case that a home- and family-centred mode of existence is one clearly more compatible with a concern for maximising the economic returns from work than with an orientation to work which embodies important wants and expectations of a non-economic kind (Goldthorpe et al. 1968a: 155).

The solidaristic orientations of the 'traditional' working class had given way to instrumentalism. Work was not a central life interest and source of identity (Dubin 1956) but was valued only for its extrinsic, rather than intrinsic, rewards. While the occupational group of 'persisting social

relations' between fellow workers had been 'responsible for the rein-
forcement and reaffirmation' of 'social bonds' in the past (Dennis *et al.*
1956: 79), social relations with colleagues from the workplace were no
longer valued. They were not the preferred companions outside work.
Once again, the Luton team stressed the interconnection between
instrumentalism and privatism.

THE DEBATE ON INSTRUMENTALISM

As was noted earlier, numerous commentators (Argyris 1972; Brown
1973; Daniel 1969, 1971; Goldthorpe 1970, 1972; MacKinnon 1980; Whelan
1976) debated the Luton team's key findings on instrumentalism. A
somewhat trenchant debate ensued between Daniel (1969, 1971), who
emphasised the importance of experiences at work in shaping attitudes
to work and work relations, and Goldthorpe (1970, 1972), who insisted
on the importance of non-work correlates on instrumentalism. Beyond
the stalemate between the two protaganists, however, commentators
agreed that both work and non-work factors interacted with each other to
produce an instrumental orientation to work. As Brown recently argued:

doubts have been expressed as to the extent to which orientations
are shaped solely or mainly by non-work situations and experiences: yet if they are influenced in part by workplace experiences
the technology and structure of the employing organisation must
be granted a much greater explanatory importance than
Goldthorpe and his colleagues gave them (1988: 47).

The 'structural properties' of a person's work situation (Newby 1977:
119), therefore, inform industrial attitudes and behaviour as well as prior
orientations to work. More recently, for example, it has been argued that
the increasingly international nature of markets, which has witnessed a
further loss of control over paid work, also contributes to an instrumental
attitude towards paid work (Newby *et al.* 1985: 93). The sources of
instrumentalism, in other words, are many and varied.

Debate also centred on the form and content of instrumental
orientations to work. Numerous studies (Beynon and Blackburn 1972;
Blackburn and Mann 1979; Brown 1973) of industrial workers rejected
the neo-classical assumptions of the 'orientations to work' approach
(Gallie 1988: 14). They failed to find the clearly and coherently expressed
instrumentalism evident among the Luton workers. Again, a consensus
of opinion emerged to the effect that workers are instrumental but they
are not as single-minded or as narrowly focused in the pursuit of economic rewards as the Luton team suggested (Brown *et al.* 1983).
Instrumentalism does not preclude instrinsic concerns, nor is it all pervasive. Again, Brown (1988: 48) concluded that the orientations approach
had value in underlining the social construction of workers' industrial
attitudes and behaviour, but the uses of the framework, with its inad-
equate account of constraints, were now limited.

The notion of instrumentalism has been challenged still further recently. In their sample survey on the British class structure, Marshall and
his colleagues (1988: 207–8) found that nearly two-thirds (64 per cent) of
their respondents viewed their jobs as more than simply a way of earning
a living. The overwhelming majority (82 per cent) of them found their
work enjoyable, over a third (36 per cent) recognised work to be an
important site for socialising with other people, while just under a quarter (24 per cent) found their jobs presented them with opportunities to
use particular skills. That said, the responses were obviously shaped by
social class. Well over half (63 per cent) of semi- and unskilled male
workers viewed work as simply a means to an end, as did just under a
half (48 per cent) of skilled male workers (according to Goldthorpe's class
schema). From these findings, Marshall *et al.* (1988: 210) conclude that
working-class instrumentalism is evidence of the fact that

> where proletarians do treat work simply as a source of income,
> more commonly they do so because they lack sufficient skills to
> secure a more interesting job, or because they are trapped in labour
> markets offering only a restricted range of job opportunities (1988:
> 210).

In other words, the structure of the labour market rather than pecuniary
orientations to work from outside the workplace account for working-
class instrumentalism.[3]

Marshall *et al.* (1988: 215) also found considerable amounts of sociability between fellow workers in their free time.[4] Just over half (54 per cent)
of their respondents considered some of their workmates as friends, the
overwhelming majority (82 per cent) of them seeing these people socially
outside work. Once again the answers were heavily influenced by class,
since members of the working class was less likely to socialise with
workmates who had become friends than their service-class counterparts
(67 per cent compared with 91 per cent) Despite these class differences,
however, the Essex team conclude that

> What seems to us to be striking about the data is…the extent of the
> coincidence between relationships formed at work and those pur-
> sued in spare-time activities. Given the degree to which residence
> has become dissociated from local sources of mass employment in
> post-war Britain, it is striking indeed to find that half of those in
> employment can number friends among their workmates, and that
> over 80 per cent of these friendships are subsequently pursued in
> non-work contexts. There is scant evidence for structural privatism
> in this finding at least (Marshall *et al.* 1988: 216).

Of course, Marshall and his colleagues readily concede that their
survey data have their limitations. They are unable to provide any detail,
for example, on patterns of sociability among fellow workers in general
and working-class workmates in particular. What are the opportunities
and constraints which structure working-class patterns of sociability

with colleagues from paid work? How might those opportunities and constraints vary across the family life-cycle? In what contexts do fellow workers meet, and what significance do people attach to their relations with colleagues from paid work? Their survey was unable to unpack these issues.

These issues have been neglected with regard to women in particular. Discussion of the 'traditional' worker invariably focused on men working in exclusively male occupations (Dennis *et al.* 1956; Tunstall 1962; Walker 1950; Zweig 1952). It was certainly the case, as Alexander (1976) points out, that female employment was less visible than male employment since women were often engaged in paid work at home, in other people's homes in the case of domestic service, or in small workshops rather than large factories in the nineteenth century. However, many commentators largely assumed that employment was not an important dimension of a woman's social identity. On the contrary, it was accepted that women were defined in terms of their role in caring for their husbands and children in the home. As a consequence, accounts of the demise of the 'occupational community' focused exclusively on the movement of men into the arms of the immediate family in the home. Yet married women's increasing participation in the labour market over this century suggests that they have been moving out of the home and local community (Franklin 1989), and that the workplace is an important site of social interaction for women. Rather than view work in strictly pecuniary terms, women enjoy the sociability of the workplace more than men (Cavendish 1982; Coyle 1984; Marshall *et al.* 1988; Martin and Roberts 1984; Pollert 1981). Once again, therefore, the form and content of sociable contact with fellow workers, be they men or women, need to be explored further. The rest of this chapter explores these issues by considering in turn the patterns of sociability of the men and women interviewees.

MEN AND INSTRUMENTALISM

All of the men worked full-time at the main Vauxhall plant in Luton. With the wide age range of the interviewees, their length of service with the company ranged from three to thirty-four years. On average, the men had worked for Vauxhall for seventeen years, the implication being that, unlike the Luton team's respondents, the majority of them were long-standing employees of the company. Some of the older men of the sample described their previous low-paid jobs and how they had had to work long hours to earn a decent wage on which they and their families could survive. Lawrence Atkinson had worked as a cutter in Luton before entering Vauxhall and he explained the decision to get a job with Vauxhall:

> I worked for seven years as a cutter. I was the only employee. I left when I asked for a rise but didn't get one. I'd worked very long

hours as the pay was very low on a flat week and I felt cheated. Money was important in going into Vauxhall. I also thought about the pension. In Vauxhall, they had an established pension scheme which you just joined and the company took a contribution from your wages. I was making sure that my wife and family would be secure.

Working for a large company which offered secure wages, a favourable pension scheme and other entitlements was an opportunity which he could not afford to miss. This was especially the case for three of the older men – Richard Graves, Kevin Jackson and Daniel Knight – who had experienced job insecurity, redundancy and short bouts of unemployment over the early part of their working lives, and two of the younger men – Anthony Dodd and Colin Burgess – who had been unemployed at a time of record levels of unemployment in the mid-1980s. Again, the data suggest that members of the working class were making the best of employment opportunities which arose in the post-war period of prosperity and were not rampant pecuniary instrumentalists. There is little evidence to suggest that the 'traditional' working class would not have taken the opportunity for secure, well-paid manual work if it had been available to them as well.

The only cases of strongly pecuniary orientations to work, if they may be called that, were to be found among those men who had given up apprenticeships for the high wages which Vauxhall offered. As Robert Edwards explained:

I'd done three years of an apprenticeship to be an electrician. I just got fed up and left. One day, me and a mate went there for a job for a joke. We got the job and I've been there twenty years since. It's been no joke.

Mr Edwards had subsequently regretted the decision to give up his apprenticeship because he was 'fed up' with it rather than anything else. As we shall see, work at Vauxhall offered few instrinsic rewards.

The decision to work for Vauxhall was also the source of regret for Peter Ibbotson, who had qualified and worked as a gas fitter in London. Originally, he had gone into Vauxhall as a 'stop-gap as we needed the money' when he and his family moved to Luton in search of affordable housing. However, the good wages had meant that it had never been worth giving up the job, especially when his family was growing up. In some respects, he had been trapped by his earlier decision to work at Vauxhall and he still entertained the possibility of 'returning to gas work' even though he had worked for the company for nine years. Any instrumentalism had certainly diminished over the years. All of these circumstances were far from the favourable opportunities available to the Luton team's sample of predominantly young men, although Goldthorpe et al. did not collect very detailed information on the work histories of their respondents. We do not know if any of their respondents had experienced unemployment during their working lives or if they had changed jobs in anticipation of redundancy.[5]

The men worked in a variety of skilled, semi-skilled and unskilled jobs in different departments, and their experiences of paid work, therefore, varied as well. Some of the men enjoyed aspects of their skilled jobs. Leslie Kent, for example, described himself as 'very content' with his 'good job' as a cutter on the trim shop. The men who worked as production operators on the track, however, certainly found the work monotonous and the fast pace in which they had to complete their tasks a strain. Anthony Dodd had started work as a production operator at Vauxhall after eighteen months of unemployment and he felt 'lucky to have a job'. At the same time, he also said: 'I've hated this job since the first day I started and I'll hate it until I finish.' Anhok Kasim also worked on the track and he found:

> Work is very tiring. I used to be on the side feeding the track and I was always ahead of them and could take it easier. Now, they've put the old ones on those jobs and the young ones on the track. You can't go anywhere. You can't see anyone. You can't talk to anyone. You stay where you work. You can only say 'hello'.

Indeed, many of the interviewees complained that the pace of work had increased in the factory over the last few years. Discipline was much tighter than it had been in the past and it was increasingly difficult, for example, to talk to fellow workers as they went about their tasks.

More importantly for all the men, however, were the alienating conditions of factory work in general. The noise of the machinery, the dirt of the factory, the heat and the lack of natural light meant that working in a factory all day was, purely and simply, miserable. Merely working in these conditions was tiring even if the work tasks in themselves were not exhausting or unrewarding. As Peter Ibbotson remarked: 'work was tiring for just being there'. It was for this reason, among others, that the interviewees did not want their children, especially their daughters, to work in a factory. Their very conditions of work generated an instrumental orientation to work and while the company had offered them good wages in the past, working in the car industry certainly had its drawbacks as well.

MEN AND SOCIABILITY

Some of the men worked alone, some worked alongside a small group of men, while others worked with lots of other people on the track. Irrespective of the size of the work group, however, the men's patterns of sociability varied across the family life-cycle and according to the demands of paid and unpaid work placed upon them in sustaining the household. Many of the younger men of the sample, for example, met their fellow workers to play a sport, the most popular being football and fishing.

Andrew Bennett spoke enthusiastically of his hobby which he shared with a number of fellow workers:

> I play five-a-side football every Friday with my workmates and we have a good time. A lot of the blokes used to play football at school and so we had an inter-section football match at work. We decided to take it up regularly to get fit because everyone was complaining that they were not fit to play. We've stuck it for seven months. It's a good laugh. Everyone has a chance to see how good they are. We don't just do it to win, just to run hard, see how fit we are and to play.

On the other side of the coin, some of the older men in the sample explained their low levels of socialising with younger men with reference to their different hobbies. As John Mills suggested:

> We have the occasional function but we have different interests. The younger ones play squash together and go out with their girlfriends. We just don't go to the same places.

However, as was the case with Stephen Underwood and his love of fishing, these activities took them way from home and family only once or twice a week during the sporting season.

These sporting activities often generated contact with other Vauxhall workers extending beyond the immediate work group. This was especially the case where the men pursued their hobbies through a club organised by the company. There was a fishing club and members were able to use a number of waters owned by the company. These Vauxhall workers were casual acquaintances whom the interviewees met only when they used company facilities. Stephen Underwood spoke of Vauxhall workers in these terms:

> I see them when I go fishing. I go to Vauxhall water so I see all the Vauxhall workers. I haven't been for a while but as soon as I go fishing again, they'll say 'hello, how are you, long time no see'. If I don't know them, it only takes five minutes.

A shared hobby, therefore, brought the men into contact with other Vauxhall workers but only on a very casual basis for their company was enjoyed in the context of the hobby. They did not appear to socialise in other contexts with these men. They were not a closely attached group who enjoyed spending a lot of their spare time together. It was the hobby which took away them from 'family time' rather than contact with a group of Vauxhall workers.

Socialising with workmates and their wives and children was found, however, when the men knew their fellow workers from other contexts.[6] As Grieco (1987) found, the roles of kin, neighbour and fellow worker sometimes overlapped. This was especially the case among the young, native Lutonian men of the sample who knew workmates from school or the neighbourhood in which they had grown up. Michael Clark spoke of a workmate who had been a neighbour when he was young:

I went to school with him. We're really good friends and we went to their wedding. They often come to dinner. We see them at weekends and go out for drinks. The wives have got to know each other too.

Neil Palmer spoke of a friend whom he had known for many years and who also worked at the Vauxhall plant when he explained: 'We meet for lunch and play games and dominoes but I've known him for a long time anyway. We played cricket together in our youth.' Anita Palmer added:

They have young children so we visit each other's homes on a Sunday afternoon. When you have children, you mix with couples with children. You do the same kind of thing being in the same situation as themselves. We went with them to a fireworks display for example.

These companions were of a similar age and shared the same position in the family life-cycle. They shared similar preoccupations as well as opportunities and constraints on what they could do with their free time. These friendships had been sustained over the years and they had come to incorporate wives and children, too. They were joint friendships which were not detrimental to the family. These men were not isolated from their workmates even if they only socialised with them occasionally rather than on an extensive basis. They were neither privatised workers nor traditional workers in their patterns of sociability with fellow workers.

For many of the men, however, sporting activities had dwindled with age and, more importantly, they had had to do as much overtime as possible to support their young families. Many of the older men in the sample recalled a time when paid work almost completely dominated their lives, when their wives were not in formal employment, their children were young and there were numerous bills to pay. This was true of the men currently in this stage of the family life-cycle, albeit with less opportunity to do overtime in a depressed economic climate. They had responsibilities as the 'major' breadwinner of the family. Speaking of his workmates, Martin Farrell suggested: 'They're married men, with wives, families and homes. You have to live like a married man, not like a bachelor, and look after your home and your children.' The meaning of marriage for the interviewees and its impact on their life-styles will be discussed more fully in the following chapter.

Nevertheless, the men were not entirely isolated from their fellow workers. Occasional social activites like visits to a theme park or zoo with wives and children were mentioned. These excursions were planned to cater for all members of the family but especially the children. It was a way of extending good relations at work, being able to meet family members and 'having a chat'. They were able to enjoy the company of fellow workers and their families away from work and work concerns. As Michael Clarke noted:

That's a bit of socialising with the workmates but it's not really a socialising friendship. It's just more of a group activity to extend our workmate relation- ship outside the factory but not really a friendship sort of thing.

For the most part, however, the men emphasised the different constraints on sociability with workmates. They did not share the same interests or they did not live in close proximity with fellow workers. As Timothy Merrick said:

Some of the people live in places like Milton Keynes and I don't see them around Luton. The people I work with, we do go out for an occasional dinner or drink but it's not the case of casual meetings in the pubs because they don't live in Luton.

Furthermore, their normative guidelines legitimised these structural constraints. The men preferred to come away from the factory and leave their workmates behind. After all, they worked together all day and they did not want to spend more time with colleagues when their working day had ended. They wanted to go home and relax with their families. Daniel Knight felt that 'Once I leave Vauxhall, that's it as far as I'm concerned.' Similarly, Leslie Kent reflected:

People don't have much to do with each other outside work. In work, we get on well except one or two. It's an exception to find contact with workmates outside work. They keep themselves to themselves. I've no aversion to contact with workmates. I've never had call to communicate, not on a regular basis. I'm very contented with home life, being on my own. I've had no inclination to be in contact with workmates.

Edward Cass also argued: 'I carry on my life and they have their own lives, it's as simple as that', while Richard Graves noted that he, along with his fellow workers, liked doing their 'own things at weekends'. In other words, they underlined their independence.

On the whole, therefore, the men referred to their fellow workers as a group of people, like neighbours, with whom they enjoyed pleasant but not extensive relations. They had their 'ups and downs', one or two people were less sociable than others, but otherwise people got on well together. A comfortable atmosphere was sought and enjoyed at work. People were relaxed and easy going and there were no tensions between them. The majority of the interviewees had one or two people whom they considered as closer friends. They were workmates to whom they could talk to more intimately about their worries, fears, hopes and plans. They were fellow workers who had perhaps started work at the same time, occupied the same position in the life-cycle or shared a hobby. They did not know a wide group of people on an intimate basis. Given these circumstances, they had neither the time nor the inclination, to socialise extensively with colleagues from work. The factory was not a place where close personal attachments could be initiated and sustained to any great extent. The circumstances and conditions in which paid work was performed, the demands of unpaid work and the interviewees' personal preferences regarding sociability with fellow workers interacted to pattern the form and meaning of the men's social relations with their colleagues from work.

WOMEN AND INSTRUMENTALISM

As Table 3.4 indicated, twenty-four of the thirty-two women interviewees were engaged in formal employment. Unlike their husbands, they worked in a variety of 'typical' female jobs for different employers in the town. Six women worked for Vauxhall. Four women – Bridget Underwood, Elizabeth Adams, Anita Palmer and Julia Farrell – worked full-time as production operators at the main Vauxhall plant in Luton. Carol Sawyer worked as a full-time production operator as well at another Vauxhall factory in Dunstable, while Sandra Davies worked as a part-time cleaner in the main Luton plant in the evenings. Indeed, a further six women had worked for Vauxhall, in one way or another, in the past. Jane Bennett, Uma Kasim, Christine Merrick and Karen Osborne had all worked as production operators while Marion Capel and Daphne Foulds had worked in the office at Vauxhall. Indeed, it was at work that they had met their husbands, illustrating the overlapping of roles, as Grieco (1987) also found. Finally, after her first child was born, Uma Kasim had worked on a temporary evening shift after her first child was born for A.C. Delco, a subsidiary of General Motors, where car components are made. In sum, therefore, just under half (fourteen) of the women worked or had worked for Vauxhall. To put it another way, nearly three-quarters (fourty) of the sample worked or had worked for the car company.

Four of the twenty-four women – Kim Dodd, Bridget Underwood, Marion Capel and Irene Cass – had no children, and they had worked full-time continuously thoughout their working lives. The remaining twenty women had interrupted work histories as they had taken time off to raise their children. The length of time which they had been economically inactive ranged from the statutory minimum of six months to eighteen years in the case of Pauline Graves, who cared for her mother and then raised a son until he went to work at 16. On the whole, the older women had been economically inactive for a longer period of time than their younger counterparts, waiting until their children went to secondary school or left school altogether before resuming work, if their financial position permitted, while the younger women of the sample had returned to formal employment somewhat earlier. Of the twenty working women with child-care commitments, thirteen worked part-time and seven worked full-time. However, there was no neat relationship between hours of work and stage in the family life-cycle because some of the young women – like Alison Clark, Elisabeth Adams and Anita

Palmer – worked full-time since they only had one child each, while the hours of those who worked part-time ranged from two to six hours a day. The women's attitudes to formal employment, as others have noted before (Cavendish 1982; Dex 1985, 1988; Martin and Roberts 1984; Yeandle 1984), differed from their husbands'. They stressed both the push and pull factors which had propelled them back into paid work after caring full-time for their children. Barbara Wright had looked after her two children at home full-time for thirteen years. She returned to formal employment, as a part-time clerk/typist, over seven years ago. She recalled the desire to return to employment, especially as child care responsibilities became less time consuming:

> I felt I was beginning to get so that I didn't think there was enough in just doing housework. You want to get out and broaden your mind a bit, give yourself something to talk about when your husband comes in, in the evening, rather than just domestic chores.

It seemed that Mrs Wright was escaping from the 'privatised character of contemporary domestic labour' (Allan 1985: 40), although not necessarily from her home and family life altogether. Formal employment offered her the opportunity to get out of the house and local vicinity; to undertake some intrinsically rewarding work tasks other than housework; and to meet other people, be they colleagues from work or customers. Being employed meant she was involved in a wider social world beyond the immediate family in the home. Formal employment, despite its accompanying stresses and strains, was enjoyed for all of these things.

Other women stressed the financial pull into work. They recalled a time when there had been almost no extra money left over once the mortgage and weekly household bills had been paid. At one of the most demanding stages of the family life-cycle – raising young children – they could not afford to rely on one wage. Anita Palmer, for example, returned to work at Vauxhall full-time six months after her son was born. As she stated: 'I had to go back to full-time work after my son was born or otherwise we wouldn't have been able to afford the house. I didn't want to.' She would have preferred to stay at home until her son started primary school before returning to paid work. Like a number of the other women who worked full-time, she would have liked to work part-time as well, enjoying work for the same reasons as Barbara Wright stated rather than be forced to work full-time for financial reasons. Again, whether these attitudes reflect an unfettered instrumentalism is open to debate. It appeared that issues of choice and constraint interacted in different ways for the women engaged in formal employment. These issues will be discussed further in relation to child-care and domestic responsibilities in the following chapter.

WOMEN AND SOCIABILITY

Like their husbands, some of the women worked alone, some worked alongside a small group of people, while others, notably the women who worked at Vauxhall full-time, worked with a large group of people. On the whole, however, they worked with small groups of other women for much smaller employers than Vauxhall in Luton. Irrespective of the size of the work group and establishment at which they worked, the women's patterns of sociability altered across the family life-cycle and according to the demands of paid work – either full-time or part-time – and unpaid work. For the economically inactive women, for example, the ability to sustain contact with colleagues from their previous workplace depended on availability on both sides. Jane Bennett found that sociable contact with her friends from her last job had declined since she had left formal employment. Her free time did not coincide with that of those work-mates whom she considered friends, all of whom were still in their same jobs. She had worked at Vauxhall before the birth of her first child but her fellow workers shared the same shift as her husband. Their free time coincided with the time when her husband was free, Ultimately, she wanted to be at home when her husband was free although she would have liked to have enjoyed the company of her friends from work as well. It was a source of frustration which increased her desire to return to a job after her second child was born.

Circumstances were not quite as constraining for Dorothy Atkinson, who, at the other end of the family life-cycle, was retired and without child-care commitments. She met her colleagues from her last job regularly every two or three weeks. Together, they talked about work, passed on information about fellow workers and discussed their own home and family lives. As Mrs Atkinson explained: 'Two women come round in the evening and we catch up with all the news. It's usually when my husband is at his swimming club.' Structural factors, therefore, played a very significant part in shaping these women's opportunities and constraints for sociable contact with friends from their last jobs.

The opportunities to share the company of fellow workers beyond the workplace were enjoyed, not surprisingly, by those women who worked part-time and especially if they worked only a small number of hours. Karen Osborne worked as a school helper for two hours at lunchtime from Monday to Friday. She had two particularly close friends with whom she socialised outside working time: 'We go to each other's houses for coffee. We're very friendly and get on well together. We just talk generally about lots of things.' Like their husbands, the women made reference to one or two colleagues from work who had become friends. They did not socialise with all of their fellow workers. These friends tended to occupy similar positions in the family life-cycle. Heather Jackson, who worked as a clerical assistant in the afternoons during the week, had one close friend from paid work and she ventured: 'We're of a similar age with children of similar ages. I tend to identify with her.' Occupying the same stage in the family life-cycle meant that they shared the same worries and concerns. They were mothers raising families within certain financial constraints, whose children were in the education system or who might be looking for jobs. They were people who worked for a living and who wanted to have a happy and comfortable home and family life. They were 'ordinary people' leading the same sorts of lives.

Nevertheless, these women did not socialise with their fellow workers extensively. After all, they had domestic duties to fulfil, to which they attached considerable importance. They could enjoy the company of fellow workers as they went about these tasks – shopping on the way home from work and so forth – and at home – enjoying a coffee break and a chat – at suitably convenient times. However, they were responsible for the smooth running of the household and socialising with fellow workers was not allowed to interfere with this responsibility. While the women undoubtedly enjoyed their jobs for the opportunities which it offered them to socialise with other people, they did not work simply in search of close affiliations. Barbara Wright enjoyed the company of one or two women friends on a regular basis and the arrangement suited both her and her fellow workers. As she explained: 'I work with people all day and I enjoy it for that point. Then it's nice to just come home to family life really.' Similarily, echoing these sentiments and those of the male interviewees, Pauline Graves enjoyed her 'little job' as an early morning cleaner for getting out of the house and meeting people, but she added that 'as soon as I come away from work, I never think of it'. While socialising took a different form from their husbands' patterns of sociliability since it invariably took place in the home, both the men and women enjoyed regular contact with fellow workers who had become friends.

For the women who worked full-time, the opportunities for socialising with fellow workers outside working time were restricted still further. Like their male counterparts, they socialised with colleagues from work only occasionally in their free time. The women mentioned special occasions in the life-cycle like birthdays, engagement parties, weddings and so forth when they might meet. Anita Palmer described her relations with four other women workers at Vauxhall in these terms when she said 'we go out as a group to weddings and engagements and occasionally we club together and have a meal out'. Similarly, Marion Capel, who worked as a computer office manager spoke of the occasional meal or drink together if her group felt low-spirited:

> I do feel close to them. Occasionally we might arrange a night out if we feel down hearted. We go out for a meal at the same place and we do all go; across the age groups and seniority.

Once again, these activities were seen as a way of maintaining good relations at work. The impression the women gave was of knowing and taking an interest in each other's lives and of sharing a concern for colleagues' well-being. As Gullestad (1984: 257) also found, these women talked about their home and family lives, relationships with kin, neighbours and other colleagues at work in a more personal way than did their husbands.

There was little evidence of an instrumental attitude towards fellow workers, either in work or beyond it. Returning to Anita Palmer and her friends and acquaintances at work, she felt:

> You do get to know them because you work so closely together. We're always together for tea-breaks and dinner. You work so closely together that you can't help but ... well if you don't talk and don't get to know a person, you're a pretty miserable person. We do still have disagreements but we get on because we're all in the same boat. We're there for the money and you've got to have money to live. It's very boring work so if we have a laugh and a joke too, it releases the boredom and you forget about the job you're doing and think about what you'd rather be doing.

Thus, a shared approach to work brought people together even though work was seen as a means to other ends. This finding implies that an instrumental orientation to work does not necessarily prohibit a sense of solidarity with fellow workers, nor does it preclude sociable contact with colleagues from work outside the factory as the Luton team suggested. The interviewees did not positively seek to limit their attachments to fellow workers because they saw work as providing only extrinsic rewards. Fellow workers were not deliberately excluded from the interviewees' lives in this way, but the work involved in sustaining the household acted as a limiting force on sociability.

Given that these structural factors influenced the opportunities for, and constraints on, sociability, the interviewees neither expected nor necessarily wanted to see any more of their colleagues from work in their free time. They stressed the importance of leading their own lives. Irene Cass, who worked full-time as a machinist, maintained that

> Workmates are workmates and that's it. I see more of them than I do my own family. I wouldn't like to see them outside work too. I have my own life. We have a laugh and a chat but that's as far as it goes.

Frances Hills, who worked part-time as a cook but worked a twenty-eight hour week, said 'we've done our own things, been involved in our own lives and gone to other places'. Finally, like their husbands, they had responsibilities as family 'breadwinners' and extensive socialising with fellow workers was not compatible with these responsibilities for, in the words of one woman, when you are 'buying a house and getting things together... you can't be out enjoying yourself as well'. The meaning of marriage and establishing an independent household among the women interviewees will be discussed in the following chapter.

CONCLUSION

On the whole, the interviewees socialised with their colleagues from work in their free time. They enjoyed occasional excursions with their work group and regularly enjoyed the intimacy of one or two colleagues from work who had become friends. Thus, contrary to the Luton team's findings, the interviewees were not entirely family centred to the point of excluding all sociable contact with fellow workers. The interviewees' non-work lives were not entirely insulated from paid work or their workmates.

Once again, the evidence suggests that paid and unpaid work shaped the men's and women's patterns of sociability differently and the way in which it shaped the opportunities to socialise with fellow workers beyond the workplace changed across the family life-cycle. These structural factors rather than an instrumental orientation to work influenced the interviewees' patterns of sociability with fellow workers. They did not approach work in a singularly instrumental fashion but derived intrinsic rewards from their jobs as well. Indeed, an instrumental orientation to work was found to be a source of solidarity rather than schism. Neither did they view fellow workers instrumentally. The interviewees did not consciously seek to limit sociable contact with colleagues from work in pursuit of the material well-being of the immediate family in the home. There was little evidence of such rational economic calculation as the Luton team implied. As we have seen, the interviewees enjoyed the company of their fellow workers at work and in their spare time as well.

That said, the interviewees were clearly not immersed in the occupational community of extensive socialising with workmates associated with the so-called 'traditional' working class. To repeat: paid and unpaid work militated against that kind of extensive sociability with workmates. Moreover, for the most part, the interviewees were not unhappy with the level of contact with their friends and acquaintances at work. They valued their independent lives instead. The interviewees' normative guidelines, it seemed, legitmised the structural forces shaping the patterns of sociability.

As has been suggested, the interviewees' attitudes to their jobs and their patterns of sociability clearly varied between the men and women of the sample and across the family life-cycle. That is, the opportunities and constraints on sociability were not static but dynamic. Some of the young men of the sample, for example, enjoyed regular sporting fixtures with their workmates, while some of the women who worked part-time enjoyed talking to and confiding in fellow women workers in their free time. Given the domestic division of labour, it was not surprising to find that the men usually socialised with their workmates outside the home, while the women tended to meet in each other's homes. Nevertheless, both the men and women alike socialised with their fellow workers as a group only occasionally because of the demands of paid and unpaid work, and their preference to lead their own, independent lives.

This chapter concludes the examination of the interviewees' patterns of sociability and the extent to which their daily lives may be aptly described as family centred. Contrary to the Luton team's conclusions, the data suggest that the interviewees' lives did not centre on the immediate family to the exclusion of wider kin, neighbours and colleagues from work. There was little evidence to support the view that the interviewees' norms and values emphasised instrumentalism and individualism at the expense of sociability and solidarity. Rather, the demands of paid and unpaid work involved in sustaining the independence of the household structured the opportunities and constraints on sociable contact with fellow workers. These demands certainly militated against the kind of extensive sociability associated with the 'traditional' working class, but it did not preclude socialising with people beyond the immediate family altogether. Given that the portrayal of 'traditional' working-class life-styles has been hotly contested, these findings suggest that working-class patterns of sociability may have not altered over the twentieth century as much as the Luton team argued. Moreover, changing working-class norms and values alone do not account for any alterations in life-styles which may have occurred. With these arguments in mind, the following two chapters examine the extent to which the interviewees' life-styles could be accurately described as home centred. Chapter 7 explores the interviewees' conjugal roles, while Chapter 8 focuses on their patterns of leisure.

NOTES

1. Indeed, Zweig (1961: 12) went on to argue that the pursuit of money to buy consumer durables generated a responsible attitude to work and the company. As consumers, workers would tolerate work in a positive fashion. Overall, however, Zweig was unclear about workers' attitudes to employment. While he argued that they had become more responsible in their approach to work than in the past, he also referred to their contradictory or ambivalent attitudes to paid work as a result of the monotonous and boring nature of work tasks. This confusion arises from his failure to clarify the causal processes which generated the decline of the 'traditional' working-class community and the emergence of a home- and family-centred existence.

2. Goldthorpe and his colleagues, therefore, preferred Chinoy's (1955) analysis of consumer aspirations and leisure patterns among factory workers to that of either Blauner or Mallet.

3. Furthermore, the Essex team found that their working-class respondents, along with the rest of the sample, saw paid work as being as important as any non-work activity which they enjoyed. They concluded that 'alienation at work' is 'not counterbalanced by a wholesale retreat into the home as an alternative or compensatory source of meaning and fulfillment' (Marshall *et al.* 1988: 218).

4. Despite the plethora of empirical studies on industrial workers in the late 1960s and 1970s, the majority of researchers, with a

few notable exceptions (Hill 1976; Salaman 1974), took little interest in patterns of sociability beyond the workplace.

5. The lack of work history data and, indeed, any biographical details on the respondents, was a shortcoming of the Luton team's survey method.

6. This overlapping of social roles could, of course, have applied equally to women. It was particularly evident among the men because they worked for one of the largest employers in Luton where the situation was more likely to arise.

7

CONJUGAL ROLES

Emphasis has been placed on the ways in which the interviewees' lives were inextricably bound up with the lives of their wider kin, neighbours and colleagues from work. The interviewees did not lead family-centred life-styles as Goldthorpe and his colleagues predicted. That said, the interviewees were not engaged in extensive sociability with wider kin, neighbours or colleagues from work like the so-called 'traditional' working class. On the contrary, their opportunities for, and constraints on, sociability were structured by the demands of paid and unpaid work which had to be met in order to sustain their independent households. These work demands varied between the men and women and across the family life-cycle, and subsequently shaped their different patterns of sociability. Furthermore, the interviewees were largely content with the amount of sociable contact which they enjoyed with kin, neighbours and fellow workers since they valued the independence of the household. Their normative guidelines regarding sociability underlined the importance they attached to determining their own lives and the autonomy of the household.

This chapter turns to the issue of home-centredness in general, and to men and women's conjugal roles inside the household in particular. Are men more involved in child-care and domestic tasks than they were in the past as the Luton team argued? Is the domestic division of labour between husbands and wives still unequal? How do the interviewees define and feel about the conjugal roles they fulfil? Are they part of a 'companionate' marriage? In opposition to the Luton team's findings, the data suggest that women remain primarily responsible for child-care and domestic tasks. The sexual division of labour, whereby men are employed outside the home and women fulfil unpaid work inside the home, accounts for the segregation of conjugal roles. Even so, men are not aloof from the daily routine as was alleged of 'traditional' working-class men. The men interviewees contributed, albeit in different ways from their wives, to the undertaking of child-care and domestic responsibilities. Their involvement, however, was the product of necessity as their wives returned to formal employment, and was not exclusively the result of the husbands' desire for a home- and family-centred existence. Structural factors, such as the increasing participation of married women in the labour market since the Second World War, rather than a new instrumentalism among working-class men explained the nature of the interviewees' conjugal roles and the ways in which they varied across the family life-cycle. The interviewees' normative guidelines reflected the exigencies of their daily lives.

CHANGING WORKING-CLASS MARRIAGES

Studies of the 'traditional' working class emphasised the distinct work roles which men and women played in sustaining the household. Men were primarily engaged in paid work outside the home, while a woman's life was devoted to the 'most sacred responsibility' of the 'health and happiness of her husband and children' in the home (Spring Rice 1981: 14).[1] Similarly, just as paid work dominated the lives of men, women's lives centred on domestic and child-rearing tasks. In poor housing conditions and without modern appliances, domestic chores were time-consuming and often involved hard physical labour (Slater and Woodside 1951; Spring Rice 1981). Both working-class men and women led hard lives.[2]

Moreover, since men were in paid work all day and socialised with their workmates in the pubs and clubs in the evenings, women turned to the company of other women in similar circumstances to themselves to relieve the 'almost unredeemed drabness of their lives' (Spring Rice 1981: 94). In other words, their most intimate attachments were derived from different groups of people. There was, as a result, little intimacy between partners (Bott 1957; Dennis *et al.* 1956: 227–9; Kerr 1958). Instead, marriage was about work and the practicalities of life, and not about intimacy and romantic love (Slater and Woodside 1951: 148).

Embourgeoisement theorists claimed that the strict sexual division of labour and its impact on married life was undermined by economic prosperity. Husbands were enticed away from the company of workmates to spend their free time with the immediate family in the 'comfortable and well-equipped home' (Zweig 1961: 10). They became more involved in the domestic routine of the household, jointly sharing the tasks which had to be completed. Wives, therefore, no longer had to perform domestic chores alone and, coupled with better standards of housing and domestic appliances, their workloads lightened considerably (Newson and Newson 1963). Finally, this life-style generated a 'new' intimacy between members of the conjugal family. Husbands and wives no longer existed in separate social worlds with different interests and concerns. Instead, they shared the same hopes and plans for their individual household. As Young and Willmott argued:

> Whatever happened in the past, the younger husband of today does not consider that the children belong exclusively to his wife's world, or that he can abandon them to her (or his mother) while he takes his comfort in the male atmosphere of the local pub (1983: 6).

Economic well-being, it seemed, led to a number of favourable developments in home and family life (Klein 1965; Young and Willmott 1975).

The Luton team sought to distance themselves from what they saw as the embourgeoisement theorists' exaggerated claims of shifts in working-class norms and values. However, the Luton team did not differ significantly from them in their description of changing conjugal roles within working-class marriages. They found that the majority (62 per cent) of their male respondents spent most of their spare time 'in and about the home itself' undertaking mostly 'chores and odd-jobs – including gardening' (Goldthorpe *et al.* 1969: 102), which they completed either alone or with their partners. As evidence of 'familistic values', their male respondents were involved in or had taken over some 'women's work' within the home. While they found evidence of gender segregation of domestic tasks, they emphasised that most of the fathers were involved in a variety of child-care activities. Just under half (48 per cent) of the men put the children to bed, two-thirds of them read to the children, while the overwhelming majority (80 per cent) took their children out on various excursions (Goldthorpe *et al.* 1969: 105–6). These arrangements, they stressed, were valued in themselves and were not the product of necessity. While never claiming that men and women shared their conjugal roles equally, the Luton team argued:

> Nevertheless, at least among the couples included in our critical case, it would certainly appear that some of the values that sustain the communal, kin-based sociability of the traditional type of working- class community were no longer dominant. Specifically, on the evidence we have been able to present, one could assert that primacy was clearly given to the material well- being, the social cohesiveness and the autonomy of the conjugal family over against the demands or attractions of wider kinship or community ties; and one could at least suggest that probably the one most important concomitant of this changed emphasis was the acceptance among these workers and their wives of the ideal of the 'companionate' marriage (Goldthorpe *et al.* 1969: 108).

By 'companionate' marriage, the Luton team referred to closer, more instrinsically rewarding, partnerships between husbands and wives and parents and children than was evident in the past. Workers' 'expressive and effective needs' were no longer met in the workplace but in the immediate family in the home (Goldthorpe *et al.* 1968a: 175–6). This argument endorsed Bott's (1957) finding that the form of conjugal roles is related to families' informal social networks and that people with loose-knit networks of kin, neighbours and fellow workers (as a result of geographical mobility) tend to have relatively joint conjugal role-relationships.

The Luton team's findings were certainly based on very crude measures of the degree to which the respondents' conjugal roles were segregated or joint. In a separate paper, Platt (1969) made this point, highlighting three major difficulties with the methodology and the research findings. First, Platt expressed her unease about the limited focus of the questions which were put to the respondents. Critical questions on who usually does the housework and who makes the household decisions were never asked. Nor were penetrating questions asked about who usually looks after the children rather than just entertaining them. Secondly, she was critical of the assumption that either people had segregated or joint conjugal roles. There was no recognition that couples might undertake some tasks separately and other tasks together. In other words, the notion of jointness was never properly conceptualised or operationalised. Thirdly, Platt was critical of the analysis of conjugal role behaviour alone. The survey data did not tap norms and expectations and the processes by which they translate into actions, the perceptions and effects of constraints and the meanings and feelings of the issues at stake. She argued:

> One needs to know not merely what norms are expressed on each issue, but also what the meaning and relative importance of the issue is to the people concerned. Some items of behaviour may have different meanings for one couple from those they have for another, and issues may vary in their relative significance (Platt 1969: 293)

Subsequent research and commentary (Allan 1985; Edgell 1980; Hunt 1980; McRae 1986; Oakley 1974; Pahl and Pahl 1971) on conjugal roles has largely echoed Platt's misgivings and confirmed her suspicions of the findings which emerged from the *Affluent Worker* series. Even though they were more cautious than embourgeoisement theorists, the Luton team still exaggerated the degree of jointness in conjugal roles. Research has shown that the domestic division of labour between husbands and wives remains unequal. Given the institutionalisation of work roles and unequal power relations, it is not surprising to find that women take on the bulk of day-to-day domestic and child-care chores, while men choose to do certain, masculine, tasks. For example, even among middle-class couples, who are often assumed to have a more equal domestic division of labour than working-class couples, Edgell found little evidence of jointness in domestic and childcare tasks. He concluded:

> This overwhelming evidence of conjugal role segregation, especially in domestic task be- haviour, could be said to reflect the profound influence of the sexual division of labour in which men are typically responsible for the breadwinning role and women for home making (Edgell 1980: 35–6).

Indeed, studies (Leaver 1987; McKee and Bell 1986) have shown that people subscribe to traditional models of the sexual division of labour where men are unemployed and are no longer the main breadwinner of the family. Thus, despite affluence, better housing conditions and the advent of domestic appliances, it appears that the division of labour between men and women has proved remarkably resilient over the course of the twentieth century (Bose 1982; Collins 1985; Maynard 1985; Oakley 1981; Wilson 1980).

Despite this consensus of opinion, avenues of research on conjugal roles remain open. Studies of domestic and child-care tasks have tended to be very narrowly focused on the issue of who performs which different tasks as a way of overcoming the fuzziness of the conceptualisation and operationalisation of jointness. In other words, successive studies have focused very particularly on 'who does what and when', but, echoing Platt's remarks, the attitudes and feelings towards domestic and child-care responsibilities have still been largely ignored. Little time has been devoted to men's and women's experiences of their paid and un- paid work roles in general, and their feelings about these responsibilities and duties. How do they define their roles? What do their roles mean to them? How important are the different responsibilities and duties they fulfil? Do they change over the life-cycle as a result of circumstances and experience? What are their satisfactions and dissatisfactions? Are wives satisfied with the amount of work their husbands perform in and around the home? Do husbands think they do enough domestic and child-care work or do they feel they should do more or less? Do they share hopes and plans for the immediate family in the home as the Luton team suggested? These issues will be discussed in relation to the family life- cycle to illustrate how, in the context of perceived opportunities and constraints, norms and values and attitudes and feelings translate into action, and, in turn, are adapted to the circumstances in which people find themselves.

ESTABLISHING AN INDEPENDENT HOUSEHOLD

Both the men and women interviewees automatically associated early marriage with establishing an independent household of their own. In- variably, marriage meant buying a house and items of furniture like beds and three-piece suites, and domestic appliances such a a cooker, refrig- erator and washing machine.[3] Marriage was associated with decorating the house according to their own style and taste. It was about creating a comfortable home in which to live (Devine 1989). All of the items re- quired were deemed essential for the smooth running of the household according to prevailing domestic consumer standards. They could be afforded when both partners were engaged in full-time paid employ- ment.

The interviewees stressed the importance of establishing their homes before the arrival of children since it was presumed that wives would leave the labour market to raise their young children on a full-time basis.

Depending on one income while raising a young family would be difficult so it made economic sense to establish the home before their arrival.
Newly-married Anthony Dodd and his wife, Kim, intended to have
children in a couple of years' time. As Mr Dodd explained: 'It has to be a
time when Kim can afford to give up work and have children. We
couldn't do that now. We can't afford it.' Bridget and Stephen
Underwood were also in the same stage of the family life-cycle and
Bridget felt

> I would like to start a family but not just yet. I don't want to leave
> the burden of money, the mortgage and things like that on
> Stephen. It won't be too long I hope but I will work full-time up to
> then. It's a lot of money not to have all of a sudden. Now we're
> buying and decorating and we need more money. I hope we would
> be able to manage.

The contribution of the wife's wage to the family income was recognised
as extremely important at this time.[4] It was not considered rational to
coincide the peak earnings of the husband in the early years of marriage
with child-rearing, as the Luton team found (Goldthorpe et al. 1969: 127–
9). Rather, women would contribute to the household income after marriage, and both incomes would secure the financial position of the family
later on.

Thus, the interviewees, in their roles as husbands and wives, shared
an aspiration to establish and secure an independent household of their
own. They hoped to achieve a standard of living which other 'ordinary
working people' around them also enjoyed. Both partners contributed
financially to establishing the home. As we shall see, the interviewees
were also clear about the path which their lives would take. That is, they
would fulfil different work roles in order to sustain their homes during
their lives.

As Hunt (1980) and Mansfield and Collard (1988) found, the period
before the arrival of children is a time when household tasks are shared
most equally across the family life-cycle. This was evident among the
interviewees of this study. They believed that if both partners were
working full-time, it was unfair of a husband to expect his wife to undertake domestic tasks alone. After all, they would both feel tired after a
day's work and would be in need of relaxation. As Stephen Underwood
suggested: 'I couldn't have me and Bridget coming in from work and me
sitting down while she is doing all the cooking.'

Couples recounted the ways in which they both cooked, cleared away
and tidied up after a meal together. They stressed that there was not a
huge amount of housework to be done, especially if both partners were
not at home during the day. Husbands and wives undertook day-to-day
domestic chores together before they both relaxed for the evening. Rachel
Edwards remembered when a time when 'we'd come in together and I'd
start cooking while he did the tidying up. It didn't get that untidy then

anyway with just the two of us.' As Mrs Edwards's comments also suggest, however, the type of domestic tasks which husbands and wives undertake is, even in this stage of the family life-cycle, obviously gendered. Substantial domestic chores were not undertaken during the week when paid work dominated the day. Instead, time-consuming domestic tasks – like washing and ironing clothes, shopping for groceries for the following week and cleaning the house thoroughly – were left to the weekend. As Hunt (1980) also found, it was these tasks which the women interviewees performed alone. Bridget Underwood described a usual week in these terms:

> After a day's work I feel shattered. We have a meal, wash up and hoover. Then we watch telly and read. We don't do much really. In the summer we might go out for a drink but in the winter we don't go out during the week. We just like to come in and relax. At the weekends, that's when all the housework gets done and the shopping.

At the weekend, however, Stephen Underwood spent Saturday or Sunday fishing.

Thus, even though wives worked (or had worked) full-time, they undertook more than their fair share of substantial domestic tasks, especially at weekends. Different types of domestic tasks were also gendered. This inequality, however, was neither a source of considerable grievance for the women nor the cause of marked conflict between husbands and wives. Even though they worked full-time, the women still saw domestic duties as ultimately their responsibility rather than their husband's duty. They appeared to subscribe to a strict sexual division of labour. Kim Dodd described her husband as 'very good' about domestic work because he proved 'willing to help me out' during the week. Yet the fact that she worked as well led to some dissatisfaction about the division of domestic chores in her household:

> I don't expect him to do much more. I would like him to do more on Saturday when I'm at work and he is at home. I'd like to come home to a meal and a tidy house rather than a group of blokes watching videos.

For the most part, the women interviewees did not harbour a great sense of dissatisfaction about the unequal amount of domestic work they did in comparison to their husbands. Both the men and women alike constantly emphasised that there was not a huge amount of housework to be done. Housework, it seemed, did not seriously curtail any weekend activities – sports or hobbies – which the women might have enjoyed.[5]

ASSUMING CHILD-CARE DUTIES

The interviewees presumed that one parent, namely the mother, would care for young children on a full-time basis while the husband would provide financially for the family. It was women, for biological reasons (Cornwell 1984; Edgell 1980; Oakley 1972), who stayed at home to rear young children and men who provided the family income through paid work outside the home. The interviewees, then, defined the sexual division of labour within the household in terms of distinct responsibilities, relating them to the biological make-up of men and women.

All of the women who had children had assumed full-time child-care responsibilities in some point at their lives. The interviewees believed very strongly that a mother was needed at home to provide full care and attention to her children. She should provide a secure and loving home in the most formative years of their life. Rita Malik was at home looking after her young son and she felt: 'When he's young, I wouldn't want to leave him. The early years of a child are very important. You need to have contact with your parents. You need to know them.' Both the men and women interviewees continually emphasised the importance which they attached to their parental responsibilities. As parents, they and they alone were ultimately responsible for the well-being of their children. Thus, Lisa Smith felt

> I think if you have children, you should look after them. I think it is nice if they know who their Mum is and not have babysitters everyday or go from this person to that person.

In other words, the interviewees, and especially the young women interviewees, echoed popular theories about parental care and the well-being of children embedded in women's networks in working-class areas in the early twentieth century (Roberts 1984) and promulgated by Bowlby (1953, 1969) among others.

Thus, all of the women interviewees had taken on the bulk of direct, day-to-day rearing of children when they left the labour market. Husbands were not involved in routine child care because they were engaged in paid work away from the home. Indeed, some of the older men recalled a time when they had seen little of their young children during the day. With only one wage coming into the household, they had had to work as much overtime as possible to manage. In this way, and to the men's regret, the children had become their wives' sole responsibility. Geoffrey Hayward stated:

> At the time, I was working twelve hours a day, seven days a week so I didn't see a lot of them when they were young. I would have liked to have seen more of them but money was the main thing, making ends meet.

The younger men of the sample also faced similar constraints on the amount of time which they could spend with their children, although overtime was clearly not as abundant as it had been in the past. They spoke enthusiastically of the time which they spent with their children. Andrew Bennett, whose wife was at home all day looking after their 2-year old child, described how his daughter gets me up at six. I'm at work all day and I only see her for two hours during the day. I make up for it at the week- ends as I'm always with her. I would like to spend more time with her. I do when I'm on nights and I have long week ends. When I get home in the mornings, she's up and I stay up with her for an hour. I'd like to stay home all day if I could but I don't get paid for that so I can't. She can be quite a handful as she is always mischievous but she's all right, she's no bother.

Stressing the importance of a close relationship between himself and his son, Neil Palmer stressed 'I want to be involved with my son. One parent is not enough. I want to know everything he does as well as his mother.'

Undoubtedly, the fathers enjoyed time spent with their young children. Given they were away from them for most of the day, the company of their children and their relationship with them was greatly valued. The young men's comments, however, indicated that time spent with children centre on entertaining them. This finding concurs with the Luton team's data. However, what the Luton team ignored and what was evident in this study was that the men did not usually undertake routine child-care tasks. Indeed, entertaining the children when they got home from work freed their wives to complete domestic chores uninterrupted. Matthew Smith, who had an 8-month-old daughter cared for on a full-time basis by his wife Lisa, described how 'When I get in, I take over our daughter to give Lisa a break as she's been with her all day.' Usually, 'a break' meant that Mrs Smith could cook the dinner uninterrupted by her child.

These findings, of course, confirm the well-known fact (Comer 1974) that men do the more agreeable household tasks such as child-care rather than domestic tasks, and the more enjoyable aspects of child-care such as entertaining children rather than the mundane activities like feeding them, washing and ironing their clothes and so forth. The findings highlight the processes by which these circumstances, both unintentionally and intentionally, emerge and the important structuring influence of paid work on men and women's different child-care tasks. Contrary to the Luton team's findings, women continue to fulfil an unequal burden of child-care responsibilities.

HOUSEWORK

It was also presumed that since wives were based in the home for most of the day, they should perform the majority of domestic tasks. Again, this was perceived as 'natural' and the most obvious means of organising the division of domestic labour when husbands were absent from the home. The bulk of housework tasks should be completed during the day alongside child-care responsibilities. Lisa Smith reflected these attitudes when she stated:

When I worked full-time, we did the house- work together: washing up at the end of the day and day-to-day clearing up. I used to
say to him that once I was at home, he wouldn't have to do any of
that any more which he doesn't now. Now I'm at home all day, I do
all of it. Matthew doesn't do anything but he does take over the
baby when he comes in from work.

Even so, there were few instances where women did all the housework while their husbands did nothing. Both the men and women felt
there was a lot of housework to complete in this stage of the family life-
cycle. Housework, as Oakley (1974) has aptly described it, had a never-
ending quality in that once all the necessary tasks had been completed, it
was almost time to begin the various chores all over again. The men
helped their wives to complete housework so they could 'take a break'
before the daily routine began once more. While Aziz Malik's wife, Rita,
was at home all day, he said 'If she's busy or there's too much to do, I'll
give her a hand. It is important to help. That's what it's all about, sharing.'

The men interviewees stressed the importance of helping their wives
so that they could both relax at the end of the day. Peter Ibbotson stated:

During the week, Sheila does all the cooking and things like that
because I'm at work and she's at home. At the weekends, if I'm not
working, I muck in and we get all the work done so that we can
relax together and go out.

Similarly, Roberts Edwards suggested:

If I come in and the wife hasn't finished, I muck in. There's no set
pattern. I always try to say to her that when I finish work, you
should finish work. If we're going to sit down for the evening, we
should all sit. I think it's wrong that one should be slogging away
and the other one can be sitting down. You're supposed to be a
family so you should help each other.

The men emphasised that it would be unfair to expect their wives to
complete housework alone. They also wanted to share their free time
with their wives in the evenings. If household chores had not been
completed when they got home from work, they would help their wives
so that the family could enjoy their evenings together. This is, of course, a
very different picture of daily life from that contained in studies of
'traditional' working-class life-styles (Dennis et al. 1956; Zweig 1952).
That said, the findings are not all that different from the communal
nature of home life portrayed by Hoggart (1957). He noted the way in
which communality often precluded individual members undertaking
independent activities in the home. All of these findings, therefore, raise
the question of whether men in the past were as aloof from the routine of
family life as some commentators of the 'traditional' working class led us
to believe.

Overall, the men interviewees felt quite satisfied with their contribution to domestic work in the home. After all, they were at work all day

and exhausted by it in the evenings. For these reasons, they were not prepared to undertake substantial domestic tasks at the end of the day. They were, however, willing to assist their wives as they completed their day's work. That is, they were flexible about helping their wives to finish household chores. The domestic division of labour in their households, as they saw it, was not rigidly defined. Echoing this benign view, Andrew Bennett suggested:

> I'm more domesticated since I got married. I don't leave it to the wife because she is pregnant but I wouldn't anyway. Since we've been married I've been good around the house. I will do anything. I don't mind just so long as it keeps the house tidy. I do the washing up, wiping up, hoovering, looking after the baby. I'm not bothered.

Other men conceded that they tried not to do housework if they could avoid it. Robert Edwards helped his wife with housework but he also felt: 'Still if I can have a lazy life I'll have one. Women won't let you have one. If they think they can get you to do something they'll get you.' Given the demands of paid work, therefore, the men felt they played a fair role in the domestic routine. Although they preferred not to do any housework, they were flexible in doing what their wives asked of them.

Many of the women spoke favourably about their husbands' contributions to the housework and particularly their willingness to undertake work which was asked of them. They appreciated the help which they received. They also perceived that the division of domestic labour was flexible. Rachel Edwards felt her husband was 'very good' because 'he does help out a lot'. In a similar vein, Margaret Kent felt:

> I never expected my husband to do domestic work but if I wanted him to do anything, he wouldn't hesitate. He doesn't give a second thought to doing the washing up which he does without me asking.

While the interviewees defined the division of domestic labour in a traditional way, with men and women having distinct and quite strictly defined responsibilities, their daily lives did not conform to this picture. Their conjugal roles were not entirely separate.

Other wives, however, were disgruntled about the unequal amount of housework which they did in comparison with, to husbands. Some dissatisfaction was expressed. They noted that while their husbands might be quite willing to help when asked, they were poor about performing such tasks on their own initiative. Many of the wives felt that their husbands did not think along the same lines as themselves, seeing and thinking about what needed to be done next. They often had to be cajoled into doing housework. As Jane Bennett stated:

> If he's asked, he'll do it but he's not one of these people who gets up and automatically says I'll go and wash up or I'll go and make a cup of coffee or I'll go and do this or that. If I say go and put the kettle on, he'll do it but he's got to be prompted.

In a similar vein Brenda Richards described a frequent situation which annoyed her:

> When my husband is on nights, he looks after himself cooking wise. He is good cooking wise but he doesn't clear up after himself. It annoys me when I come home from work to find it all there and I want to use things. I don't consider that it's my thing to do. I just get lumbered. My husband's argument is that he does the decorating and fixes the car but my argument is that he doesn't do that every day. I just get on with it now. I can't be bothered.

Furthermore, a number of women expressed their dislike of the way in which their husbands persuaded them to leave tasks which needed to be done. Speaking about her husband, Elisabeth Adams suggested 'He is always trying to get me to sit down and leave it but to me there isn't another day.' Similarly, Jane Bennett reflected 'I try to do housework at night but he says sit down, we'll do it at the weekend. Of course at the weekend I have to do it.' There was a sense, then, that husbands dictated when domestic work was done. Women were expected to be free when their husbands were free. Ultimately, housework was completed when husbands were absent from the home, undertaken by wives alone. Husbands would help their wives complete domestic tasks at the end of the day but as Jack Foulds, who was one of the older members of the sample, suggested, 'if a woman is anything of a housewife, the work would be done before the husband came home.'

Women in the sample, therefore, recognised that they performed a considerable amount of work in the home while their husbands made a limited contribution in comparison. There was a sense of injustice and they did not fully accept that paid work should exclude their husbands from domestic work. There was a constant, tiresome need to cajole their partners to help with domestic duties. As we shall see, the husband's contribution to the domestic routine changes as women return to formal employment. Before turning to this issue, it is important, once again, to reiterate the different circumstances in which the women returned to formal employment.

THE RETURN TO FORMAL EMPLOYMENT

Attention has centred, so far, on the interviewees' reflections on the organisation of child-care and housework in the early stages of the family life-cycle. The majority (twenty four) of the women were in formal employment in the labour market. While all of the mothers had cared for their children full-time, the length of time out of the labour market varied from six months to twenty-six years. Only one women – Maria Knight – had remained a a mother and housewife full-time for the twenty-six years of her married life.

As was noted in Chapter 6, the women returned to the labour market for a variety of reasons. Some women were pulled into the labour market, others were pushed out of the home and often both factors were at work. The lure of paid work as a way of getting away from being at home and doing housework all day and meeting people in a different setting was described by numerous women interviewees. Elisabeth Adams described the sheer boredom of staying at home when her only child started school:

> My child was at school all day and my husband was at work all day. Once I was up with Natalie, had taken her to school, made the beds and done some general housework each day, I didn't have a lot to do. I was bored by ten in the morning. I was totally cheesed off. All the family was working and my day was really monotonous. When my husband came in he was tired and I was lively and raring to go.

Obviously, these experiences were particularly acute for Mrs Adams with only one daughter. As survey research (Martin and Roberts 1984) has shown, the extent to which child-care and domestic demands dictate women's daily lives and allow them to return to paid employment depends on the number of children in a family and the closeness of their ages. The survey data, of course, suggest that changing working-class patterns of fertility (Gittins 1982, 1985) have altered the amount of child-care and associated domestic tasks for which women are responsible over the course of the twentieth century. While some commentators have argued that household standards and tasks have increased, the women in this sample could distinguish between routine tasks and housework which filled up their spare time. There was a time in the day when housework could be said to be complete, allowing them to do other activities like going out to work.

Other women stressed the financial 'pull' into work. They spoke of the difficulties of managing on one wage at one of the most demanding stages of the family life-cycle. Once the mortgage and weekly food bill had been paid, there was little additional money for the quarterly heating and lighting bills and even less cash for clothes or leisure activities. While they would have liked to stay at home with their children (as their earlier remarks implied), many of the women had been forced to seek employment earlier than desired. Uma Kasim, for example, had stayed at home for sixteen months after the birth of her son. She then worked on a temporary contract in a local factory in the evenings, doing fifteen hours a week for eight months. She had earnt £50 a week, which she felt was good in comparison with other jobs involving similar hours. She explained the circumstances in which she started work and her child-care arrangments:

> When I was looking for work, my mother started at the same place. I went along too. It was convenient as she could look after him while I was working. We swapped him when she went into work and I was coming out.

At the time of the interview, she was looking for evening work with a small number of hours. If she was called back to the same factory, it 'would be ideal', as would

> any evening job which would allow my mother to look after my son. I wouldn't like to leave him with a childminder for the whole day. I'd be paying out a lot of money to the childminder so it wouldn't be worth going out to work anyway.

Working a small number of hours in the evening was a 'convenient' way of making some extra money while her mother looked after her son. This example is in line with Marsh's (1991) findings on the growth of people working a small number of hours.

Indeed, part-time employment was considered as the ideal way of combining child-care and domestic commitments with paid work. The women interviewees presumed that they, rather than their husbands, would remain primarily responsible for the children. Sheila Ibbotson had also had 'small jobs' while raising her two children, and she felt, 'I never wanted to be working when the children were on holiday. I like to be at home as much as possible with the children.' Her own father had been unable to work due to ill-health and she reflected:

> All I remember of my mother was that she was forever working. She didn't seem to have any free time at all. She was either out at work or slaving away at home. I wouldn't do it.

While Mrs Ibbotson had recently ventured into self-employment in catering (which she combined with her job as a school helper), the other women were dependent on the employment opportunities in the local labour market. The search for part-time work, in close proximity and with hours which coincided with school hours and holidays led a number of women, like Uma Kasim, to work unsocial hours in the evenings or at weekends.[6] Given their dislike of babysitters and their strong sense of parental responsibility, they took on work when either their husbands or mothers were free to look after the children. Sandra Davis had worked at weekends for six years as a domestic at the local hospital. Her husband looked after the children so there was always one parent at home with them. Although it meant that she and her husband were forced to 'keep different hours', she explained that 'we desperately needed the money and it fitted in with the children. One parent was out but the other was in.' This finding coincides with Beechey and Perkins's (1987) research on part-time employment, which highlighted the role of the labour market in structuring the opportunities for, and constraints on, economic activity. What were the implications of these structural factors and normative guidelines for the organisation of child-care within the households concerned?

FATHERS AND CHILD-CARE

Undoubtedly, the women undertook a substantial amount of preparatory child-care and housework before they went out to work. The food shopping would be done, the house clean, clothes washed and ironed and so forth. Nevertheless, both the men and women interviewees discussed the way in which husbands were forced to look after children in a more substantial way than was suggested earlier. They actually have to oversee their children's activities in a responsible fashion rather than merely enjoy their company for a short period of time. They were responsible, if their wives worked in the evening for example, for organising their meals, leisure activities in and outside the home, overseeing homework and preparation for bed. They had to perform the less enjoyable and the more mundane aspects of child-care while their wives were at work.

The interviewees stressed the importance of husbands being 'capable' of caring for their children. Wives should not have to worry about the welfare of their children. Anita Palmer, who worked full-time at Vauxhall but on the opposite shift to her husband, suggested:

> I do nightwork and I'm not worried that my son won't be looked after properly. He can look after him just as well as me. My father wouldn't have been able to look after me or my sister because he never did it. It was not the done thing. It's a change for the better. Father used to sit us on his knee and read stories but he didn't wash nappies or bath us as babies.

Neil Palmer expressed similar sentiments in his interview:

> I think you should do more really because it not only helps your partner but you're helping yourself as well. It is better for men. If the wife wasn't in, nothing would get done because the husband couldn't do it. It just gets done. It's also made me closer to my son.

Again, these remarks must be placed in the context of the interviewees' sense of parental responsibility for their children. Julia Farrell recalled how, before she returned to full-time work, her husband:

> looked after the children in the evening when I was working parttime. They were only five and seven. We'd never leave the children alone or with someone outside the family.

Thus, there was some evidence of men performing routine child-care tasks when their wives went out to work in comparison to time spent with children when their wives were at home all day. The findings do not, however, detract from the fact that it is still a mother's life which is most closely meshed with her children's daily lives. They remain primarily responsible for their children's well-being. It is women who care for their children on a full-time basis in their early years and any paid work which they do centre on their children's needs. As Backett (1982: 72–3) suggests, the withdrawal of women from the labour market to care directly for young children subsequently influences the organisation of child-care responsibilities in the household. It is women who are substantially involved with 'direct' parenting and who have a the greater understanding and knowledge of a child's needs. Husbands still depend on their wives to inform them about their children. Knowledge and understanding of a child and the care that is needed is more gradually learnt by fathers, who have a less direct parenting role than their wives (Backett:1982: 198–9). As Michael Clark conceded:

> My wife does tend to do more. She is more involved and knows more about what is going on with our daughter at school. Alison seems to have a very good knowledge of the way the school programme goes. I wouldn't be very good with school things. She tends to spend more time with our daughter. When she is home early, she can be with her for quite a while.

Men, as fathers, are not aloof but are part of a child's life, albeit in a different way from their wives. Mothers, are inextricably bound up with the day-to-day lives of their children.

HUSBANDS AND HOUSEWORK

Similarily, both the men and women interviewees stressed the necessity of husbands helping more substantially around the home when wives worked than might have been the case in the past. The women emphasised that they 'needed' more help because they had less time to perform the work themselves. It implied that help from husbands had to be a regular contribution. They had to participate more fully in the domestic routine, completing mundane tasks as well as the pleasanter side of housework. Most of the women who worked felt that assistance from their husbands had been forthcoming. Obviously, the extent to which this was the case depended on the demands of paid work on women. Where women worked on a full-time basis, they had only as much time as their husbands to perform domestic duties, and relied on greater help from their husbands than others. As Daphne Foulds explained:

> When I went out to work, I went out on condition that I had help in the home. I don't think a housewife should do two full-time jobs. That's not fair to a woman to be honest. If they expect you to earn money, they must be prepared to help in the house. We've been most fortunate. We've done that.

A contractual view of marriage was in evidence once again (Cornwell 1984: 95). Since women were taking on some aspects of the breadwinning role and contributing to the family income, men should take on more responsibilities around the home. It was fair.

For the most part, husbands concurred with these views, although they stressed the sheer necessity of helping their wives. If their wives had less time to do housework because they were working and contributing to household income, they had to do housework regularity. Margaret Kent worked as a machinist at home to contribute to the family income. In the past, she had worked very long hours to supplement the family income. Her husband, Leslie, felt

When you see that your wife has had to work very hard – she was doing a lot of outdoor work at home – it just wasn't fair with her having to do the washing up and then do the sewing. Helping comes through necessity more than anything else really.

Circumstances, therefore, demanded that men did more domestic work in the home. While much preparation was done before they went out and wives still did different types of household tasks from their husbands, husbands were expected to maintain order and tidiness while they were away.[7] The domestic routine should not falter merely because wives were engaged in paid work and were not there to oversee everyday household activities.

'COMPANIONATE' MARRIAGE

Finally, it will be recalled that the Luton team argued that members of the working class increasingly seek the ideal of a 'companionate' marriage. Unlike the 'traditional' working class, they have high expectations of marriage whereby a spouse is a person's most 'significant other'. No other relationship can match the close personal relationship between husband and wife (Goldthorpe *et al.* 1969: 108). A number of commentators (Hart 1976; Leonard 1980; Mansfield and Collard 1988; Morgan 1985), on the other hand, have argued that these ideals of marriage are no more than an ideology of romantic love which emphasises the compatibility of two people in a married relationship. It is these socially constructed definitions of marriage which permeate society and give meaning to married relationships.[8] Against this background the interviewees were asked about their overall feelings towards marriage.

The interviewees did not perceive of marriage in this idealised way and it was discussed in a much more mundane fashion. The notion of marriage as an intimate relationship was underplayed. Teresa Mills felt:

Well, everbody's life is much the same. You get up, go to work, come home, watch telly, go to bed, get up. It's more or less the same for every couple in the world I should think but we seem to get on all right. We have rows and that but I'd say we're an average couple. I think it's how you go along yourself. There's no guarantee of anything. I've known couples who were married thirty or forty years and then they divorced and were off with someone else. There's no ideal partner I think. You go along and take it as it comes I suppose.

Kim Dodd stressed the importance of friendship over and above notions of romantic love.

You don't marry just for love. You're also best friends. If you can't be that there's nothing there. It is true that love isn't always there. If you're friends you can still do things and come to agreements.

It may well be the case, of course, that notions of romantic love are taken on board in courtship and early marriage but this ideology is much less meaningful to people who have been married for a number of years. Their experiences of marriage counteract the impact of this ideology. As Mansfield and Collard (1988) also found, the high expectations of marriage are somewhat different from reality.[9]

Indeed, the interviewees stressed that living so closely and in reasonable harmony with another person was something that was learnt over the years. Intimacy did not exist naturally between two people but emerged from the hard work required if a relationship was to work. Partners have different demands on them throughout their lives and it is important to be sensitive to each other's needs. How they felt about different things, especially when they were tired, did not always coincide. Thus, understanding was deemed important for a successful working relationship. Aziz Malik felt:

> Marriage is all about understanding. If you understand each other, everything else comes later. If I want something and I'm rushing about but Rita's had a bad day or in the middle of something, that's going to start an argument. You feel each other nagging. Little things can start an argument. Understanding is important.

Geoffrey Hayward felt marriage involved 'give and take' and he went further to say:

> There are times when things get on top of me and times when things get on top of Judith. You've got to realise what is going on. It's no good saying pull yourself together. You have to look after each other and pull each other through.

Although their lives were closely meshed, they still had different demands, concerns and worries in their lives. Marriage meant relying on, and confiding in, each other about hopes and fears, more so than even the closest of friends outside the married relationship. Finch found that this 'self-reliant view' of the household is one of the distinctive features which makes the meaning of marriage different in Britain from that in other European countries. She argued:

> there appears to be particular emphasis upon the more 'private' relationships within the household, especially the marriage relationship (a feature which also tends to characterise Australians). British husbands and wives seem more inclined than their married counterparts elsewhere to turn to each other when they need practical help, and rather more likely to keep personal problems within the family or to themselves (Finch 1989b: 102).

As with kin, the strong feelings and emotions attached to the married relationship derive from the long history of the relationship, even if the relationship has not always been easy. The interviewees did not, therefore, uncritically subscribe to the ideals of a 'companionate' marriage as the Luton team alleged, for the reality of married life was much more complex than they described.

CONCLUSION

In contrast to the Luton team's findings, the interviewees' conjugal roles were, for the most part, segregated. Above all, women remain responsible for child-care and housework and their husbands help them. The sexual division of labour, whereby men are employed outside the household for all of their working lives and women fulfil unpaid work at home full-time, albeit for a dwindling amount of time, accounts for this segregation. However, as the women interviewees had invariably returned to the labour market after they had had children, their husbands had become involved in some of the mundane tasks associated with child care and housework. In other words, within the overall framework of segregated conjugal roles, the degree of segregation and jointness of conjugal roles varied across the family life-cycle and according to whether the women were in gainful employment or not.

These findings suggest that the men interviewees' involvement in child-care and housework was the the result of exigencies rather than a desire for a home- and family-centred life-style as Goldthorpe and his colleagues asserted. Once again, structural factors, such as the men's and women's patterns of employment and the lack of child-care provision in Britain in comparison to other European countries, played a significant part in shaping the degree of segregation and jointness of conjugal roles, interacting with the interviewees' norms and values. Both the men and women continued to adhere to a contractual view of marriage, with a strict division of domestic labour. These views meant that women with children sought jobs with hours which sat as comfortably as possible alongside their chief and all-important responsibility of securing the welfare of their children. The difficulties of finding convenient part-time jobs in the labour market, however, dictated that many of the women had to work unsocial hours and to rely primarily on their husbands to mind the children.

Doubts have been raised, once again, about the Luton team's account of changing working-class life-styles over the course of the twentieth century. Their description of the causal links in the chain and the extent of change which they predicted have been found wanting. Despite their more cautious stance on the degree of working-class normative changes in comparison to embourgeoisement theorists, the Luton team still exaggerated the move from segregated to joint conjugal roles and the emergence of 'companionate' marriages. Interacting structural and normative factors have altered the form and nature of conjugal roles over the last ninety years, but the extent of change should not be overstated since many continuities persist. In this chapter, for example, it has been stressed that even though married women with children have increasingly returned to the labour market since the Second World War, they have returned to part-time jobs, thereby retaining their overall responsibility for the well-being of their children and the household as a whole.

Their husbands' changing contribution to child-care and housework must be seen in this context. With these continuities in mind, attention now turns to the interviewees' leisure patterns.

NOTES

1. Of course, it was 'traditional' for married women to work in some industries and labour markets in the late nineteenth century and early twentieth century. Women, for example, had a long history of employment in the textiles factories in Blackburn and elsewhere as the Pilgrim Trust (1938) highlighted in its study of unemployment in the 1930s. The Luton team recognised that studies of the 'traditional' working class, with their emphasis on the almost complete segregation of men's and women's lives, were not representative of working-class life as a whole. However, they still took such portrayals of men's and women's working lives as indicative of working-class life-styles and the bench-mark from which the degree of change could be ascertained.

2. Poverty also accounted for the domestic violence which characterised working-class marriage as Ayers and Lambertz (1986) show in their analysis of marriage relations in inter-war dockland Liverpool. Davies's (1992) remarks on rows over money among working-class couples living in Salford in the early twenieth century imply that domestic violence was a fairly widespread fact of married life among members of the working class. None of the interviewees discussed domestic violence so it was impossible to examine, from the interview data at least, whether married relations have changed in this respect since the first half of the twentieth century.

3. The interviewees' consumer aspirations in general and their desire to own their homes in particular will be discussed further in Chapter 9.

4. This is not to say that securing their future standard of living was the sole consideration in life for the interviewees. They were not pecuniary instrumentalists. With both partners working full-time and without child-care commitments, they had money and the free time to enjoy themselves. Thus, Anthony Dodd said: 'We're trying to get as much out of life before the children come along as then everything changes.' The younger interviewees knew from their parents and friends that rearing children would change their life-styles considerably. Their financial position and their leisure would be greatly curtailed.

5. The question as to why the women did not have a hobby or sport which they enjoyed outside the home like their husbands raises the issue of the patterning of leisure by gender which will be discussed in Chaper 8.

6. Four women worked early in the morning or in the evening, while a further two women had done so in the past.

7. As Michael Clark suggested: 'My wife thinks that I should know all about the car and how it works and I should deal with that. I tend to think a bit that she should do the cooking. I don't think she should do the cooking. She's just a lot better at it than me so I let her do it.'

8. While notions of romantic love might be powerful ideals, it

should not be assumed that men and women uncritically accept an ideology of love and marriage (if such a coherent ideology exists at all). To do so is to presume that these ideals are adhered to irrespective of how meaningful they are for people in their daily lives.

9. The characterisation of marriage as a practical arrangement raises the issue of who controls the family budget. In the first half of the twentieth century, Roberts (1984) found that women took full responsibility for managing the household's financial affairs. These issues were not, unfortunately, discussed in the interviews so the extent to which the gendered management of household finances has changed over the course of the twentieth century has not been examined.

8

LEISURE

The daily routine of the interviewees was, for the most part, dominated by the paid and unpaid work necessary to sustain the individual household. The husbands participated in the domestic routine of the household, albeit in a different way from their wives. While they did not undertake the bulk of domestic and child-care tasks, this was not to say that they played no part in the day-to-day routine of the household. They made an important contribution to the smooth running of the household, especially when their wives worked a substantial number of hours outside the home. This chapter explores the form of the men's and women's leisure. Has leisure become more home- and family-centred for men than it might have been in the past, as Goldthorpe and his colleagues argued? Is their leisure less segregated from women's leisure than it might have been in the early part of the twentieth century? Is privatised leisure the product of 'new' aspirations for the material well-being of the immediate family in the home?

Unlike the Luton team's conclusions, it will be shown that leisure, for men at least, is not exclusively home- and family-centred. While paid work curtails leisure, men continue to enjoy a range of leisure pursuits, from sports to drinking in the local pub, which separates them from their wives. Women's leisure is much more confined to the home than is their husband's leisure, although as child-care tasks diminish they also enjoy leisure activities like keep-fit. Again, patterns of leisure were structured according to the unpaid and paid work demands of the men and women in the sample and, especially for women, according to their stages in the family life-cycle. Work shaped the opportunities for, and constraints on, the amount of leisure time available and the kinds of activities which could be pursued. Neither the men's nor the women's leisure had the consequence of instrumentalism.

The interviewees' leisure patterns, however, could not be described as either extensively communal or highly segregated like 'traditional' working-class leisure. While the men pursued various leisure activities on their own, they also participated in leisure with their families, like barbecues and picnics, which centred on entertaining their children. Similarily, the women's leisure activities were not exclusively confined to the home for as the burden of child-care declined they could also enjoy themselves beyond the home. The interviewees' leisure patterns, in other words, could not be accurately described as jointly privatised or separately communal. If the truth lies somewhere in between these mutually exclusive life-styles, the Luton team's account of the causes of changing working-class leisure, and the extent of these changes, is placed in some doubt.

WORKING-CLASS LEISURE

Commentators on the 'traditional' working class emphasised that men's and women's lives were strictly segregated. Given their different work roles, leisure also took a segregated form. While leisure was segregated between men and women and husbands and wives, however, it was a communal activity as well. Thus, men usually spent their free time with fellow workers drinking in the local pubs and clubs, while women, who had less tangible free time, gossiped with women neighbours, including kin, on the doorsteps and streets close to the home (Bailey 1978; Dennis *et al*. 1956; Kerr 1958; Roberts 1984; Zweig 1952).

On the presumption that women did not really have leisure pursuits, analysis of patterns of leisure among the 'traditional' working class focused on the nature of men's leisure. It was argued that as a consequence of dangerous and physically hard work men sought to enjoy leisure to the full. Drinking, gambling and conversation with fellow workmates in the pubs and clubs was pursued with vigour. Leisure was gregarious, frivolous and excessive, to achieve maximum enjoyment (Dennis *et al*. 1956: 130–1). Little thought was given to the future and the only aim was to enjoy pleasure in the short term. Hoggart argued that 'the immediate and present nature of working-class life puts a premium on the taking of pleasure now, discourag[ing] planning for some future goal in the light of some ideal' (1958: 133). In sum, leisure was an escape from their harsh lives dominated by work to secure only a meagre existence. Excessive drinking and gambling allowed men to cope with their daily lives, allowing them to remain 'cheerful' in site of everything (Zweig 1952: 124).[1]

Embourgeoisement theorists (Klein 1965; Zweig 1961) argued that, as a result of growing consumer aspirations among the working class in the post-war period of prosperity, leisure took a more privatised form than had been the case in the past. The search for the well-being of the immediate family in the home meant that men were no longer so care-free in their leisure (Zweig 1961: 127). They did not want to waste their money on drinking and gambling with fellow workers. They preferred the company of their wives and children in the home instead, and to spend their money more carefully in securing the future well-being of the individual household (Young and Willmott 1983: 118). As a consequence, men spent their free time pottering around the home undertaking DIY tasks, gardening and watching television. Despite these different patterns of leisure, it was still an escape from the harsh world of paid work, but it was now the home, rather than the pub, which acted as a haven. Men enjoyed non-work lives which were quite distinct from their work lives (Klein 1965; Mogey 1956; Zweig 1961).

In yet another change in emphasis, the Luton team distanced themselves from embourgeoisement theorists by highlighting not so much instrumentalism but the consequences of instrumentalism on leisure. Paid and unpaid work curtailed the extent of leisure time and the types of activities which could be pursued. While underlining that their 'respondents' objectives as producers and the conditions of work they experienced did in fact carry implications for their lives outside work', they noted (Goldthorpe et al. 1969: 96) that overtime and unsocial hours, undertaken to secure a high wage, left very little free time for leisure. They argued:

> an active and varied social life within their present community was, we would suggest, made difficult to establish because of the exigencies experienced by our affluent workers in the daily performance of their jobs... We have seen that in the plants in which these men were employed overtime working was the normal practice, and that the majority were required to work according to some sort of shift system. Consequently, leisure hours were frequently curtailed and occurred at unusual and often varying times of day; in addition, energy and what could be perhaps be termed 'social vitality' were likely to be unduly sapped. In these ways, therefore, obstacles must inevitably have been created not only to the acceptance of distinctively middle-class styles of sociability – such as, say, evening parties or extensive participation in clubs and societies – but indeed to *any* kind of frequent and regular association with persons outside the immediate family group (Goldthorpe et al. 1969: 97 emphasis in original).

If wives worked, the opportunities for leisure were limited still further since housework had to be completed at weekends.

Asked to account for their 'main spare-time activities', the Luton team found that nearly two-thirds (62 per cent) of their respondents enjoyed their leisure 'in and about the home itself'. Men spent most of their time doing odd jobs, including gardening and watching television, while women often combined television watching with knitting. These activities were carried out either with or without other members of the immediate family in the home. Thus, Goldthorpe and his colleagues found among their sample of respondents a routine whereby

> after finishing work and carrying out their various chores and familial obligations, our affluent workers and their wives wanted only to 'take it easy' and 'relax' before the daily round began again (1969: 102).

They led home- and family-centred lives with 'husband, wife and children forming together a highly "individuated" and self-reliant group' (Goldthorpe et al. 1969: 101). Thus, the Luton team stressed that force of circumstance, arising from instrumentalism, led to home- and family-centred patterns of leisure.[2]

Somewhat paradoxically, these accounts of changing patterns of working-class leisure described two seemingly different types of leisure as forms of escape from paid work. Yet the ways in which these varied forms of leisure helped people to escape from their jobs were never elaborated upon by either commentators of the 'traditional' working class or the 'new' working class. It was never really explained in any detail, for example, why 'traditional' working-class leisure took the form of gregarious, frivolous socialising rather than any other form of leisure as compensation for hard work. Similarly, it was never explicitly examined how and why patterns of leisure centred on the home and family as a result of 'new' consumer aspiration rather than take a different form altogether. In other words, the very nature of people's leisure activities and why they might enjoy them; what meaning leisure held for them and so forth were never properly examined.

As Moorhouse (1989: 17) has noted, the failure to explore the nature of leisure in itself arose from the way in which it was theorised within the sub-field of the sociology of leisure. Early commentators in the field emphasised the dominance of paid work on leisure and the causal relationship between the two (Cotgrove and Parker 1963; Parker 1964, 1965, 1976; Roberts 1970; Wilensky 1960). The form, nature and meaning of leisure were always defined and described as an adjunct to paid work. It is only more recently that commentators have moved away from focusing on the relationship between leisure and work. One of the major reasons for this shift in analysis came from a recognition that the nature of women's leisure could not be explained with reference to paid work (Bell and Healey 1973; Burns 1973; Moorhouse 1989; Parker 1976; Smith 1973). Indeed, the way in which leisure had been theorised meant that women's leisure had been neglected altogether. As Deem correctly pointed out:

> the *sexual* division of labour's impact on women's lives and leisure
> has been much less researched than the social (that is mental/
> manual) division of labour's impact on men's lives (1986: 5).

Subsequently, feminist sociologists (Deem 1985, 1986; Maynard 1985) and social historians (Davies 1992; Roberts 1984) accounting for women's leisure have raised conceptual issues of how leisure should be defined. Leisure, for women at least, is not a distinct part of their daily lives where they are entirely free from obligations and able to choose what they want to do. Rather, leisure is embedded in their day-to-day existence. Moreover, the amount of leisure available and the form which it takes are not exclusively shaped by paid work but by gender, stage in the family life-cycle and other limiting factors (Bell and Healey 1973; Horne and Jary

1987; Rapaport and Rapaport with Strelitz 1975; Rojek 1989; Smith *et al.* 1973; Smith 1973; Smith 1987; Talbot 1979). Applying this analysis to men's leisure, Brown and his colleagues (1973) and others (Marshall 1986; Marshall *et al.* 1988; Moorhouse 1983) have noted the way in which the workplace can be a site for leisure. It is where people often enjoy the company of fellow workers, customers or whoever. Work and leisure are not distinct areas of women's or men's lives since the boundaries between the two are often blurred.

Against the background of this wide remit, this chapter examines the form and meaning of the men's and women's leisure across the family life-cycle. Is leisure exclusively home- and family-centred for men and women alike, as Goldthorpe and his colleagues argued? Is privatised leisure the product of instrumentalism and the consequent exigencies? How do husbands and wives feel about each other's leisure? Is there any sense of injustice if one partner enjoys more leisure than the other? It will be stressed, as the Luton team also emphasised in their analysis of leisure patterns, that men's and women's work roles in perpetuating the household allowed different opportunities for, and constraints on, their free time across the family life-cycle. However, contrary to the findings of Goldthorpe and his colleagues, it will be argued that exigencies *per se* accounted for the interviewees' patterns of leisure and were not themselves the product of instrumentalism. Moreover, the data illustrate that men still enjoy a measure of independence in their leisure, while women's leisure is closely bound up with their family work role. There are continuities in working-class leisure from the early twentieth century.

MEN AND LEISURE

Obviously, paid work curtailed the amount of leisure which the men in the sample could enjoy and the form which it took. Over half (sixteen) of the men interviewees worked shifts which involved a month of day work and a month of night work. The remaining thirteen men worked on the day shift only, while one man – Simon Sawyer – had opted to work nights permanently. Just under half (thirteen) of the men worked overtime, usually an additional hour at the end of the day, if only, some suggested, to miss the congestion in the factory car plant at the end of the day. Of the other seventeen men who did not work overtime, eight of them mentioned that the opportunities for additional work did not exist in their departments of the factory at all. Unlike the Luton team's respondents, therefore, extensive overtime working was not the norm.[3]

Undoubtedly, the men cited their jobs as the greatest constraint on their leisure. Nightwork certainly curtailed their free time and what they could do with it. Stephen Underwood, for example, noted the dominance of paid work when he worked nights in particular:

I sleep all day. All I do is wash, have dinner and I'm back out to to work. There are no free hours at all and no social life. I do sometimes think I want to go out or not go into work. It is constant work. While they might have free time during the day if they got up early, more often than not they were exhausted, tiredness militating against even 'pottering' around the house and garden. The overwhelming majority of the men disliked nightwork intensely.

They also disliked shiftwork in general. It excluded them from socialising even with other members of the household. While others were relaxing, they might be leaving for work. Their free time did not always correspond with the free time of others, excluding them for the daily routine of their wives and children. At the time of the interviews, Vauxhall management were trying to abolish the 'month about' shift system and to replace it with a 'double-day' shift. This change was being contested by the trade unions, who were concerned about the loss of earnings resulting from the abolition of the night shift. This concerned the men, too, but they also expressed their misgivings about the unsocial hours which they would have to work in the early mornings and late evenings. This was the time they were most likely to spend with their families. Furthermore, the new shift system would disrupt their social lives even more than the exisitng shifts because it would alternate on a weekly rather than a monthly basis. Working a month of days and then a month of nights, despite its drawbacks, was preferred to the proposals for a 'double-day' system.[4]

The men spoke at length about their feelings of tiredness and lack of energy at the end of a working day. As Robert Edwards suggested: 'I just don't want to do anything. I haven't got the energy.' Paid work militated against the 'active' pursuit of hobbies or socialising in their free time. They merely looked forward to quiet and undemanding relaxation. Moreover, the men stressed that, during the week at least, they had little free time anyway. Having completed domestic chores and odd jobs in the early evening, they had only a couple of hours to themselves. Their free time was not all that distinct from the daily routine of sustaining the household. Finally, the prospect of work the next day curtailed their activities in their free time. Their jobs would be even more arduous than usual if they had been out enjoying themselves the previous evening. While tiredness had not mattered in their youth when they were single, it seemed to catch up with them as they became adults and had domestic and child-care responsibilities.

Like the Luton team's respondents, the men felt that they did not 'do a lot', especially during the week and in the winter months. They 'pottered about' in and about the house doing a little gardening, painting and other DIY activities, odd maintenance jobs, reading the national and local newspapers and watching the television. Their leisure activities centred on the home and family. As Roy Mayes suggested:

I haven't got much free time. I stay at home in the week and visit the family at weekends. Work is very tiring and I prefer to stay in.

I might go out for a walk in the summer but in the evenings during
the week I watch television or a video and read the papers.

In a similar vein, Bruce Capel explained:

I do feel tired and I don't do much. I do gardening in the summer
and decorating which I enjoy. I just relax and watch TV. I don't like
going out so much in the week. I prefer people coming in.

There was neither the time nor the inclination to partake in extensive
socialising or to pursue hobbies during the week. After spending the day
in the company of others, they did not want to socialise with other
people, least of all their workmates. They wanted only to relax at home in
congenial surroundings without interruption.

These findings concur with some of Goldthorpe's and his colleagues'
conclusions. The men's jobs certainly curtailed their leisure time and
shaped what they could do in their free time. However, contrary to the
Luton team's explanation of changing leisure, these circumstances were
important in themselves in structuring the men's patterns of leisure.
There was little evidence to suggest that the exigencies they faced were
the consequences of pecuniary instrumentalism.

The data also confirm, in part, Pahl's (1984) more recent study of
working-class lives in the 1980s. He found what he termed extensive
'self-provisioning' on the Isle of Sheppey, household members spending
a lot of their free time maintaining their homes and engaged in a variety
of DIY activities. He argued that self-provisioning is not merely a response for those people who cannot afford to employ the services of
others but 'it also provides aesthetic satisfactions, pride in workmanship
and a sense of domestic solidarity (Pahl 1984: 105). He linked informal
work around the home, in other words, to working-class domestic respectability. However, the interviewees of this study did not speak of
their home-centred leisure activities in such fond terms or as a compensation for the drudgery of their jobs. Instead, they continually emphasised
the ways in which paid work constrained the amount of free time they
had and what they could do with it.

These remarks are supported when the men's leisure activities at the
weekend are considered. The majority of the younger men in the sample
enjoyed (playing or watching) a sport in their free time. Football and
fishing were the favoured sports, although cricket, golf and squash were
also mentioned. Invariably, they had enjoyed these hobbies from their
youth. Gerald Mills, for example, explained that he 'started sea fishing
when I was a young boy. I used to go with a school friend and his father.'
Andrew Bennett played football regularly and he enthused:

I'm a sports fanatic. I don't do anything else except sport. I don't
mind doing a bit of gardening or decorating but if I've got any free
time sport will come first. If I got the chance to play I would rather
do that than gardening or anything else.

Various sporting activities, therefore, dominated many of the men's leisure. They were, of course, largely segregated sports, football and fishing being almost exclusively dominated by men. They enjoyed the games in themselves, for the social contact with other men who enjoyed the same hobbies and as something different from work. Returning to Gerald Mills, for example, he enjoyed deep-sea fishing because 'its just getting away from everything, the change. When you're out at sea, you can't even see the land. It's all peace and quiet.' Escaping from work was an aspect but not the sole reason why they enjoyed their leisure pursuits.

Contrary to the Luton team's findings, therefore, there was evidence of continuities in working-class men's leisure patterns. Like working-class men of the early twentieth century (Bailey 1978; Davies 1992), the men enjoyed a sport with other men, be they kin, workmates or childhood friends. Their leisure was segregated and took them away from the immediate family in the home. When they had some tangible free time, their leisure patterns were not exclusively centred on the immediate family in the home.

However, this is not to suggest that the men were immersed in their hobbies for extensive amounts of time. Like Andrew Bennett with his football, Kevin Jackson played golf once a week mostly in the summer, while the anglers of the sample might spend Saturday or Sunday fishing in the season. There was little evidence of their hobbies seriously detracting from time spent with their wife and children. Nor did the men necessarily want to devote all of their time playing or watching sport, since there were other things to do and other people to socialise with. Stephen Underwood, for example, used to spend almost all of his weekends fishing with his father and brothers when he was single but now that he was married, he felt 'I don't think Bridget minds and I could still go off. She knows where I am but I wouldn't want to go off and leave her so much.' He enjoyed his hobby but it did not dominate his free time, excluding him from other pursuits.

Many of the men also enjoyed a regular drink when they had some tangible free time from work. They might casually pop into the local pub on a Friday night or more formally arrange to go to a pub or club on a Saturday night, usually with kin or, in the case of the younger members of the sample, old school friends and other friends from their youth. They might also casually meet their neigbours and other Vauxhall workers using the local pub as well. The men emphasised that they needed and deserved a drink at the end of a hard week's work. They felt 'entitled' to a 'break' away from the routine of paid and unpaid work. After a hard week's work in the factory and at home, it was quite legitimate that they should enjoy some tangible leisure time away from the daily routine entirely. At least they could relax without work intruding into their spare time. Matthew Smith went to a club at the weekend with his father and brothers, and he argued 'I give my attention and time to my wife and child all week so the Saturday evening is my free time.' While never explicitly stated, it seemed that the men felt that the burdens of work fell more heavily on their shoulders than on their wives, especially working in the dirt and grime of the factory, and that they should be able to enjoy a drink while their wives stayed at home with the children. The men played down the importance of other regular users of the pub. They were acquaintances. They might 'pass the time of day' with them and chat about local news and sport but these men were not close friends. Neil Palmer enjoyed the company of people he knew from his youth at the pub close to his parents' home on a Friday night but he also ventured to say 'there are quite a lot of people I know but there's not much to it. I leave them to come home after a quick drink.' Malik Aziz also stressed the casual nature in which he met people from his bachelor days:

At the weekends I might pop out and have a few drinks with friends from the old days when I was single. I know them to have a chat. I don't tell them everything just say I've been busy when they ask where I've been. I still go but I don't go as much as I used to. I just go up to the pub and if some are not there I know someone else will be. I know where they gather so I go there on my own.

Once again, however, it appeared that the men went out for a drink at the end of their working week. They did not spend a lot of time in the company of other men in the local pub to the detriment of their wives and children at home. Accordingly, time spent at the local pub was not resented by the wives in the sample even though they did not enjoy the same freedom as did their husbands. They did not enjoy drinking in the local pub so they were not especially aggrieved when their husbands went out and they did not. As Teresa Mills explained:

I don't go out in the evenings. I like watching the telly and sitting in and knitting. Occasionally I go to bingo. My husband likes a pint. I don't mind going out with him for an hour for a drink. I don't like drink really and I'm not one for sitting in pubs.

Her husband, as the most regular drinker in the sample, liked to catch the last hour of drinking time once or twice during the week as well, but his excursions to the local pub did not stop Mrs Mills watching television and knitting, which she would rather be doing.

Frequenting the local pub, therefore, meant that the men's leisure was not exclusively home- and family-centred as the Luton team alleged. Unlike their wives, they went out and invariably enjoyed the company of other men, not unlike working-class men in the early part of the twentieth century. Nevertheless, the picture which emerges falls far short of the extensive sociability between men in the pubs and clubs of the 'traditional' working-class community (Dennis *et al.* 1956; Zweig 1952). Nor was their any evidence to suggest that these men held a strong sense of belonging to the group of men whom they casually met in the pub or allegiance to a common set of norms and values. Sociability, in this limited form, was not the bedrock of working-class solidarity.

Then, of course, doubts have been raised about the portrayal of extensive drinking by men in the pubs and clubs in the first half of the twentieth century. Was it representative of working-class men's leisure as a whole or was it only to be found in particular regions? There are studies of the 'traditional' working class which offer a somewhat different picture of men's leisure activities from that of segregated leisure in the pubs and clubs. For example, Rich's study (1953: 307) of leisure in the Black Country noted the way in which men were often involved in informal social activities around the home in the early evening, and enjoyed a visit to the pub only in the latter part of the day. Women would remain at home with the children. While women spent more of their free time at home than men they also occasionally joined their husbands in the pubs and clubs. Joint or family leisure was enjoyed in the clubs where a range of activities were undertaken. They were not exclusively male enclaves. These findings suggest that men's patterns of leisure have not altered as much as the Luton team led us to believe.[5]

Of course, the extent to which the men played sport or frequented the local pub varied according to age and stage in the family life-cycle. Some of the older men recalled how they had stopped playing football, for example, in their early thirties as their physical fitness had declined. Many of these older men, not unlike the Luton team's respondents, had worked overtime when it was available and when their children were young and household expenses high. Their leisure had been particularly home- and family-centred at this stage of the family life-cycle. This was evident among the men with dependent children. The weekend was also a time when they socialised with both the immediate family and extended kin. With some tangible free time, the opportunities existed for 'active' pursuits with partners and children beyond the home. Roy Mayes, who had four children, described how he and his family 'often see the wife's family and go out for the day to different places with them. We go out for a meal with the kids too and try different places.' Similarly, Robert Edwards, who had two young daughters, suggested, 'we go out for picnics, take a blanket and go out anywhere and the children think it's wonderful'. While Mr Edwards loyally watched Luton Town playing at home every other Saturday, family activities and entertaining the children in particular took up much of his free time as well. It appeared that the men in the sample were not aloof fathers who took little interest in other members of the immediate family. Leisure activities were enjoyed with them and one type of leisure did not preclude the other. There was little evidence of family neglect.

As has been suggested, most of the women interviewees were not especially unhappy with their husband's leisure patterns and their freedom to leave the family home for an uninterrupted drink or a football match. As Deem also found in her study in Milton Keynes:

> Even among women who felt no sense of resentment about this, there was in the research an awareness that most men were able to

enjoy leisure in a much more unfettered way than most women (1986: 40).

Indeed, some of women spoke of the advantages of their husband's absences. Mrs Kasim, for example, got 'fed up' with the 'waiting around' for her husband to come in after an afternoon's cricket. On the other hand, his absence also meant that 'it gives me the chance to catch up with work and bits round the house. I pop into my mum or go shopping.' While Mrs Kasim referred to the work she could do while her husband was playing cricket, as we shall see, many of the women interviewees enjoyed being on their own at home, doing odd jobs at their own pace.

However, there was tension between the partners of two couples over the men's freedom to do 'their own thing' in their free time. Interestingly, both of the men enjoyed quite different hobbies from the rest of the men in the sample. They were or had been time-consuming hobbies as well. Leslie Kent was involved in St John's Ambulance and he had been active in an amateur dramatics group.

> I gave it up when it was getting too much. Margaret was getting depressed being on her own so much as I was out all the time rehearsing. I would like to do more duties for St. John's but I would feel guilty because I couldn't go out with Margaret. Therefore, I don't take it up. On the Saturday she likes to get out of the house and go shopping or visit markets.

Although she had worked almost all of their married life, Mrs Kent had worked alone as a machinist at home. She disliked spending so much time alone in the house while her husband pursued his own hobbies. As a result of her husband's frequent absences, she had joined a choir.

> I got involved when I was fed up with my husband always being out. He encouraged me and I now enjoy singing in the group. I hadn't the confidence to do things on my own before.

Similarily, George Stone spent a considerable amount of time researching his family tree and he belonged to a local history society. He talked about the constraints on the amount of time which he could devote to his hobby:

> In any hobby that I want to do it's awkward because apart from weekends you're either at work or miss out. At weekends my wife wonders what I'm doing because I want to relax and do a hobby myself and go out and it upsets her while most of the time I'm at work I miss my hobbies and I can't get involved because I'm either working or tired out.

Speaking of his wife's leisure he noted that she did not have any hobbies. He went on to say:

> She enjoys the garden and her animals but other than that she hasn't really got a hobby. We differ because she's got her own things and I've got mine so we go different ways at weekends. She's got a home as well and the children to look after.

Going 'different ways' in this case clearly meant that Mr Stone was free to pursue his leisure activities while Mrs Stone was restricted to the home. He was unfettered by domestic and child-care obligations. Unlike the other men's hobbies, his leisure detracted from family time. As we shall see, women do not enjoy to the same extent hobbies which free them from the domestic routine and all of its responsibilities.

Overall, it was found that paid work and, to a lesser extent, unpaid work limited the amount of leisure which the men enjoyed and the range of activities which they could enjoy in the time free to them. Tiredness at the end of the day and a limited amount of spare time confined their activities to DIY, gardening and television watching, as the Luton team also found. Unlike the Luton team's findings, however, paid and unpaid work were important structuring influences on the men's patterns of leisure in themselves and were not merely the consequence of working-class instrumentalism in the post-war period of prosperity. Moreover, the men's leisure activities were not exclusively confined to the home in a 'highly individuated' fashion as the Luton team argued. Especially at the weekends, they enjoyed leisure activities beyond the domestic routine of home and family life in a manner, as we shall now see, that their wives did not. In this respect, some of their leisure activities were segregated.

However, the extent and nature of these independent leisure pursuits fell far short of the kind of extensive socialising with other men in pubs and clubs associated with the 'traditional' working class. Their independent leisure activities did not preclude joint family outings and excursions which usually involved entertaining dependent children in the most demanding stage of the family life-cycle. Their leisure could not be appropriately described as 'privatised' or 'communal' for the truth appeared to lie somewhere in between.

WOMEN AND LEISURE

Like those of their husbands, the women's leisure patterns were shaped according to the demands of paid and unpaid work, which were in turn structured by the family life-cycle. The women rearing young children at home had the most home- and family-centred leisure of all the women interviewees. The women described how they tried to set aside different parts of the day for work and leisure. The bulk of domestic work was completed in the morning and the afternoon was kept free for their leisure activities. Preparations for the husband's home-coming were begun again in the late afternoon and early evening when the children were also prepared for bed. With the children in bed, they could then relax with their husbands in the evening. In this respect, the women spoke of the freedom to organise their own routine. On the other hand, they conceded that it was extremely difficult to confine domestic and child-care tasks to the morning and evening, and usually they worked intermittently throughout the day. While they had some room to manoeuvre, they recognised that their leisure was curtailed by their role as mothers of young children. These findings support much of the literature illustrating the ways in which women's lives, including their leisure, are dominated by their role in the family (Gavron 1966; Hobson 1978; Holme 1985; Rapoport and Rapoport with Strelitz 1975).

Unlike their husbands, the women found it difficult to define their leisure. After some thought, they cited time spent with their children in the afternoon, when domestic work was temporarily complete, as their major source of leisure. Undoubtedly, the women derived great pleasure from entertaining and playing with their children, who in turn entertained them. As Rita Aziz suggested: 'these days I am mostly with my son playing with him. Since he came along my leisure time is playing with him.' At the same time, they acknowledged that the joys of parenthood were tempered by the stresses and strains of child-care. Their children could be very demanding and hard work. As Jane Bennett noted: 'I'm at the stage when my daughter is a handful. She is into everything, and being pregnant I do get tired.'

These findings go some way to confirm the time budget analysis conducted by Gershuny and Jones (1986: 30), who argued that time spent looking after children has increased over this century as time spent on domestic work has declined. The women's accounts also hint at the ways in which work and leisure are so closely intertwined for women in a way that is not the case for men. Since both work and leisure are undertaken at home, work time and leisure time are hard to distinguish as they intrude into each other. Invariably, for women with dependent children at least, leisure is enjoyed within the context of work. It is not a distinct time in which they can pursue their own hobbies unfettered by domestic and child-care demands (Hobson 1978: 88–9).

When they were not entertaining their children or seeing their female kin and neighbours (whose company, as we know, was usually enjoyed in the afternoon), the young women might watch television, listen to the radio, play records or do some knitting, sewing or dress-making. Lisa Smith described how she would usually 'sit and play cards, watch TV or go out for a short walk', while Rita Malik suggested:

> I'm not stuck with my son all the time. When he sleeps I carry on with housework. If I finish that and there's nothing else to do I can sit down and watch TV for an hour or something else. I try to do some sewing or dress-making if I have time.

Thus, they had small amounts of free time – usually not more than an hour or so – which limited what they could actually do. Moreover, they were confined to the home by their children which curtailed their activities still further. It was not surprising to find that many of their leisure activities encompassed a domestic side as well (Hobson 1978: 85–6). Just as paid work shaped and patterned the men's leisure, so unpaid work structured the women's range of leisure activities.

Unlike their husbands, therefore, none of the young women pursued independent hobbies beyond the home. Once the household routine had been temporarily completed in the evening, they, like their husbands, watched television or busied themselves in and around the home. Their weekend activities did not differ significantly from during the week. They might visit kin, go shopping or take their children out on an excursion with their husbands. They certainly did not go out alone to enjoy themselves with other women on a Friday or Saturday evening. Securing the physical, social and psychological well-being of their children was literally a full-time occupation.[6]

As their children become more independent, however, women's child-care tasks decline and they have more free time. which, in turn, increases the range of activities in which they can engage. Of course, the extent to which this is the case depends on such factors as the number of children in a family, the age of the youngest child and, importantly, whether a woman returns to work full- or part-time. Like their husbands, those women who worked full-time found their leisure was seriously curtailed by their jobs. What little leisure time existed was confined to the home during the week, especially since they carried the 'double burden' of paid and unpaid work (Cavendish 1982; Coyle 1984; Pollert 1981; Yeandle 1984).

Like their husbands, these women suggested that they were tired from paid work and they wanted only to relax quietly in the home. Kim Dodd described these feelings: 'Work is mentally tiring. I very rarely go out in the week. I come in and cook which I hate. I do some knitting and watch television.' In a similar vein Irene Cass suggested:

> With work I am standing all day and it is very tiring. When I come in I don't want to move. I feel exhausted. I'm entitled to a little relax. I sit down with a cup of tea and a fag. That time belongs to me. Sometimes I just go to bed after a meal if I feel like it. I don't go out during the week. I don't feel like bothering to see people as I'm just so tired.

Home, as has been argued elsewhere (Devine 1989; Marshall *et al.* 1988; Saunders 1990), was a haven from the busy world outside for the women as well as for the men of the sample. It was the place where they could sit down and relax, albeit briefly, from the demands of other people. After a 'hectic' day's work the women did not want to undertake any strenuous or demanding activities in the evenings. Reading, watching television and knitting were activities which the women mentioned as relaxing.

Similarly, weekends were spent completing large domestic tasks and relaxing with the family. As Anita Palmer explained:

> I've not got any hobbies away from the family. I would love to but I haven't got the time. My idea of weekends now is to be with Neil and my son. I don't see much of them in the week so that is my pleasure to be with the family.

It was also a time when they could visit their extended kin or take children out for the day to a zoo, theme park or similar establishments. Their leisure patterns, in many respects, were not fundamentally different from the women raising their children at home full-time. Bar the occasional night out with colleagues from work, they did not, for example, have a 'break' from the domestic routine like their husbands.

For those women whose free time was not subsequently swallowed up by their jobs, a slightly wider range of activities was open to them in increasingly tangible amounts of free time. Particularly during the day, these women were able to enjoy a hobby and meet other people outside the home. Sheila Ibbotson, who had two school-aged children, had an unusually flexible day since she was self-employed in the catering business and demand for work varied. She described a typical day:

> I fit in the shopping and housework around work. I might see a few friends for coffee. It has lapsed but we did do a lot of keep-fit together – swimming and jogging. If I'm out having a coffee or at yoga that is leisure time.

Pauline Graves, who had a 26-year-old son living at home, worked as a cleaner for two hours every day in the early morning. She suggested:

> I don't stay at home. I have as much freedom as I want. I do keep-fit or go into town. In the mornings I get most of my housework done then and I take the dog for a walk. My free time time begins when I want it. I don't restrict myself at all. There's no strict routine if I want to do something earlier. I do a lot of walking, knitting, keep-fit and dancing.

Inevitably, leisure still included activities normally associated with women, including visiting family and friends, knitting and watching television. The additional hobby which seemed to take up women's time was keep-fit, which included activities such as swimming, jogging and yoga. This was enjoyed with other women in the same situation as themselves who were also available. Women with independent children also found they could attend evening classes since their children no longer demanded they be confined to the home at night. These findings confirm many of the findings of Deem's (1986) study of female patterns of leisure across the life-cycle.

That said, the women found that much of their day was filled with paid employment, domestic tasks and child-care duties. Leisure activities were not enjoyed endlessly but squeezed into a full day, and not all of the women could enjoy hobbies to the same extent, if at all, away from the home. Catherine Mayes who had four children at school, worked part-time as a home-help. She explained her daily routine:

> I finish work at half past one and I spend the afternoons cleaning, and preparing the dinner. I don't have much free time. I have half an hour before the children come in from school when I have a cigarette and relax.

Indeed, some of the women found that catering for their independent children was as strenuous as coping with dependent children too. Karen Osbourne had four sons in their late teens and early twenties living at home, two of whom were working. She felt:

I don't have very much time. It's seven thirty before dinner is finished and all the things are done. I had more free time when the children were small. With four boys at home that's six large meals and a lot of washing.

For other women, evenings were often spent facilitating their children's leisure. Angela Stone had a 13-year-old daughter who demanded much of her time:

I do the tea and then I might sit and watch television. I take my daughter to dancing three times a week so a good part of the week has gone. I have to stay there for two of the classes which are one hour each so it's too long to do anything else in the evenings.

Indeed, it was mothers rather than their fathers who took children backwards and forwards to their hobbies, while the men relaxed at home. Thus, in the evenings and at weekends, they were not always free to relax in a way that their husbands did as they continued their 'mothering duties'. While they took pleasure from seeing their children enjoying themselves, they always felt so 'busy' with the children. They had little free time to themselves. This illustrates, once again, the way in which women's lives are so closely intertwined with family activities, leaving them with little freedom to enjoy an individual hobby independent of the immediate family in the home. Only when husband and children left the home during the day did they have some time and space for themselves.

Furthermore, other women found that their activities were curtailed because their part-time employment still dominated the day, leaving only limited amounts of free time. Judith Hayward worked as a cook at school and noted this problem:

My work hours are spread across the day. In the morning I can't do much with going to work and in the afternoons I can't do much with coming home to prepare the meal. If I had morning hours I would have the afternoons free.

Barbara Wright resented attempts by her employers to get her to do overtime, knowing it would intrude into her small amount of free time:

I like to know I can come away at two and have the rest of the afternoon to myself. I know in advance what I'm doing. That time between my job and my family coming home is the part of the day I have to myself. It gives me a little time to think and maybe do a little something on my own.

For these women, being on 'one's own' was an important source of relaxation when they were not caring for the needs of others. Pleasure was gained from having time when they could do as they pleased, even though it often involved 'pottering' around the home or occasionally visiting friends. It was a time in the day when their activities were uninterrupted and they could do things at their own pace. This small amount of time was jealously guarded as a tangible period which women could devote to themselves. This was their leisure when they could 'look after themselves' rather than anyone else.

To a greater or lesser extent, therefore, as parental responsibilities diminish, women have the opportunity to enjoy a broader range of leisure activities than in earlier, more demanding, stages in the family life-cycle. While not wishing to over-state the differences between the leisure patterns between women in and out of formal employment, their leisure was certainly influenced by the number of hours which they worked. It dictated the amount of free time which they enjoyed and what they could do in the spare time.

CONCLUSION

Paid and unpaid work structured the opportunities for, and constraints on, leisure of all of the interviewees. It determined the amount of free time available, which in turn influenced what feasibly could be done in their spare time. For the most part, work left the interviewees with little free time during the week or the energy to engage in extensive socialising with other people at the end of day. On weekdays at least, free time was in short supply, confining men and women to 'pottering' in and around the house and garden. It was not a way of spending their free time which the interviewees embraced enthusiastically but the brute facts of sustaining their material existence meant their preferences for a different type of life were at best secondary

Some of the data arising from this research confirm the Luton team's findings. A similar range of activities, including watching the television, reading the national and local daily newpapers, gardening, DIY and knitting, was common to the respondents interviewed by the Luton team and the interviewees of this study. Goldthorpe and his colleagues also highlighted the major structuring influence of both paid and unpaid work on leisure patterns. However, the Luton team was keen to show that work, and particularly paid work, was a dominant influence on people's lives because they wanted to secure high standards of living. As members of the working class, their respondents could earn high wages to attain these ends only by shiftwork and overtime (Goldthorpe *et al.* 1969: 101–3). On the other hand, this chapter has highlighted the ways in which both paid and unpaid work, in itself and irrespective of consumer aspirations, was a major structuring influence on patterns of leisure. Securing their basic material standard of living and not new norms and aspirations for material well-being governed these people's daily lives. This suggests, contrary to the Luton team's findings, that leisure patterns have not changed as a result of 'new' consumer aspirations among members of the working class in the post-war period of prosperity.

Nor, indeed, have working-class leisure patterns changed as dramatically as the Luton team and embourgeoisement theorists before them alleged. The interviewees' leisure patterns and especially the men's leisure were not exclusively home- and family-centred. A range of sporting activities and drinking in the local pub, for example, took many of the men away from the company of the immediate family in the home at the weekend. Some of their leisure, therefore, was segregated and spent in the company of other men. Their wives, on the other hand, were far more confined to the home in comparison, their leisure being closely intertwined with their children. Thus, the way in which paid and unpaid work shaped the form and meaning of leisure varied between the men and women in the sample. It also varied across the life-cycle, confining men as well as women during the most demanding stage of the family life-cycle and freeing women as well as men as child-care tasks gradually diminished.

In some respects, therefore, the segregated nature of the men's and women's leisure was not unlike 'traditional' working-class leisure as portrayed by numerous commentators (Dennis *et al.* 1956; Zweig 1952). However, unlike 'traditional' working-class men, the male interviewees were not engaged in extensive leisure pursuits which took them away from the home and family for considerable periods of time. For the most part, their segregated leisure pursuits did not prohibit joint family activities. Indeed, the majority of the male interviewees, alongside their wives, enjoyed family leisure, often facilitating and sharing the leisure pursuits of their children. Similarly, the women were not entirely confined to the home, enjoying hobbies like keep-fit as their children became more independent of them.

This chapter concludes the examination on the extent to which the interviewees' lives could be accurately described as home-centred. Unlike the Luton team's findings, the evidence suggests that the interviewees' lives were not exclusively home-centred. The men were not totally involved in the domestic routine of the household and continued to enjoy leisure activities in the company of men beyond the home. Their daily lives were not entirely home-centred. Nor, for that matter, were the women's lives confined to the immediate family in the home. Many of the women worked outside the home and, if their jobs did not swallow all their free time, they enjoyed some leisure on their own as well. Rather than men moving into the home, the data indicated that women are moving out of it.

This chapter also concludes the analysis of the interviewees' styles of life in general. The interviewees' daily lives were neither privatised nor communal. While the paid and unpaid demands of sustaining the individual household shaped their day-to-day existence, it did not prohibit the interviewees socialising with other people or participating in activities beyond the home. In other words, both the Luton team's causal account of the demise of the 'traditional' working-class community and their explanation of the rise of home- and family-centred life-styles since the Second World War have been placed in some doubt. Goldthorpe and his colleagues identified 'new' wants and aspirations among members of the working class in the post-war period of prosperity as the major catalyst of change in people's life-styles and socio-political proclivities. It is to the interviewees' consumer aspirations and social perspectives that this study will now turn while the final empirical chapter will examine their industrial and political attitudes and behaviour.

NOTES

1. This argument implies that the 'traditional' working class found ways of living with the harsh realities of their daily working lives.
2. The Luton team's emphasis on the impact of paid and unpaid work on leisure is not, of course, unlike the central argument of this book. As we shall see, however, it will be argued that work in itself, and not as a consequence of instrumentalism, shaped the men's and women's leisure patterns across the family life-cycle.
3. Other men had worked overtime in the past but now chose not to work additional hours. As Malik Aziz explained:

   I work eight to five, days only. I don't do overtime. I'm not a grabber. I used to be when I did shift work. I often did seven nights a week when I was single. I just did it to make myself secure when I married. I had a big wedding which cost a lot of money. We lived at home for five months until we found a house to buy of our own. I don't need the money now. I've got everything.

   Unlike the Luton team's respondents, even those men who worked additional hours were not singularly instrumental.
4. After much detailed discussion, the new shift system was introduced in 1988 (The *Luton* News: 3 November 1988)
5. The Luton team (1969: 106) contrasted their own findings with Rich's study of leisure patterns in the Black Country, although Rich's findings were quite similar to their data. The leisure patterns of her men and women interviewees were not entirely separate and were not nearly as segregated as those found by Dennis and his colleagues (1956).
6. The women without children usually went out with their husbands at the weekend but, given their dislike of baby-sitters, the women with young children went out only occasionally.

9

ASPIRATIONS AND SOCIAL PERSPECTIVES

While the interviewees' daily lives revolved around the household, their life-styles could not be accurately described as privatised. Their lives were neither entirely family-centred, nor exclusively home-centred. Sustaining the well-being of the household demanded much of their time but it did not completely prohibit sociability with kin, neighbours and colleagues from work. Nor did it exclude leisure activities beyond the home for the men and women interviewees, either separately or jointly with their children. Moreover, there was little evidence to suggest that the interviewees consciously chose their home- and family-centred life-styles to secure the 'material well-being, the social cohesiveness and the autonomy of the conjugal family' (Goldthorpe *et al.* 1969: 108). Instrumentalism did not account for their life-styles. Rather, the form and nature of their daily lives was the product of the work involved in sustaining the continued existence of the household. The work required, be it paid or unpaid, shaped the opportunities for, and constraints on, sociability and leisure. The interviewees' norms and values reflected and, in part, legitimised, the structuring influence of work on their lives.

This chapter focuses on the interviewees' aspirations, and their perceptions of and feelings towards the social order. These two issues are considered together since, as the Luton team argued (1969: 116–7), the meaning of people's aspirations can be understood only in the social context and life experiences in which they are formed.[1] It will be seen that the threat of redundancy and unemployment hung over these families' lives and the Vauxhall workers hoped to hold on to their jobs for as long as possible. In the meantime, all they could do was carry on with their daily lives. This included striving for improved standards of living like other 'ordinary, respectable families'. However, the interviewees did not look to general economic advancement or industrial and political struggles (to be discussed more fully in Chapter 10) for economic improvements, as the Luton team found. Rather, they expected to enjoy small, cumulative gains as the household moved through the family life-cycle. Not surprisingly, the interviewees did not share the optimism of the Luton team's respondents. That said, neither were their consumer aspirations fixed despite the difficult economic circumstances under which they lived their lives.

Turning to the issue of social consciousness, the interviewees proffered a pecuniary model of the class structure. This finding concurs with the Luton team's data on images of the social order. However, sharing similiar standards of living and striving for more improvements was an important dimension of class solidarity. In other words, the interviewees' consumer aspirations were not the source of schism or individualism. Moreover, it was a source of great dissatisfaction to many of the interviewees that their lives were dominated by the dull complusion of economic necessity, while others, especially the upper class, enjoyed a freedom away from purely instrumental, material concerns. They occupied the lower echelons of a class-based society which was deemed both unfair and unjust. In this respect, they were class conscious rather than conservative. Indeed, these consumer aspirations and class identity were the source of wider ideals for a different, freer and more democratic society than existed at present. Contrary to the Luton team's findings, the interviewees' aspirations did not lie exclusively within the capitalist system.

WORKING-CLASS ASPIRATIONS

It was argued (Dennis *et al.* 1956; Hoggart 1957; Kerr 1958; Zweig 1952) that working-class aspirations were fixed in the past. Members of the working class had no desire to improve their economic circumstances, and their concern was focused on maintaining their current standards of living. They accepted life fatalistically, emphasising the present rather than looking forward to the future. Kerr's study of a Liverpool slum, for example, found little desire among its inhabitants to improve their standard of living even though their housing was poor and they enjoyed few facilities.[2] She found 'little money is spent on making the home more comfortable to live in, though in some cases, a parlour is kept for ritual occasion' (Kerr 1958: 27). These attitudes, it was argued, derived from a dichotomous view of society, a perception of an unchanging social order strictly divided between 'them' and 'us'. Given their fixed class position, members of the working class did not expect their economic circumstances to improve in the future. Unchanging economic and social circumstances, in other words, shaped working-class wants and expectations.

Various commentators (Black and Simey 1954; Jennings 1962; Kuper 1953; Mogey 1956; Young and Willmott 1957; Zweig 1961) argued that economic prosperity in the post-war period fuelled 'new' economic and social aspirations among the working class. Enjoying secure employment and improved standards of living for the first time, working-class people no longer expected their material lives to stay the same. They looked to the future with optimism, expecting further material improvements and improved social standing. Moreover, they viewed the social order in a different light. They no longer saw the class structure and their own class position as unchanging, rather the opportunities for mobility were open. Working-class solidarity, it was argued, was thereby undermined in the pursuit of individual material well-being and status enhancement. The Luton team distanced itself from the embourgeoisement theorists' arguments. They agreed that the new working class aspired for economic prosperity. They wanted more money to spend to attain a 'high standard of domestic living'. In the sphere of consumption rather than production, they could enjoy 'autonomy and creativity'. Their respondents, with little experience of unemployment, had few anxieties about job insecurity. There was little evidence of fatalism as they looked to the future without fear or doubts. With a clear majority (62 per cent) having experienced improvements in their standard of living in the previous ten years, they optimistically looked ahead to achieving further economic advance. The basis of these aspirations lay in a belief that economic progress would continue. The Luton team stated:

> Our conclusion must then be that the attainment of progressively higher standards of domestic living represents the typical 'project' among the workers we studied. For these men and their families, we would suggest, there are no longer well-established patterns of consumption with which they are content to conform, but rather they are aware of a wide range of possibilities out of which many different life-styles may be created. The recognition of such possibilities generates the desire for ever-increasing consumer power (1968a: 142).

However, Goldthorpe and his colleagues stressed that the 'manner' in which these aspirations were pursued was different from middle-class practices, shaped by the fact that the men were still wage-workers. Their respondents did not seek promotion or to set up their own business as a viable way of making further material advances. They were realistically aware of the objective barriers to advancement by these means. Their economic future would not be shaped individually by themselves but collectively, either by the economic progress of the country as a whole or by industrial and political struggles.[3] Contrary to embourgeoisement theorists, the Luton team argued there was little evidence of rampant individualism in the pursuit of economic advancement or a search for status enhancement.

The Luton team found that their respondents did not discuss their family finances together or plan them over time. Saving was done to pay the bills or to buy particular items in an *ad hoc* way. They were not financial planners who made long-term decisions on spending and saving. These attitudes and behaviour, the Luton team concluded, arose from the 'conditions of service and occupational opportunities' of the manual worker

> who is primarily dependent upon general wage increases for his material advancement and whose further income will tend thus to

be less progressive and also less certain and predictable – even assuming that his continuity of employment is unbroken (Goldthorpe *et al.* 1969: 126).

Finally, finding no evidence to suggest that workers and their wives restricted family size as a way of increasing their consumer power, the Luton team examined the respondents' educational and occupational aspirations for their children. They found that their respondents wanted their children to go to grammar schools for a good education, high-level qualifications and further educational opportunities. They also wanted their children to enter non-manual jobs, not only for the economic rewards and prospects which they offered but also for the inherent attractions. Again, the Luton team placed these aspirations in the context of the life experiences of their respondents:

> The relevant experience in this respect, we would suggest was not the failure of our affluent workers to secure while-collar status, but rather their confrontation with the distinctively working-class dilemma... of having to choose between work which provides them with some degree of instrinsic satisfaction and work which afforded the highest going rate of economic return. If one accepts the subjective significance of this dilemma in the case of a sizeable proportion of our respondents, then it is readily understandable that, for their children, they should hope for occupations that offered a high level of material reward *and* of inherent attractiveness, and for the type of education that is generally necessary in order to open the way into such occupations (Goldthorpe *et al.* 1969: 133–4, emphasis in original).

The inability to meet these aspirations in comparison to their white-collar counterparts derived from persistent normative differences – such as the value placed on vocational rather than academic subjects – between the working class and middle class. The evidence suggested that the respondents still held a working-class outlook on life with regard to their aspirations for their children.

PRODUCTION ASPIRATIONS

Against the background of stagflation outlined in Chapter 1, the aim of this research was to explore the nature of the interviewees' aspirations. Did the interviewees strive for and expect to enjoy improvements in their material standard of living in the future like the 'new' working class? Or, given the very different economic climate from the post-war period of prosperity in which the *Affluent Worker* study was conducted, did they presume that their social and economic circumstances would remain the same? Were they content to accept their lot as was said of the 'traditional' working class? What was the basis of their optimism or pessimism about their economic futures? Did the interviewees seek to improve their economic circumstances by individual or collective means? Of course, whether fatalism aptly describes people's perceptions of Britain's economic problems in general has been widely debated throughout the 1970s and 1980s (Alt 1979; Marshall *et al.* 1988). However, the extent to which fatalism has re-emerged among members of the working class in particular has not been fully considered. Had the interviewees of this research abandoned their production and consumer aspirations and the means by which to achieve those ends?

The optimism found among the respondents of the *Affluent Worker* study was not prevalent among the interviewees of this study. As earlier chapters have shown, many of the older interviewees had been forced to move to Luton in the face of unemployment in their youth, while some of the younger members of the sample had experienced unemployment in the late 1970s and early 1980s.[4] The interviewees had not unequivocally enjoyed favourable economic conditions over the course of their working lives. Moreover, as was noted in Chapter 1, the threat of redundancy and unemployment existed once again in the poor economic climate of the mid-1980s, particularly for those men and women who worked at the Vauxhall plant. The interviewees were, of course, worried about the threat of redundancy which hung over their jobs and were fearful about the consequences of unemployment on their lives. Their pessimism was grounded in these harsh life experiences.

The interviewees identified a number of reasons why they might be faced with redundancy. They cited the poor fortunes of the British economy and the world-wide recession as a threat to their jobs in general. More specifically, they refered to the poor trading conditions of the car industry within this economic context, the impact of new technology on jobs and investment in other plants in the General Motors group as having a detrimental impact on Vauxhall in Britain. Many of the Vauxhall workers could talk at length about the implications of car production at the new Nissan car plant in Washington, Tyne and Wear, on the company's share of the domestic and European market now that the Japanese car producer had overcome import controls. The list of reasons for Britain's poor economic performance and the uncertain economic climate within the car industry was extensive. The interviewees were certainly well informed, in both general and specific terms, about the economic situation in which they lived.

Many of the Vauxhall workers were fearful of the possibility of redundancy and unemployment for they had no control, either individually or collectively as members of a trade union, over some of the apparently immutable forces at work. For example, on the issue of new technology in the car industry, Malik Kasim expressed this sentiment:

> I could be out of a job tomorrow. I live in fear of new technology and what's happening to the car industry. I've been with the company eleven years and I've seen them take on people and now they are making people redundant. I've seen the start and I'll see the

end. With new technology, they have no need for people. I only work a basic thirty-nine hour week now. There is no weekend overtime which means I don't have that money going into my wages anymore. Originally, the work was there and the money was there to be earnt but now it isn't there. Standards have changed. The car is better and less people are required.

Whereas the car industry had once offered seemingly vast employment opportunities and 'a job for life', this was no longer the case. Sharing these thoughts, Simon Sawyer reflected upon a time when 'you could see a factory bursting with activity while now you can only see it slipping down. You know its closing in and sometime you're going to be cut off. You can't then be sure what tomorrow holds.'

In these economic circumstances, keeping their jobs for as long as possible was the dominant concern of most of the Vauxhall workers. That said, on a day-to-day level there was no point in worrying about or anxiously waiting for redundancy to happen. They could only continue their normal lives in these uncertain circumstances. As Anthony Dodd suggested: 'I would be worried if I was made redundant. I wouldn't know what to do. It is worrying but I just take it as it comes. If it happens it happens.' In a similar vein, Bruce Capel stated:

> I just work day to day, week to week. You don't know when they'll come out with demands for redundancies and you'll have to go. I used to worry a few years ago but I'm not worried now. You get used to it. If I have to go I'll just go.

The interviewees had learnt to live with the continual threat of redundancy and unemployment which hung over their working lives. They had no choice but to soldier on. They could only wait until 'their time was up' and they had a 'tap on the shoulder'. As we shall see, leading 'normal' lives in the meantime meant striving for improved standards of domestic living as far as possible.

There were, of course, variations in the sense of insecurity among the Vauxhall workers. Some of the older men, for example, mentioned their seniority as a source of security in the Vauxhall factory.[5] Many of these same men, however, said they wanted to take the offer of a lump sum in the next wave of redundancies. After more than twenty years at the Vauxhall plant, they looked forward to escaping from the pressures of their jobs. Having raised a family and equipped their homes, they could live off the lump sum and they could always get a 'little part-time job' to bring in some extra money if and when they needed it. Indeed, many of the men in their thirties and forties also wished they could leave Vauxhall with a lump sum. They certainly wanted to retire earlier than the statutory requirement of 65. As Robert Edwards suggested:

> I don't believe in working until you're 65. Its far too long for a man to work all his life and until he's nearly dead. Jesus, if you've not got enough money at sixty you'll never earn enough.

These aspirations for redundancy among the older men in particular and early retirement among all of the men in general have been noted elsewhere (Laczko and Phillipson 1991) as the proportion of men in the late fifties and early sixties in paid employment has fallen in the last twenty years. They indicate, as the Luton team also found, that paid work was not the site of the Vauxhall workers' hopes and aspirations. Promotion and self-employment were certainly far from their minds at the time of the interviews. However, while they had resigned themselves to the prospect of redundancy and unemployment, they still hoped to continue to improve their standards of domestic living.

CONSUMER ASPIRATIONS

Undoubtedly, the interviewees' consumer aspirations had centred, and continued to centre, on the economic, social and psychological well-being of themselves, their partners and their children. As was suggested in Chapter 7, the early years of marriage were devoted to establishing a home. With both partners working, and without the financial burden of children, they could afford to pay a mortgage on their own home and to buy the necessary fixtures and fittings. The interviewees attached considerable importance to owning their own homes. For many of the older interviewees, the achievement of buying their home was a source of great pride. Their own parents had not owned their homes, nor had other 'ordinary working people'. In so doing, they had improved their economic circumstances in comparison to their parents. Daphne Foulds and her husband Jack had lived with his parents for a short period when they married in the early 1950s. They moved into a council house, and bought the first home seven years later. Mrs Foulds explained how she had 'bettered herself':

> I found out about some cheap houses which were being built and that's where we started off. We saved all our money and used it for a deposit. There are some old neighbours in the council houses who are still there. They've paid for their houses over and over again and they've got nothing to show for it. This house is ours. It's paid for. We worked hard and we've achieved something out of life like the people around us. They are ordinary working-class people who bought their own homes. We were not like people who had money left to them to buy. We did it off our own bat through hard work. We've achieved what we have around us.

Even among the younger members of the sample, there was immense satisfaction that they had bought a house. Kim Dodd and her husband, Anthony, had lived in their own house for a year, and she explained her feelings about buying her home:

> After our engagement, we never thought about buying. We just thought we'd find somewhere to live but there was a huge council house waiting list. We hadn't done any saving so it was spur of the

moment when we went to Wimpey. It has been a struggle over this first year but I'm not prepared to let go. Once you've got something, you're not prepared to let go.
Buying a house had many advantages. It meant that they did not have to rent from unscrupulous landlords. They, rather than landlords, enjoyed the fruits of their labour since they owned a home after paying a mortgage for much of their lives. It was a secure home in that they could not easily or unjustly be evicted unless they failed to meet their mortgage repayments. It was a source of economic security if they lost their jobs. As Kevin Jackson suggested:

I look on my house as my security for the future meaning that if things get bad I've always got the house to fall back on. I can sell it and have a nice little lump sum and live in rented property.

They could be sold at a profit to buy a bigger, more valuable house or to generate money for other expenditures. Finally, houses could eventually be passed on to children in order to help them advance. Thus, the advantages of home ownership were deemed particularly important. By owning their own homes, they had some control over their economic circumstances.

As Marshall and his colleagues also found (1988: 214), the intrinsic desire of owning one's own home noted by some commentators (Saunders 1984, 1990a) was rarely mentioned by these working-class interviewees. The economic advantages of home ownership were emphasised instead. While recognising the difficulties of distinguishing between the intrinsic and extrinsic desires of home ownership, it appeared that the interviewees were instrumental in their attitudes to home ownership. The individual 'desire' to own one's home and the meaning of such aspirations should be placed in the wider economic context of the lack of alternatives to rented housing, as Harloe (1984) has correctly pointed out. The promotion of home ownership in the political sphere by successive Conservative governments especially since 1979 should also be taken into account. The context in which people 'choose' to own their own homes should not be neglected by concentrating exclusively on individual aspirations.

The interviewees spent much of their money on the attainment of a higher standard of domestic comfort. Money was used to buy what were considered to be the basic requirements of a household, such as a cooker, fridge, washing machine and numerous items of furniture. They also bought what were considered the more luxurious items of the household, such as videos and microwave ovens, and what might be recognised as newly affordable domestic products on the market. Of course, the growth of mass markets for electrical gadgetry and other domestic goods for the home such as the washing machine, television, video and microwave oven, which has occurred since the Second World War should be taken into account in the formation of material aspirations (Gershuny

1983). Individual aspirations for consumer goods should be placed within the wider context of these markets and the opportunities which have arisen to buy these goods which were unavailable in the first half of the century.[6]

Money was also spent on decorating and improving homes as Pahl (1984) found in his study of Sheppey. Home improvements such as redecoration and the installation of central heating or double glazing were undertaken to achieve comfort in a clean and bright home in line with the post-war domestic ideal (Crow and Allan 1990). As Leslie Kent suggested:

We both work very hard. We like our home comforts. We're not lavish but we like to be comfortable. People we visit seem to lack what we consider the necessities in life. You feel comfortable in comfortable furniture. Other people buy cheap things to save money for other, what we would regard as silly things. They're not concentrating on their home comforts and nice settee. It's not for people to come and see what we've got but to actually feel comfortable. They're not necessities but they are not luxuries either.

The interviewees also spoke of spending their money on new clothes, going on holiday or on family excursions. Peter Ibbotson described how

We save as much as we can to go on holidays abroad and in England. The rest of our money goes on a nice car and a nice home and everyone enjoying themselves as much as possible.

Reiterating these points, Sheila Ibbotson stated:

We like to spend money on holidays. We're mad keen on them. We save almost every penny and spend it on holidays. We like to get away once a year and go abroad so we have to save a lot of money towards that and do without other things.

Indeed, almost all of the interviewees spoke of the pleasures of holidays, of visiting kin who had emigrated to Australia, Canada, America or South Africa, and travelling and 'seeing the world' in general.

Many of the older interviewees had enjoyed improved standards of living in the period of economic prosperity in the 1950s, 1960s and, to some extent, the 1970s. However, since the mid-1970s, the lack of general economic advancement had slackened the pace of improvements in their domestic standard of living and also those of the younger members of the sample. Not surprisingly, therefore, the majority of the interviewees did not emphasise general economic advancement as a collective means of improved levels of domestic comfort. Instead, they expected material advancement to result from the hard work in sustaining the well-being of the household over the years. As the cost of raising children and mortgage repayments declined, they would have more money to spend than they had enjoyed previously. Their stage in the family life-cycle, in this respect, was a highly salient social identity, although, as we shall see, material gains took a collective as well as an individual form.

The younger members of the sample, for example, looked forward to improved economic circumstances, while the older members of the sample were experiencing better times. Lisa Smith, a young mother at home, reflected on her situation. Dependent on one wage from her husband and expecting a second child, she felt:

It has been hard not having money to spend on what you want. We've been in the house two years so we're going through the hardest years. It should get easier. Matthew didn't want another child so quickly as it costs so much. Now he wants a girl so we can hand things down although I think she should have some new things too. If I haven't got the money I won't be able to. It is hard but we should be able to cope better after a while. It should get easier later on.

While money was tight and her husband's employment was insecure, Lisa Smith looked to the future when their lives would not be dominated by these financial struggles to pay the mortgage, bills for heating and lighting, and clothes for her children. Indeed, the prospects of a better future acted as a defence against the harsh realities of the present. While her economic circumstances were uncertain, Mrs Smith did not have a 'traditional working-class perspective', living only for the present and presuming that the future would be the same.

At the other end of the family life-cycle, Barbara Wright enjoyed a more comfortable financial situation, with two adult children living at home who contributed to the household income:

When we first married every penny was spoken for. We had to spend very carefully. It's a lot easier now. The house is paid off after living in the same one over the years as there are less expenses there. The children are working and pay some expenses so if we want a holiday we have a holiday. We don't have to worry where the money is coming from.

As Pahl (1984) also noted in his study of Sheppey, there are considerable variations in standards of living among members of the working class, as there were in the early twentieth century, of course. A family with adult children contributing to the income of the household has far more re-sources in comparison to a household where the family is dependent on the wage of one person.

Some of the older interviewees could recall a time, in the early years of establishing a household, when 'money was tight'. 'Every penny was spoken for' and they had to watch their expenditure very carefully. They could do very little saving over and above their weekly household bills. In contrast, the affluence of their later years meant having a 'few pounds to spare' at the end of the week. Extra income over and above the usual basic expenditures for the house, heating, lighting and food allowed a person to buy a new dress for a wedding rather than making do, or to fill the whole tank of the car with petrol rather than purchase merely a gallon. Even bigger items of expenditure such as a car, video or micro-wave could be bought after only a short period of saving. Affluence meant that consumer goods could be bought almost when they wanted them. They did not have to save for each single item as they had done in the past. In this respect, saving for a variety of consumer durables was *ad hoc*, as the Luton team also found, but it was a welcome release after years of cautiously accounting for their money. As Richard Graves said:

> I don't save. I just take things as they come. If I need kitchen cupboards I don't think in terms of next year. There's no forward planning, I just go out and buy them. It is up to a certain limit. You can't do everything. Bigger things which cost a lot of money I have to think a bit harder. I leave it for a few weeks and if nothing comes up I'll go ahead with it.

In comparison, these interviewees acknowledged that 'things were tough' for the young generation of people raising children in the 1980s. The abundant overtime of the 1950s and 1960s, and the opportunity to increase their wages had long since disappeared. As Timothy Merrick noted 'If the children were small now and I was getting a flat wage and Christine wasn't working, I'd find it very hard to manage. I don't think it's a great living wage.' To some extent, if they were made redundant, it did not matter too much because their homes were already well estab-lished. This was not the case for young men and women, with the prospect of long-term unemployment staring them in the face.

These comments were confirmed by the interviewees raising young families who spoke of the difficulties of 'managing on a flat week'. Moreover, the constant threat of redundancy and unemployment put a break on expenditure on 'luxuries' like buying a new item of furniture or a car or having a holiday. The only means of increasing their household income was for wives to return to work, or to work full-time rather than part-time. As Rita Aziz, at home looking after her young son, concluded: 'If things get any worse than we are now, then I shall obviously have to think about going out to work. That's the only way out if I can bring in a wage as well. Two wages are better than one after all.' At least their standard of living would not drop and their future life-style would remain the same and slowly improve as they passed through the most demanding stage of the family life-cycle. The optimism of the Luton team's respondents had certainly been tempered by the harsh economic realities which faced the young members of the sample in the 1980s.

ASPIRATIONS FOR CHILDREN

While the interviewees were, to some extent, resigned to the uncertainty which hung over their own jobs, many of them expressed grave concern about their children's job prospects. Of course, some of the older inter-viewees had adult children in their thirties and forties with well-estab-lished jobs of their own. They worked in a variety of occupations, ranging from midwifery to managing a bar. Some of their children had been occupationally mobile, while others had not.

For those parents with children seeking employment in the 1980s, however, it had been a worrying time. Kevin and Heather Jackson had a daughter and son in their late teens. Unable to get the hairdressing apprenticeship that she had always wanted, their daughter worked in a clothing factory after leaving school before entering Vauxhall as a machinist. They were happy she worked for Vauxhall and she 'earnt good money for her age'. Their son worked as a gardener for the local council but, as Mrs Jackson explained:

> He did go to college to do graphic design. I was disappointed when he left and he didn't know what he wanted to do. Initially, I was disappointed and I was worried about the uncertainity. He seems happy now.

Speaking of his son's job, Mr Jackson emphasised that 'it's not grand but it's secure'. He added:

> Like most parents, I hoped they would achieve things although I don't know what. At least they've got a job and in reasonably secure employment which I'm pleased about. To get a job is the main thing these days. You have some self-respect rather than having to sit round at home all day having to borrow money to go out.

Not surprisingly, getting a secure job was accorded a high priority by parents who had faced and continued to experience insecurity in their own working lives.

Those parents with children of school age also expressed their misgivings about job prospects. Teresa Mills, who had a son of 15 and a daughter of 6, felt 'there's no jobs. There's nothing here for kids. Sometimes I've got no hope for them at all.' As Catherine Mayes, with four children between the ages of 7 and 17, confirmed, 'the job situation is not very good. I hope it will improve but it doesn't look like it. It is very worrying.' Unemployment was seen to have far-reaching implications for the whole of their lives, making the transition to adulthood difficult. Their children might find it extremely difficult to establish independent households of their own, buy their own homes and sustain a reasonable standard of living. They might never attain the standard of living enjoyed by their parents or improve their economic circumstances as they still presumed of each generation. They feared that their children might lose hope and drift away from leading a 'normal' life. Like Mr and Mrs Jackson, many of the interviewees spoke of seeing their children 'settled' in a job which gave them a reasonable wage on which they could secure a normal life.

While some of the interviewees spoke of the importance of acquiring 'a trade' as a means of getting a secure job, others emphasised the role of education. Indeed, many of the older interviewees with adult children regretted that their children had not gone to university even though they had been relatively successful in their jobs. Mr and Mrs Foulds's son had made his way up to become a project engineer for a major company. As Jack Foulds explained:

> He didn't do very well at school originally but he got a good apprenticeship and did day-release. He came on fast then and went on to night school. I would have liked to see him at university. You can only go so far with an ordinary education. If you show promise in business and if you have a university education, you can certainly get into the higher echelons.

For Martin Farrell, education was the means of getting a 'good' job, which he defined as a 'secure job with better prospects'. Referring to his two children, aged 16 and 13, he explained these ideas further:

> I want them to have a good education. My son wants to be a pharmacist and he's going to college and then onto university. My daughter wants to be a school teacher. It's a long way off but I hope the jobs are there. At least if they get an education they can turn to something else too. They have the choice. Education gives you that flexibility.

Even leaving school with a good education was not a guarantee of a job so it was important to enter higher and further education. The life experiences of the interviewees of this study, though somewhat different to the Luton team's respondents' lives, shaped their aspirations for their children.

SOCIAL PERSPECTIVES

While the interviewees spoke of their hopes and plans for improving their standard of living, albeit very gradually, in the future, they did not talk of their consumer aspriations in exclusively singular terms. Frequent reference was made to how they were like other 'ordinary working people'. They presumed that other 'respectable people' strove to 'better themselves'. After all, it was 'natural' that people aspired to improve their families' economic circumstances over the course of their working lives. They spoke, in other words, of collective advancement. Clearly, their aspirations were shaped by an image of the society in which they lived and a perception of their position within the social order. What was the form of the interviewees' social consciousness? With whom were they identifying? What was the nature of this social identity which they so readily used?

It will be recalled that 'traditional' working-class aspirations allegedly derived from a dichotomous view of society, a perception of an unchanging social order strictly divided between 'them' and 'us' (Bott 1957; Dennis *et al.* 1956; Hoggart 1957; Kerr 1958; Zweig 1952) According to embourgeoisement theorists (Butler and Rose 1960; Klein 1965; Zweig 1961), however, affluence led to different images of the social order. Members of the working class no longer saw the class structure and their own class position as unchanging, rather the opportunities for mobility were open. In other words, working-class solidarity was undermined in the pursuit of economic and social advancement.

Again, distancing themselves (if only in part) from embourgeoisement theorists, the Luton team argued that working-class social imagery had not changed as much as social and political commentators alleged. Few of their respondents subscribed to an image of an unchanging, dichotomous class structure, based on power, which was associated with the 'traditional' working class. Instead, against the background of instrumentalism, social class was defined by over half (54 per cent) of the sample in terms of money, with differences in incomes, wealth and standards of living 'being the most important determinant of class' (Goldthorpe et al. 1969: 147).[7] Moreover, those who subscribed to a money-model image of the class structure also outlined a 'large central class' which included most workers, including themselves, and which they called either middle or working class. Only the extremes – the very rich and the very poor – were excluded. Their respondents attached no significance to the manual/non-manual divide, sometimes including professionals within this large central class. They did not emphasise social or economic inequalities between people but noted instead the similarities or equality between people. This insensitivity to life-style differences and status distinctions the Luton team associated with their respondents' life experiences of seeing themselves enjoy similar standards of living to those of white-collar workers. In other words, drawing on Lockwood's paper on variations in working-class imagery, they inferred links between these life experiences, instrumentalism and 'money' models of society (Goldthorpe et al. 1969: 153).

Goldthorpe and his colleagues went on to argue that the respondents' social imagery also accounted for their emphasis on collective means of achieving their aspirations, such as general economic progress or industrial and political struggles. Their respondents did not have a conflictual model of the class structure but saw it as a basic and necessary feature of society. Thus, the Luton team argued:

> Given such an interpretation, therefore, it is scarely surprising that our respondents should tend to think far more of advancing their welfare within the existing order of society, and as part of its general evolution, than of pursuing their goals directed against this order (Goldthorpe et al. 1969: 154).

In other words, their respondents were not class-conscious radicals 'in the traditional sense' who wanted to overthrow the system, but their aspirations lay within the system. After all, they had enjoyed material prosperity within a capitalist society.

A considerable amount of controversy, as was previously discussed in Chapter 2, has always surrounded the Luton team's key findings on social imagery. The seeming lack of working-class consciousness, for example, has been the dominant concern of subsequent class analysis in Britain (Bulmer 1975; Mann 1970, 1973a; Marshall 1988; Newby 1977, Newby 1982; Parkin 1972; Westergaard 1970). While Westergaard (1970) interpreted the Luton team's findings as evidence of opposition to, rather than acceptance of, the dominant values of capitalist society, later studies of social consciousness painted a picture of ambivalence (Parkin 1972; Newby 1977) or pragmatism (Mann 1970, 1973a) in a society lacking a moral or normative consensus. In other words, there have been many different interpretations of the data on social consciousness (Newby 1982; Marshall 1988).

Indeed, in a dissenting paper, Platt (1971) pointed to some of the ambiguities surrounding the interpretation of the evidence on social imagery arising out of the *Affluent Worker* study. She expressed her unease over the failure to distinguish whether the respondents saw money as a determinant or a correlate of class. Discussing the qualitative data derived from open-ended questions in the interview schedule, she noted

> that respondents answering the class question did not make, or did not grasp, the distinction between determinants and correlates of class; thus the references to money could mean only that it was a conveniently observable, and easily conceptualisable, correlate of class differences rather than being seen as their fundamental cause (Platt 1971: 417).

The same problems of interpreting people's feelings and the meanings which lie behind their attitudes to social inequality have also been raised more recently by Marshall and his colleagues (1988). Not unlike the Luton team, in their sample survey of social class, the Essex team found that income was one of the most widely-used criteria for assigning people to different social classes. Class conflict was seen in terms of distributional struggles over money. However, contrary to the Luton team, the Essex team argued that the data should not 'be taken as unambiguous evidence of a widespread and simple pecuniary instrumentalism' for 'it is entirely possible that statements about money are simply a shorthand form of offering wider assessments about social control, power or social justice more generally' (Marshall *et al.* 1988: 189). The interviewees of this research were given the opportunity to express their feelings about social inequality in society rather than simply map out their image of the social order as a way of exploring the meanings which lie behind their social perspectives. Had their life experiences generated a benign view of the society in which they lived and their position within it, or did they harbour any sense of injustice and a desire for change?

SOCIAL CONSCIOUSNESS

The subject of class evoked strong pejorative feelings among the interviewees and proved to be one of the most difficult topics to discuss with them. Many of the older interviewees spoke with considerable bitterness and anger about the dominance of class over people's lives in the past. Invariably, however, their remarks focused on the status system. They recalled a time when every aspect of a person's life, from their family background to their styles of dress, and speech indicated who you were and what was your social standing. The interviewees were extremely scathing of ascribed status and the snobbery which had blighted social interaction in the past. In the context of this discussion, class, therefore, was equated with status. This finding concurs with Platt's (1971) remarks on the answers to questions on class in the *Affluent Worker* study. Similar responses were also noted by Martin (1954).

However, the interviewees felt that such 'class' distinctions had now almost disappeared. People no longer judged each other as they had done in the past. People were less 'snobby' than they used to be and the interviewees did not judge people in this manner. As Dorothy Atkinson suggested:

> As far as I am concerned nothing should separate people. I don't care about background as long as they are pleasant. I treat people with respect if they are nice people.

There was one exception where a sense of 'class' was still important, and this was found at the Vauxhall plant. The men and women in the sample who worked at Vauxhall experienced a sense of inferiority. That is, manual workers at the car plant were aware of a sense of superiority and separateness held by the foremen and white-collar workers which placed them in an inferior position. The status aspects of the organisation of the workplace and people's attitudes of social superiority were a considerable source of grievance. As Bruce Capel described:

> Class is still there particularly at work. The canteen is divided into top management, staff and workers. You get a strong sense of separateness with the collar and tie brigade. Staff always tell you they are staff at Vauxhall. It seems to be important to people. You don't notice class elsewhere.

Similarly, Richard Graves suggested:

> You find class at Vauxhall especially among the foremen. He's a foreman so he thinks he's middle-class and he has to move into a big house. He doesn't realise that he's working-class. I don't know why some like to create that impression. They are concerned with being on the ladder for middle-class status and they have to buy things accordingly. Yet, they can't fit into that circle which is already there. You can only buy friendship for so long. You always get toffee-nosed people. Give me your down-to-earth people anyday. I don't begrudge people getting on but when they get there they don't have to start crowing that they're there. They should just leave well alone. It's just good fortune and they should accept it.

Thus, at work there was still a strong awareness of the prestige aspects of the manual and non-manual divide, especially between workers and foremen as the first line of management. While they were highly critical, many of the men were still angry about the pretensions of foremen and others. Contrary to the findings of the Luton team, it was at work that these interviewees had a sense of place at the bottom of both the status and occupational hierarchies. They were well aware of the manual/non-manual divide at the workplace.

While the interviewees spoke of the decline of class (or status), they still felt that a class structure existed in modern Britain. In this discussion, the interviewees talked about class rather than status inequalities. People, they argued, would always belong to different social classes. Class was a 'given' fact of life and part of the structure of society into which they were born. It existed before them and would continue long into the future as well. As the Luton team found among their respondents, the interviewees defined social class in terms of money, income and wealth, and the associated life-styles and standards of living. While a variety of names was attached to different classes: the overwhelming majority of the sample spoke of two classes; the upper class and 'ordinary', working class people. Not unlike the 'traditional' working class, or for that matter the Luton team's respondents, the interviewees held a dichotomous model of the class structure. Moreover, they felt it was difficult to be upwardly mobile from one class to another.

The upper class was described as a small group of people who had huge amounts of money. As Barbara Wright suggested: 'I think most people are ordinary. I think the upper class are much fewer and they are the ones who have fantastic amounts of money.' People who belonged to the upper class had either inherited their money from their family at birth or as famous people, like film stars or football players, they had earnt a lot of money. They did not know or elaborate on how some families had acquired wealth in the first instance and it was difficult to know since the reasons lay in the past. However, they were certainly successful in sustaining their wealth and passing it from one generation to another. Their social background, their material privileges, their private education, their dominance in top jobs, their social connections and so forth secured their wealth and dominance for the next generation. Once again, the interviewees made reference to an essentially closed, undemocratic system which many, as we shall see, felt was unfair.

Turning to the implications of inheritance, the interviewees focused on the different styles of life which the upper class could enjoy. Members of the upper class, it was argued, did not have to work to enjoy a good standard of living and, moreover, their standards of living were lavish in comparison to ordinary working people. As Rita Malik observed:

> The rich can have whatever money can by. If you haven't got money you have to struggle. You can't have most of the things the

rich people can have like luxuries, holidays, flashy cars all the time. The upper class or rich enjoyed a freedom which they did not, their lives centred on sustaining their material existence.

Asked about their feelings towards the upper class, some of the interviewees argued that it was wrong that some people enjoyed these advantages over others. Anthony Dodd was angry when he explained: 'I disagree with a silver spoon. People should work for their money, not inherit it.' Thus, it was deemed 'unfair' that people should inherit a lot of money while others had to struggle over the course of their lives to attain only a fraction of what some inherited. It was unjust that their daily lives were dominated by material concerns and they did not have the freedom to enjoy the intrinsic rewards of different aspects of their lives, be it their jobs, their homes or whatever. Why should their lives be so narrowly focused towards instrumental concerns? Why were they denied such opportunities?

Other interviewees, however, felt that they did not care what kinds of living standards other people enjoyed. They did not begrudge people who did have better standards of living than they did themselves. As Rachel Edwards said: 'I think "good luck to them'. I just wish it was me.' Similarly, Julie Farrell stated:

> I'm not bothered where someone is. People aren't snobs anymore. Nobody is better than anyone else. I don't want my kids looking up to anyone. I say 'good luck to them' if they've got it. I'm not bothered in the least.

Again, money and possessions did not concern them, so long as it did not lead people to think of themselves as superior to others. Once again, the interviewees highlighted their dislike of status distinctions as well as the actual differences of money and what it meant for people's lives.

The interviewees placed themselves in a mass, central class of 'just ordinary' families who worked for a living and had similar standards of living. The overwhelming majority of the interviewees correctly described this class and their class position as working class, although some of the interviewees talked of being lower middle class or middle class before going on to describe a large group of people as well. The terms 'ordinary' or 'ordinary working people' were particularly popular and were used interchangeably with the term 'working class'. Some of these terms were noted by Saunders (1990) in his three-towns survey of home ownership and by the Essex team, although they did not elaborate on who used these terms and what they meant by them (Devine 1992a). Once again, this class was defined in terms of money, income and wealth, and its implications for people's daily lives. Angela Stone spelt out the implications of the monetary position of the working class in which she saw herself: 'Well it is really a day-to-day existence. You've got to be careful. You just can't go out and do what you'd really like to do. This is the thing.' Thus, members of this large group used the same means to attain domestic comfort for their families. They had to work to earn their wage or income. Invariably they had a struggle to manage in the early years when they were raising a family, but eventually they might enjoy improvements in their standards of living. There were differences between 'ordinary working people', of course, according to their jobs and how much they earnt or their position in the family life-cycle. Colin Burgess suggested:

We're just starting off. It has a lot to do with the age factor. There are youngsters who have just left home and others who are past that stage. We're slowly creeping up the ladder.

Yet they were united in their desire to achieve material advancement. They desired very similar things, like their own home, domestic goods to furnish their home and make it more comfortable, a car and an annual holiday. It was 'natural' to want to improve the material well-being of one's self and one's family. They were all 'ordinary, respectable families'.

The interviewees, as the Luton team also found, did not appear to distinguish between the working class and the middle class, or manual and non-manual workers, when they mapped out the class structure. They tended to stress the similarities between people in the working and middle class in terms of income and standards of living. This is not surprising since there is no reason to suppose that they were (or needed to be) fully conversant with the different market and work situations of people whom they associated with a mass central class. More importantly, many of the interviewees felt that the distinctions between the middle class and the working class were less clear cut than they used to be. This issue was more fully discussed in the conversations on class and how it might have changed from the past rather than the interviewees' mapping out of the contemporary class structure. They emphasised the more comfortable standard of living which they enjoyed in comparison to their parents. Standards of living were enjoyed now that had been associated only with the middle class, in the past. Home ownership, for example, had once been the sole preserve of the middle class but not anymore. The so called middle and the working classes of the past now enjoyed similar standards of living. As Sheila Ibbotson noted:

There has been a change from what we've got and what I had when I was a child. I've definitely come up a rung since then. I suppose it's possessions, things that you do, going abroad on holiday, owning your own house although everyone seems to do that now.

At the same time, the interviewees also alluded to the persistence of differences between the middle class and the working class. While they talked of a large central class, many of the interviewees made further distinctions between the working class and a middle class which they identified with people in well-established professional jobs like doctors. They had 'good' jobs in that they depended on qualifications for entry; the work was interesting and rewarding; the incumbants enjoyed autonomy as they went about their work; they might hold positions of power; they had prospects for promotion and; of course, they earnt more and enjoyed a higher standard of living – a bigger house, a new car, better quality furniture and so forth – than they did.

In many respects, it seemed as if the interviewees were aware of absolute changes in income and standards of living enjoyed by almost all since the Second World War, while recognising the persistence of relative differences between classes. The growth of home ownership among the working class, for example, made it harder to distinguish between people and classes along these lines, although luxurious houses were certainly owned by the upper class. Class distinctions, therefore, were less pronounced and more subtle than they had been in the past, especially in the domain of consumption. Yet, at the same time, the interviewees knew that they were still working class. As predominantly manual or lower level non-manual workers, they would never going to earn as much as professional people nor experience the life-styles and freedoms which they enjoyed.

Thus, the interviewees exhibited some uncertainty as to the extent, form and nature of differences between the middle class and the working class, and how they should about feel about them. For the most part, they were not aggrieved about their higher standards of living. After all, they still worked for a living, many of them having come from humble origins themselves, having striven hard to attain the positions they had acheived. The interviewees' sense of injustice was confined to the upper class, the visibly rich, who did not have to work to sustain the privileged life-styles which they led.

Finally, the interviewees referred to a group of 'poor' people who had lower standards of living than they did themselves. They were unemployed or single parents. Teresa Mills suggested 'you see them on the telly – "That's Life" - and what they're getting for Christmas'. Whether this group of people constituted another class was undecided among the interviewees. They were struggling to survive like other 'ordinary' families and the difference between those with their 'heads above water' was not that significant. As Malik Aziz pondered:

> There are a lot of people struggling to make ends meet especially up North. They are like us but not quite like us. At least we are a little better off. We have a little to fall back on.

Given their own lack of job security, the interviewees saw both differences and similarities in their position with these people. These people were like themselves in that they were trying to manage and strive for a better life. At least they wanted to do better for themselves and their families and, in terms of their respectability, they were ordinary working people.

Like the Luton team's respondents, the interviewees of this research held to money models of the class structure. However, money did not always denote similarities between people but was used to explain different opportunities and constraints which people faced in all aspects of their lives as well. In this respect, the interviewees were not uncritical of the society in which they lived. They were unhappy with the essentially unjust and unfair society. Rather than expect their aspirations to be met in a society characterised by class inequalities, they wanted a different, more democratic society than existed at present. Thus, contrary to the Luton team's findings, the interviewees' aspirations did not lie exclusively within the capitalist system. They conceived of a better society, of class alternatives (Mann 1970), in their wide assessment of issues of freedom, fairness, justice and democracy.

CONCLUSION

Despite their uncertain economic future, the interviewees' aspirations were not entirely fixed. They looked forward primarily to small, gradual improvements in their standard of domestic living over their lifetime. Not surprisingly, they did not look to general economic advancement of the country as a whole as the collective means by which their own lifestyles would improve. Instead, they emphasised material improvements to be gained as they moved slowly through the family life-cycle and past the most financially demanding time of raising a young family.

However, the interviewees did not envisage these improvements in their standard of living to be exclusively individual rewards for their hard work. On the contrary, their remarks were constantly framed with reference to other ordinary, respectable people like themselves who worked for a living. They identified with other members of the working class, distancing themselves from the extremes of the very rich and the very poor. The harsh fact that their daily lives were governed by instrumental, material concerns while the rich would seemingly always have money and the associated freedom which accompanied wealth was a source of grievance. They lived, after all, in a society characterised by class inequalities. Their aspirations would not be realised in that society which they described, and they wanted changes towards a more free and democratic society in which people would be treated justly and fairly.

Discussion has been deferred on the principal means by which the interviewees believed that social change could be brought about. As the Luton team also found, the interviewees looked to the trade unions and the Labour Party as the collective means by which they might attain their aspirations. It is to these two vehicles of working-class support and the interviewees' industrial and political perspectives that the final empirical chapter will now turn.

1. The Luton team argued that the failure of embourgeoisement theorists to place aspirations within the context of people's daily lives accounted for the 'piecemeal' and 'impressionistic' nature of their data. The pursuit of status enhancement and the desire to adopt middle-class life-styles, the Luton team noted, was largely assumed by these commentators (Goldthorpe *et al*. 1969: 116–7).

2. Goldthorpe and his colleagues made reference to Kerr's study (1958) in their discussion of the 'traditional' working class on a number of occasions. However, Kerr's research was carried out among the poor in a Liverpool slum, which might explain the lack of respectable domesticity among her respondents. Moreover, like Dennis and his colleagues' study (1956) of a mining community, Kerr's research was completed in the 1950s. There is plenty of historical evidence (Davies 1992; Roberts 1974) to suggest that the daily life of the 'traditional' working class before to 1939 was a constant struggle against poverty, and people wanted to improve their lot.

3. The interviewees' attitudes and feelings on industrial and political struggles as a collective means of improving their economic and social circumstances are discussed in Chapter 10.

4. The interviewees' employment histories are explored in Chapters 3 and 6.

5. The importance of seniority as a source of security was also noted by the Luton team among their Vauxhall employees (Goldthorpe *et al*. 1968a: 118).

6. As Weberians, the Luton team was highly critical of Marxist thinkers such as Marcuse (1964) who dismissed consumer aspirations as false needs (Goldthorpe *et al*. 1969: 16-7). While embourgeoisement theorists attached considerable importance to 'new' consumer aspirations, marxist thinkers tended to deny their importance altogether. The Luton team, in many respects, sought the middle ground. As a result, they ignored the growth of new markets of domestic products, and the ways in which material needs and wants have been shaped by them.

7. The Luton team was keen to stress that they had found a much stronger emphasis on money models of the class structure than had been found in other studies.

10

INDUSTRIAL AND POLITICAL PERSPECTIVES

Despite their uncertain economic circumstances, the interviewees of this study looked forward to improved standards of living for themselves and their family in the future. However, rather than expect individual improvements to arise from Britain's economic advancement, like the Luton team's respondents, they anticipated small, gradual improvements as the costs of raising a family declined. They, alongside other 'ordinary working people' with similar standards of living, would achieve their material aspirations through determination and hard work. The means of achieving their ends were discussed, in other words, in both individual and collective terms. This chapter explores the interviewees' industrial and political perspectives. Did the interviewees collectively support the trade unions and the Labour Party merely to improve their individual standards of domestic living, as the Luton team argued? Or, did they look to these two vehicles of working-class support for more radical changes in the social order in the collective interests of the working class as a whole? Were the interviewees' industrial and political perspectives like the 'new' working class identified by Goldthorpe and his colleagues or more like the 'traditional' working class?

Overall, the findings indicate that the interviewees viewed the trade unions and the Labour Party as collective means of securing both individual and collective ends. They looked to both organisations to improve their individual economic circumstances but not in a singularly individualistic fashion as the Luton team alleged. Rather, they inextricably linked individual family and collective working-class gains. Support for the trade unions and Labour Party was not conditional upon individual material well-being alone. Moreover, many of the interviewees believed their consumer aspirations would probably be fully realised only in a different kind of society than that wich existed at present. The trade unions and the Labour Party should replace a class-based society with a more democratic and free society in which people would be treated justly and fairly. That said, many of the interviewees were critical of the trade unions and the Labour Party for their failure to improve the economic circumstances of the working class as a whole as well as their individual economic positions. It was on the basis of this evaluation that support by some interviewees had been withdrawn.

INDUSTRIAL PERSPECTIVES

The Luton team found a high level of union membership among their Vauxhall assemblers, the overwhelming majority (79 per cent) belonging either to the Amalgamated Engineering Union or to the National Union of Vehicle Builders. That said, a sizeable proportion of them, like process workers at Laporte, were 'green' unionists, having joined a trade union for the first time with their current employer. Moreover, few (13 per cent) of the assemblers had joined out of moral conviction, most of them instrumentally joining a union for the advantages of union benefits (24 per cent) and representation on pay (19 per cent) (Goldthorpe et al. 1968a: 94–7). The Luton team concluded that their respondents displayed 'a largely instrumental view of unionism which clearly reflects what we would regard as their characteristic orientation towards their working life in general' (Goldthorpe et al. 1968a: 98).

The Luton team also found a low level of involvement in branch activities – attendance at branch meetings and voting at branch elections – among their respondents where the demands of home and family life competed for their interest. Greater involvement was found at the workplace – voting for the shop steward and talking about the union informally with fellow workers. From the evidence, the Luton team argued:

> That unionism should have little significance for them other than in relation to the immediate 'bread-and-butter' issues of their own work situation is entirely consistent with their definition of work as primarily a means to extrinsic ends: their main interest in the union, as in the firm, is that of the 'pay off' ... unionism in the style of these workers can be usefully described as 'instrumental collectivism' – collectivism, that is to say, which is directed to the achievment of individuals' private goals, outside the workplace (Goldthorpe et al. 1968a: 106).

The Luton team concluded that their respondents differed from traditional workers in terms of the form of participation in union affairs and, more importantly, in the meaning of union activity to the men concerned. Unlike 'traditional' workers, they viewed unionism exclusively as a means of 'economic betterment'. It was not an end in the sense of a 'sociopolitical movement aiming at radical changes in industrial institutions and in the structure of society generally' (Goldthorpe et al. 1968a: 107). These 'wider ideals and objectives' were absent among their affluent workers.

Direct evidence of instrumentalism was deduced from the respondents' attitudes about the primary concerns of unions. The majority (52 per cent) of respondents (and 59 per cent of the Vauxhall assemblers) believed that the unions should concentrate on getting higher pay and better conditions for workers. The semi-skilled Vauxhall assemblers and Laporte process workers, in particular, attached less importance than the skilled workers to issues of worker control, authority and power as a central union objective. Against the background of their instrumentalism, they did not want a greater share in the running of the firm than they already had in relation to management. The function of the union was to concentrate primarily on 'economic protection and advancement'.

Moreover, with the exception of assembly workers, more than the national average had contracted out of paying a political levy to the Labour Party, and many of those who paid the levy did not realise the links between their union and the Labour Party. The majority (53 per cent) of respondents thought the unions and the Labour Party should be separate. Thus, the Luton team's respondents were not 'committed to the traditional idea of the trade unions and the Labour Party as forming the industrial and political 'wings' of an integrated labour movement' (Goldthorpe *et al.* 1968a: 111). Their unionism originated and focused on local economic self-interest rather than national concerns.

From the evidence, Goldthorpe and his colleagues argued that the character of unionism was changing in the post-war period of prosperity. The principled 'traditional' unionist of the early twentieth century was being replaced by 'a new type of unionism consistent with the wants and expectations which they bring to their work' (Goldthorpe *et al.* 1968a: 114). However, contrary to embourgeoisement theorists, the Luton team concluded that collective action was still the primary means of workers achieving their ends even if their goals now took an individual rather than collective form. Indeed, the Luton team predicted that the desire for monetary rewards and consumer power may lead to 'greater aggressiveness in the field of "cash-based" bargaining' (Goldthorpe *et al.* 1968a: 177).

Instrumental Collectivism

Union demands for higher pay in the 1970s appeared to confirm the predictions of intensified militancy. Indeed, Goldthorpe (1978) developed the thesis of instrumental collectivism further in his sociological explanation of the high rates of inflation which characterised the decade. Rather than apportioning the blame for high inflation on the 'irrational' actions of unions and their members, as some economists had, Goldthorpe turned to changes in the social structure to account for, and make sense of, militancy surrounding pay demands. The decline of the status order, the realisation of industrial citizenship (including the accompanying process of institutional development which the Luton team referred to in their monographs) and the demographic and socio-political maturity of the British working-class explained the lack of inhibitions among unions and their members and their willingness to exploit their market position to the full (Goldthorpe 1978). The Luton team's predictions regarding instrumental collectivism had been confirmed.

The predictions appear to have been verified still further by Marshall's and his colleagues' (1988) study of social class. Nearly two-thirds of their sample proffered the view that conflict between employers and employees was the main social conflict in Britain in the 1980s. Poor industrial relations (45 per cent) and disputes over pay (31 per cent) were the most cited reasons for industrial conflict. Like the Luton team, little mention was made of issues of worker power and control (Marshall *et al.* 1988: 151–2). Moreover, the Essex team found that, the closed shop aside, instrumental reasons predominated over principled reasons for joining a union, and few of their union members believed that unions should act altruistically. Unions should focus on the fight against redundancy (36 per cent) and for increased pay (30 per cent). Thus, the Essex team argued that 'industrial conflict' and 'trade union activity' is usually perceived 'as a distributional struggle over the national income' (Marshall *et al.* 1988: 155–6). However, rather than explain instrumental collectivism by reference to material aspirations, as the Luton team had, they concluded that it derives from a belief that a redistribution of the national income is unlikely in British society as it is presently structured.

Against the background of these findings, the interviewees of the present study were questioned about their industrial perspectives. Was their unionism directed towards largely self-interested, economic concerns, as the Luton team argued, or were they principled unionists like the (somewhat idealised) 'traditional' working class? Is the distinction between 'traditional' and 'new' unionism which underpins the Luton team's analysis of changing unionism and, to some extent the Essex team's analysis as well, valid anyway? How did the interviewees' aspirations and social consciousness shape their industrial perspectives? How did they evaluate the activities of the trade unions in the harsh economic and political climate of the 1980s (Grint 1991; Winchester 1988) in comparison with the 1960s and 1970s?

A closed shop agreement operated at the Vauxhall plant at the time of the interviews. All thirty men, therefore, were long-standing members of either the Transport and General Workers Union or the Amalgamated Engineering Union. Five of those men – Peter Ibbotson, Roy Mayes, Brian Richards, Simon Sawyer and Richard Graves – were shop stewards. The six women – Bridget Underwood, Elisabeth Adams, Anita Palmer, Julia Farrell and Carol Sawyer (who were full-time production operators) and Sandra Davis (who worked part-time as a cleaner) – were also bound by the closed shop agreement as Vauxhall workers. A further five women – Angela Stone, Judith Hayward, Heather Jackson, Barbara Wright and Christine Merrick – belonged to a trade union at their place of work. They worked either for the local authority or the National Health Service. The industrial perspectives of the forty-one (thirty men and eleven women) trade union members will be considered together. Thirteen women in employment were not union members at the time of the interview and their industrial perspectives will be considered separately. Finally, the industrial perspectives of the eight women of the sample who were not employed will not be ignored for they had previously belonged to a trade union. Indeed, despite the low membership rates of the women (eleven) in the sample at the time of the interview, over half of them (twenty) had belonged to a trade union at some point in their working lives.

Union Members

Despite some dissatisfaction with the closed shop agreement at Vauxhall, the union members insisted upon the importance of belonging to a trade union. The combined strength of workers acting collectively over a disagreement with managament was emphasised in particular. Only if workers acted in unison and in an organised fashion could they successfully challenge company policies. As Michael Clarke argued:

You've got to have a union to protect you from bad moves by management. If you don't have a union there's no real backing. With the union organisation you have backing and support.

The individual on his or her own had very little power and could easily be ignored. As Robert Edwards suggested: 'a group of people together can do something. A man on his own has had it.' The interviewees, therefore, automatically equated trade unionism and collective action as the most successful means of achieving their industrial ends.

Union organisation and solidarity among the workforce was deemed especially important in the face of a large employer. As Lawrence Atkinson stated:

In a big place like Vauxhall you can't have people individually asking for wage increases. Some would be pushier than others. The meek would inherit nothing and the bosses would get everything unless you have a body. You couldn't run the place without the union.

In a similar vein Elisabeth Adams, a Vauxhall employee, suggested 'You've got to have a trade union in a large factory and if there are any problems they will fight for you.' Workers should be effectively organised to match the power of management.

All of the interviewees spoke of the union's role in defending and promoting the interests of workers on issues ranging from better conditions at work to negotiating wage increases. Representing the interests of workers meant challenging the interests and some of the more invidious activities of management. However, the relationship between unions and management was not perceived in exclusively confrontational terms. Rather, the role of the union was to uphold good industrial relations by ensuring fair play and an adherence to established rules and regulations regarding workers' rights as well as to enhance them still further. Once again, the interviewees alluded to democratic ideals of justice and openness.

Many of the interviewees, especially the older men of the sample, spoke at length about the history of the trade union movement and the long fight to guarantee industrial rights. They had secured a position for the unions at the workplace to enter into dialogue with management. They had forced management to recognise the interests and rights of workers and to abide by them. In this respect, Jack Foulds argued, they had secured 'fair play'. Malik Aziz had had to fight for compassionate leave when his son was ill, and he felt

> That's when you need the unions. I hadn't broken the rules. There was nothing in the book to say that I couldn't take time off. I saw the general foreman and I took the shop steward. I told them to show me where I was breaking the rules. It's only fair to follow procedure. I got it. It's a matter of principle. If you know the rules and you're not breaking them it's only right to defend yourself.

Thus, the union had acted as a negotiator for an employee's rights and as a witness in the dispute. But, as Mr Aziz went on to say:

> If you're on the wrong side of the law you are going to get the sack and there is nothing the unions can do about it. They have no case to fight for you. They can only fight for your rights, not your wrongs.

The trade unions, therefore, had forced employers to talk over issues of dispute rather than act in a draconian fashion. It was not a case of two camps facing each other in a state of perpetual hostility. Peter Ibbotson, a shop steward, suggested:

> The trade unions are necessary. They do a lot of good work and they have done in the past. Without them we wouldn't be in the position we are in to-day. They have improved conditions of work and got wage rises. It's not so much us and them. It's brought us closer together.

The industrial rights won by the trade unions meant that employers could not act in an entirely unfettered fashion overriding the interests and concerns of its employees. It was the trade union movement which had changed this position and had, in this respect, curtailed the power of employers.

That said, the interviewees did not envisage that the unions should usurp the power of management. Management and unions had different roles to play within the factory, even if they were being constantly contested by each other. As Simon Sawyer explained:

> Management are there to manage. The unions are there to help get the workers better conditions at work and things like that. There-fore, both of them have got to recognise each other's position.

Thus, the interviewees did not neglect issues of power and control, as both the Luton team and the Essex team found among their respondents. That said, although they described the ways in which the frontiers of authority and control were being constantly contested, they did not envisage worker control usurping the power of managers 'to manage'.

Turning more specifically to the central concerns which trade unions should address, the interviewees invariably referred to issues which figured in their daily working lives. As Gerald Mills indicated:

> The unions should watch over things like safety and conditions at work and they should watch over the men's wages or when there's a bit of trouble. Today some bloke drove one car on the track into the back of another causing about a thousand pound's worth of damage. I think it was a faulty automatic gearbox because the car just shot forward. He should have had his foot hard on the brake and the handbrake on but as he's not from that section maybe he didn't know. I don't know. But you need a union then to make sure he doesn't get the sack.

Incidents such as this one were widely quoted by the trade union members to illustrate the role of the trade unions in resolving a variety of different problems which might arise in their day-to-day working lives. It was not surprising that they spoke of issues which concerned them in their particular working enviroment. They spoke of immediate and pressing problems, such as poor working conditions or other work-related issues, both intrinsic and extrinsic.

However, as Gerald Mill's remarks suggest, the interviewees recognised that problems and issues of contention at work were not exclusively individual concerns. They might be shared with other employees who occupied the same position as themselves in the factory. Thus, if conditions of work were bad for one individual, they could also be bad for another. Their shared working conditions meant that similar issues affected their working lives. It was these circumstances which led to collective action. In opposition to the Luton team's findings, the interviewees' local concerns were not exclusively individual but took a collective form as well.

As the Luton team also found, the interviewees placed particular emphasis on the union's role in negotiating wage increases. Undoubtedly, the interviewees looked to the unions to secure annual wage increases which would allow them to sustain or improve upon their current standard of living. Echoing these sentiments, Matthew Smith said: 'the unions are a good thing. They have got better wages for people. They've helped their standards of living go up.' However, the interviewees did not consider wage increases solely within the context of improving their own individual standards of living. Again, a number of interviewees referred to notions of fairness. All workers, it was argued, should receive a wage on which they could adequately support their families. Commenting on his wages, Timothy Merrick felt:

> There must be some way of working it out. I suppose you should be able to own your own house, possibly a car, television, telephone, central heating – certain luxuries but not luxurious. Per-

haps you could take the wife and kids out once a week for a meal and the pictures. We should be able to work it out and give it to everyone.

Once again, the search for material well-being was not couched in individualistic terms.

Similarly, the desire for wage increases was not purely an extrinsic goal. The interviewees spoke of the gruelling nature of their jobs and the unsocial hours they worked. They should be paid more money for the less favourable aspects of their working conditions. As Anthony Dodd argued: 'I'm not satisfied with the wages. Not for the work we do. On nights I feel I should be paid three times as much to appreciate going to work.' These remarks highlight the many meanings which might be attached to an employee's interests. That is, while the overwhelming majority of the interviewees highlighted the importance of securing high wages, a variety of normative reasons could be used to justify this concern. Moreover, in Anthony Dodd's case, the desire for high wages was not merely directed towards an extrinsic end, there was an intrinsic concern too. In this instance, therefore, high wages entailed extrinsic and intrinsic rewards, undermining the sharp dichotomy which the Luton team posited between the two types. This finding concurs with Hill's study of dockworkers, where he found that 'the concern with the extrinsic rewards co-exists with an interest in the intrinsic' (Hill 1976: 66). Indeed, all of the findings suggest that the strict dichotomy between the industrial perspectives of the (highly idealised) 'traditional' working class and the 'new' working class, as defined by the Luton team, is not as robust as they claimed.

Somewhat surprisingly, few of the Vauxhall workers believed that the unions should fight against redundancies. Their attitudes to the threat of redundancy and unemployment outlined in the previous chapter should be recalled here. The interviewees made a variety of different comments, but they all contained the same message: there was very little the unions could do to stop job losses. Again, some interviewees referred to the seemingly inevitable reduction of job opportunities as a result of the introduction of new technology. Others cited union powerlessness, as in the case of Wapping 'where the unions have been overrun there', while some believed strike action to be futile. As Andrew Bennett suggested: 'They turn round and say strike for your job but you're losing money. If you're going to lose your job anyway, what's the point of striking to lose more money?' The circumstances in which some of the redundancies had occurred – through voluntary redundancies and early retirements – should not be forgotten either in shaping the interviewees' attitudes. Matthew Smith, for example, remarked that:

> If the products are not doing well, obviously management will want to get rid of people. Vauxhall have tried hard with voluntary redundancies and retirements. I know someone who worked over

in Dunstable who took voluntary redundancy. He had a job to go to. He banked the money which was nice for him.

Many of the interviewees, as was noted before, would have liked the lucrative lump sums which had been on offer and which, in turn, appeared to inform their attitudes to the unions' role in preventing job losses.

While the interviewees could articulate a set of a priori reasons why they should belong to a trade union and the role of the trade unions in the industrial sphere, nevertheless the discussion evoked strong pejorative feelings towards the trade unions in general. The most frequently cited criticism, found in other studies of industrial workers (Gouldner 1965; Lane and Roberts 1971), was the charge of aloofness. Communication between union officials and union members was regarded as poor. Thus, as far as some of the interviewees were concerned, the experience of belonging to a trade union was not that dissimilar from working for a large employer. Both, it seemed, were large, bureaucratic organisations which had the power to dictate when to act and when not to act. As Anita Palmer noted:

> Trade unions have the wrong way of going about things. They don't sit down and talk and let the members know what is going on. You never know about decisions. You just pay money out to be told what to do.

Although the unions were supposed to represent and fight for workers' rights, they were seen as inept at communicating and finding out the feelings of their members on decisions and campaigns. They were not, according to these interviewees, very good at enlisting support. They were just another organisation which had power over the individual.

The failure of the unions to consult their members made the interviewees particularly angry when they were called upon to take industrial action. Many of the interviewees felt that they were ill informed about areas of dispute; about why negotiations between management and the unions had broken down; and, more importantly, about strategic issues such as the chances of success if industrial action took place. The interviewees treated the issue of strike action very gravely. Strike action should be taken only as a last resort in industrial disputes since it put considerable financial pressure on union members themselves. It was they who had to suffer financially and, therefore, the likely success of action should be carefully evaluated. If they were to be asked to take strike action, they wanted all of these strategic questions answered. They would go on strike to win an issue. Many of the interviewees, for example, were unhappy with the one-day stoppages the union had organised in protest against the company's decision not to contribute to the pension fund in the coming year (1987) because excess funds existed (*Luton District Citizen*: 20 November 1986). While the union wanted the company to increase the pensions on offer instead, it was not the most pressing issue the employees, faced as they were with the prospect of redundancy. Many of them were also unconvinced about the strategy of one-day stoppages anyway. It was for these reasons that the interviewees attended meetings specifically called to vote on strike action, while conceding that they rarely attended branch meetings or voted in branch elections.

Many of the interviewees felt that the failure to inform members of contentious issues and union strategies undermined the union overall and the potential for collective action. There was a difference of opinion here: some interviewees blaming the union hierarchy, others blamed union members, while some felt that fault lay with both parties. As Anthony Dodd argued:

> When I first started work the unions had influence. When the shop stewards called people out, they all came out. Now, despite the call, it's up to the individual. If someone is unfairly sacked I think everyone should come out. The shop stewards now are very poor. You need real leaders of men. They need to say they are for the workers rather than shy away.

Robert Edwards, on the other hand, felt:

> Things have gone backwards. There is no leadership and the membership is no good. They wouldn't back anybody. OK, I don't believe in walking out over anything but people now they wouldn't lose a pound to save anybody. But it could be them tomorrow. That's what they don't realise. They're really selfish.

Mr Edwards also conceded that the 'move backwards' had undermined his willingness to take industrial action. If only partial support could be secured in a dispute, why should some people carry the burden of industrial action when others were not prepared to do so? In this respect, the unions were on a 'downward spiral'.

Thus, among the union members of the sample, allegiance to the trade unions was not uncritical. The shop stewards of the sample were as critical as the rank-and-file members. Brian Richards, who was a shop steward argued:

> I'm not 100 per cent unionist. It gives you some protection in your job. I don't agree with some policies though. Sometimes they're good and sometimes they go over the top.

However, the lack of confidence in the trade unions was not the consequence of individual consumer aspirations undermining a solidarity once prevalent among the working class, as the Luton team argued. Rather, the trade unions were not perceived as successful organisations which informed their members of contentious issues with management and enlisted their support; which organised collective action; and which won concessions as a result of industrial action.

Many of the trade union members regretted the changed circumstances of the trade unions compared with their more successful past. A number of the interviewees described the changes in working practices, the company's plans to introduce a new shift system and the increasing heavy-handedness of management at work. Discipline over small issues had tightened and leniency had been lost. Informal social relations between workers and line managers had disappeared. Overall, the poor atmosphere at work, according to the interviewees, accounted for the high rates of absenteeism which were reported in the national press (The *Guardian*: 30 October 1986). While few lamented the loss of union power from the 1970s, many of them felt that 'things had gone too far the other way' in the hostile economic and political climate of the 1980s.

Non-union Members

Thirteen women who were in formal employment at the time of the interview did not belong to a trade union, although four had done so on an earlier occasion. Of the eight women who were not employed, five of them had been union members in the past as well. It should be noted, first of all, that the non-union members of the sample did not differ significantly from the union members in their industrial perspectives. They were not especially hostile towards trade unions. They recognised the strength which could be drawn upon from collective action, for, as Teresa Mills noted: 'If you've got a problem at work the union can step in and sort it out.' They also voiced similar concerns about the trade unions as large, somewhat aloof bureaucratic organisations which did not always consult their members on union strategies, especially in relation to strike action. Lisa Smith, who had belonged to a union for part of her working life, felt 'you should fight for your rights', but added, 'if you know you've got a really good chance of winning then it's worth it. But if not you can't afford to lose your money these days.' Against this background, why did these women not belong to a union?

Many of the non-union members of the sample had not been approached by a trade union to join. However, the women did not find this surprising because they worked part-time or on temporary contracts. Union membership was not perceived as applicable to them in non-standard jobs. They did not have industrial rights so there was nothing, as such, to defend. Uma Kasim had worked at A.C. Delco, part of the General Motors group, on a temporary contract. It involved working in the evening, which allowed her to leave her young son with her parents. She felt that trade unions:

> are not for people on an evening shift with a temporary contract. The set hours were fifteen so I wasn't entitled to anything like sick pay and holidays The company can set down the laws. We were told at the beginning so I didn't expect it.

In a similar vein, Sheila Ibbotson, who worked as a school helper and who combined her job with private catering, noted:

> I don't belong to a trade union but I will do when I've got a proper

job and go out to work. It doesn't apply with the amount of hours I do. I did belong with the GPO. I joined to be united with all the other workers. You got to know what all your rights were and you hoped someone would fight for you if something went wrong.

Union membership was equated, instead, with employees who worked in permanent full-time jobs and who were entitled to certain industrial rights. In many respects, these women were in need of greater protection from employers to protect what little they had and to fight for more employment protection. However, union membership was not perceived by the women interviewees in this way. How far this is the 'fault' of the individual women or the trade union movement is, of course, a moot point.

Indeed, joining a union would have involved considerable cost to many of the women, for they had experienced anti-union attitudes from their (often small) employers. Unlike those employees at Vauxhall, with its closed shop, and employees of the local authority and the National Health Service, which encouraged union membership, these women would meet obstacles if they joined a union. In a previous job as a cleaner Margaret Kent suggested: 'I would have got the sack if I'd joined.' Brenda Richards noted: 'It would just cause aggro with the boss if I went to a union meeting. He doesn't like unions. He always thinks we'd be plotting against him.' Similarly, Kim Dodd recognised that her employer could not stop her joining a union but 'the firm doesn't agree with them' and it would make life 'difficult'. In less than favourable circumstances, these women had not joined a union. Where a union was present at their place of work, and if it actively recruited members, they would join to act collectively in the pursuit of industrial rights. None of the women had actively pursued union membership, but then how many Vauxhall workers would have joined a trade union without the closed shop and in the face of opposition is, of course, not known.

Although the union members (who were predominantly men) and the non-union members (who were predominantly women) have been considered separately in this chapter, their industrial perspectives were remarkably similar. Different opportunities for, and constraints on, union membership confronted the men and women interviewees. These findings confirm numerous studies which have found that the low rates of union membership among women are not to be explained with reference to women's industrial attitudes. Structural rather than attitudinal differences divided the men and women in terms of their capacity to belong to a trade union. Trade unions have been absent from industrial and occupational sectors where women, and especially women who work part-time, are employed (Bain and Elias 1985; Beechey and Perkins 1987; Hunt 1982; Millward and Stevens 1986; Yeandle 1984). It is only more recently that some trade unions have sought actively to recruit women employees in non-standard forms of employment to their ranks (Grint 1991).

Overall, the findings concur with only some of the Luton team's conclusions. The interviewees' industrial perspectives centred on local issues at the workplace and questions of pay. In this sense, they may be described as instrumental collectivists. However, their local and monetary concerns were not couched in singularly individualistic terms. Their poor conditions of work, for example, would often be shared with fellow workers and this was recognised to be the case. Nor did the interviewees' pecuniary concerns preclude wider aspirations for power and control at the workplace, whereby people would be treated humanely and fairly. Similarly, the interviewees' criticisms of the trade unions did not derive solely from a single-minded instrumentalism directed towards individual material well-being. On the contrary, the interviewees discussed their evaluations of trade unions in both individual and collective terms. Support was conditional on their successful pursuit of both individual and collective issues. In other words, the interviewees' remarks suggest that the relationship between individual and collective ends is much more complex than the Luton team might have led us to expect. This issue will be reconsidered in relation to the interviewees' political perspectives.

POLITICAL PERSPECTIVES

The Luton team also employed the concept of instrumental collectivism to explain their respondents' political attitudes and behaviour. Contrary to the embourgeoisement thesis (Butler and Rose 1960), a 'large and stable' majority of their repondents were Labour Party supporters. Nearly three-quarters (70 per cent) of the sample voted Labour in both the 1955 and 1959 General Elections and almost the same percentage again (68 per cent) had never voted for another political party (Goldthorpe *et al.* 1968b: 13–5). The major reason for voting Labour derived from a perception of Labour as the party of the working class. However, when they explored their respondents' political orientations further, the Luton team found economic and social advancement was the more important reason for supporting Labour. Goldthorpe and his colleagues concluded that such calculations of the economic 'pay-offs'

> suggest that our affluent workers' support for Labour is probably less solidaristic and more instrumental than that of the many traditional workers from whom the Labour Party has in the past received almost unconditional allegiance (Goldthorpe *et al.* 1968b: 31).

Once again, the Luton team turned to an account of the changing social bases of working-class political perspectives to explain the replacement of the solidarism of the class-conscious 'traditional' working class by a weaker and more diffuse socio-political orientation among the new 'working' class. The 'natural' uncritical allegiance to Labour fostered by the 'traditional' working-class occupational community had been undermined by changes in industries and occupations, geographical mobility and privatism. The primary concern with economic advancement engendered a more critical form of support, conditional upon economic advancement. In other words, the quality of working-class allegiance to Labour had changed (Goldthorpe *et al.* 1968b: 77–9). That said, the Luton team also concluded that changes from 'traditional' communal sociability to a new home- and family-centred life-style did not militate against collective action entirely for it was still the most important means available for workers to improve their economic position.[1]

The relationship between class and party has, of course, continued to generate controversy in the field of election studies. One of the most trenchant of these debates has centred on class dealignment. It is widely agreed that absolute class voting (the overall proportion of the electorate who vote for their natural party) has declined, although disagreements persist as to whether relative class voting (the relative strength of the parties in different social classes) has also diminished. Crewe (1983, 1986, 1987, 1989) insists that economic self-interest underpinned the political beliefs and attitudes of an increasingly fragmented working class in the 1980s, which explains Labour's electoral decline during the decade. Heath and his colleagues (1985, 1987, 1991) among others (Marshall *et al.* 1988; Devine 1992b), however, argue that Labour's decline is not the product of changing working-class proclivities but is the result of negative evaluations of the Labour Party among all social classes in the 1980s. The debate, in other words, echoes the earlier controversy between embourgeoisement theorists and the Luton team, the contributors in each case seeking to explain Labour's successive electoral defeats at the hands of the Conservative Party in the two periods in question.

The Findings

In the context of these debates, what were the political attitudes and behaviour of the interviewees of this research? Were they long-standing supporters of the Labour Party or did their allegiances lie with other political parties? What were the reasons for their support? Were they critical, like the 'new' working class or uncritical, like the rather idealised 'traditional' working class, in their allegiances? What was the basis of their critical evaluation of the political parties? Was support instrumental and conditional upon economic advancement? How did they rate the parties' performances in government and opposition? In conversation with the interviewees, it was possible to discern the cognitive and evaluative processes by which their political perspectives were formed, the influences on their political attitudes over their lives and they ways in which they had changed or remained the same.[2]

The interviewees have been divided into three categories according to their political affiliations. As Table 10.1. shows, an equal number of interviewees were either Labour Party or disillusioned Labour supporters.

TABLE 10.1: Political Allegiances of the Interviewees

Political allegiance	Number of interviewees
Labour Party supporters	24
Disillusioned Labour Party supporters	24
Non-Labour Party supporters	14
Total	62

Both groups of interviewees spontaneously identified Labour as the political party which represented the interests of ordinary working-class people like themselves. Both groups were critical of Labour over a similar range of issues but the latter group had decided to abstain or vote for another political party at the forthcoming General Election. A smaller number of interviewees were Conservative Party supporters who, like the Labour Party supporters, inherited their party allegiance from their parents. They were also critical in their support of the Conservatives and a number of them were intending to vote differently at the next election.

Despite their differing party allegiances, voting histories and future voting intentions, it is important to stress that the sample as a whole held one overriding opinion about the current political scene. Like the Luton team's respondents, neither the political parties nor politicians were held in high regard by the interviewees. They disliked the squabbling between the parties and the extravagant promises which were made but never fulfilled. The interviewees were highly cynical about promises of economic prosperity. Indeed, despite all the furious debate, electoral promises, and changes of government, their daily lives went on as before and, for the most part, their economic circumstances remained the same. The world of politics was remote from their more mundane, material existence.

Labour Party Supporters

These interviewees spontaneously identified Labour as the political party which represented the working class. As members of the working class they supported and voted for the Labour Party. As Uma Kasim explained: 'I've voted for Labour in the past as a working-class party. They are the party for us. I think of us and our child as working-class.'

Similarly, the Conservative Party was automatically associated with the rich. There was, then, a strong sense of 'them' and 'us' underlying the interviewees' perceptions of the political parties and whom they represented in class terms. The data confirm the findings of the Luton team and the more recent work by Robertson (1984), Heath and his colleagues (1985, 1991) and the Essex team (Marshall *et al.* 1988), who also noted the continued importance of this class/party association.

The interviewees used the term 'working class' more readily when they spoke about their political perspectives while they had preferred, at times, to describe themselves as 'ordinary working people' in the more abstract discussions on class. They associated themselves with the working class rather than with the more diffuse category of 'ordinary working people'. In other words, their working-class identity was clearly salient in the political domain (Devine 1992b). This is hardly surprising since the history of the Labour Party is of a party seeking to represent the interests of the working class (Cronin 1984; Hinton 1983) but the finding suggests that the Labour Party continues to be more successful in mobilising political support along class lines than the Luton team and, more recently, Marshall and his colleagues (1985), have argued.

However, when the interviewees were asked to elaborate on these spontaneous remarks to explain the formation of their political allegiances, the form of working-class interests and the ways in which Labour stood for those interests, many of them could not do so. The younger members of the sample, in particular, felt they could not elaborate upon their political allegiances. In explaining their allegiance to the Labour Party they simply referred to the political affiliations of their parents. Matthew Smith, who claimed to have no interest in politics or to know the differences between the political parties, suggested 'My Dad has always been Labour and I put a cross there but that's only because my Dad has always been Labour.' While politics and the political parties had not dominated conversations in the household and parents had never directly told them how to vote, the interviewees knew where their parents' allegiances lay. Given their own lack of interest in politics, they took their parents' lead and voted Labour. Parents, it seemed were the first source of guidance, albeit of an indirect kind. These interviewees appeared to inherit their party political allegiances although, despite their cynicism about politics, they had formulated opinions about political events of the day as well.

The older interviewees, who were undoubtedly more politically- informed than their younger counterparts in the sample, referred to different experiences during their lives which had led them to identify themselves as working-class and to vote Labour. Richard Graves emphasised both the influence of his father's political allegiance and his childhood experiences:

I remember the baliffs throwing out poor people who couldn't pay rent. It doesn't happen now but I remember that it did. I'm guarding that that doesn't happen again. I don't want to see those days back.

Similarly, David Osborne referred to the impact of his working life on the formation of his perspectives:

I suppose my opinions come from my working life. In the factory I saw the way in which the average working man gets treated. If it wasn't for the trade unions we wouldn't be in the position we're in today. We'd still be in the bad old days. That's what made me follow the Labour Party too.

Thus, their daily lives, at home and in work, generated a working-class identity which led the interviewees to identify with Labour. Many of the interviewees saw it as 'natural' that they should identify with the Labour Party as the party for the working class. It seemed, for these interviewees at least, that the milieu in which they lived generated and sustained a strong identification with the Labour Party. Yet, it will be recalled that their daily lives took a home- and family-centred rather than communal form. A home and family-centred life-style did not preclude identification with the working class or the Labour Party among these interviewees.

The interviewees were keen to play down the influences of other people's opinions on their own political ideas and to highlight their independence. Politics was not a topic of conversation which they particularly enjoyed. Political discussions only led to heated arguments as people asserted their own views. Ultimately, people had their own opinions and supported different political parties and these had to be respected. In relation to discussions of politics at work, Robert Edwards noted: 'I don't think it's worth talking about. I don't discuss it very much. Some people can't talk. They get upset and excited about it. I just leave it alone.' It seemed that the interviewees did not belong to solidaristic work groups which avidly discussed politics.

At the same time, however, the interviewees felt that other people in their lives, such as family, neighbours and fellow workers, shared the same outlook on life as themselves. Politics were not explicitly discussed but they talked about the daily news, features on television and articles in the newspapers. The day-to-day events of their own lives and the world were discussed, and other people largely shared their views as they mulled over different issues. They shared a similar outlook on the world which derived from their position as 'ordinary working people' but that outlook, of course, did not necessarily translate into a particular party political allegiance.

Returning to the question of working-class interests, the interviewees did not hold an a priori set of clearly defined class interests. Some of the interviewees preferred the modest proposal that Labour stood for giving working-class people 'a little bit more' and of being 'more inclined' towards the working class.[3] In this respect, Labour would try to achieve a fairer or more equal society. Other interviewees placed greater emphasis on these ideals. Simon Sawyer suggested: 'They give people opportunities. Nobody wants to be under the feet of other people. You should give people the opportunity to prove themselves, look after themselves.' Numerous abstract ideals like 'freedom', 'opportunity', 'fairness', 'justice' and 'equality' were discussed in relation to the type of society in which they would like to live. Some interviewees, in other words, aspired, albeit in a highly idealised manner, towards a transformation of the social order.

When the interviewees elaborated upon what they meant by a fairer or more equal society, they usually focused on improved standards of living for the working class. They wanted higher levels of domestic comfort than they enjoyed at present. Labour, David Osbourne argued, was the

> only party which will bring people's standard of living up to what I would like to see it. I think the average person should be able to afford to buy a house, have fridges, television sets, a car if they want it.

Thus, as Marshall and his colleagues (1988: 153) also found, the interviewees wanted distributional justice, seeking a fairer and more equitable distribution of income and wealth and associated life-styles. Furthermore, while the interviewees looked to Labour to improve their economic circumstances, their aspirations were not couched exclusively in terms of individual material well-being to the detriment of other.[5] They wanted a fairer, more democratic society in which they as individuals and collectively as members of the working class could enjoy good standards of domestic comfort. Improved standards of living could be enjoyed by all the individual households of the working class. Their individualist and collectivist ideals were not mutually exclusive but coexisted with and complemented each other.

However, the Labour Party supporters were also highly critical of Labour, having evaluated the party's record in power and found it wanting. They were not particularly impressed with its performance in opposition either. Political events and not just social factors had shaped and informed their political proclivities as well.[4]

Earlier in the chapter it was noted that the interviewees, including the long-standing Labour supporters, were extremely cynical of the political parties. All parties promised to generate economic growth and prosperity and to improve people's standards of living. The interviewees were highly sceptical about such claims and they did not believe that any political party, Labour included, could overcome economic stagflation. Brian Richards, who was a long-standing Labour supporter, still felt

> They are full of promises to get what they want but I'm still working for a living, paying high taxes and high interest rates. It doesn't really matter who gets in. It doesn't really affect your way of life except you probably dig a little deeper into your pocket.

Despite their allegiance to Labour, therefore, many of the Labour supporters were unconvinced that the party would improve their standards of living.

Invariably, they elaborated upon this view by referring to the last Labour government of 1974–9, and the 'winter of discontent' of 1978–9 in particular. Their evaluation of the Labour Party's record in office in the 1970s and the events surrounding the 'winter of discontent' remained a salient political issue in 1987. Indeed, a number of interviewees discussed the events of that period at length, recalling the conflict between the government's incomes policy and the competing claims of various unions for higher wages. Against this background, refuse disposal services had come to a halt, there were empty shelves in the shops, and levels of unemployment and inflation were high. The interviewees recalled the 'fiasco' of this period, when it seemed that the economy was in a mess. There was much confusion and despair about the whole period and how the situation had arisen. However, while some interviewees apportioned blame on the unions, others blamed the Labour government for the turn of events.[5] Simon Sawyer, for example, was highly critical of the trade unions:

> I was very disappointed. Callaghan was telling us the truth about the condition of the country but the unions didn't believe him. They thought the Conservatives were offering them better opportunities with free collective bargaining. What is there to bargain for now? Nothing.

While he was critical of the unions' demands for more pay for their members, Richard Graves highlighted the impact of wage constraints on poorly-paid workers:

> They had percentage wage increases and the person at the bottom was still out in the cold. They were still as badly off after 10 per cent. There was no light at the end of the tunnel. If everyone had got a 5 pound rise irrespective of their wages it would have been OK. Instead we had a big gap created and the bottom were left where they were.

The 'winter of discontent', therefore, was perceived as a period when numerous groups of workers were clamouring for pay rises and the Labour government could not meet everyone's demands. Most importantly, the interviewees were not convinced that the same circumstances would not arise again. Given their greater affinity with the trade unions, they would make more wage claims once again and the Labour Party would not be able to meet them. The economy would not prosper in such circumstances and nor would their own standards of living improve.

Thus, while these interviewees supported Labour as the party who would improve the economic and economic circumstances of the working class, they doubted Labour's ability to achieve these ends as well. Past performance in government and the poor economic climate suggested they would fail. It reminded them of Labour's mismanagement of the economy and the collapse of the special relationship between Labour and the other vehicle of collective working-class support, the trade unions. As Whiteley (1983) found, their subsequent performance in opposition, including the divisions within the party in the early 1980s, left them feeling that Labour could manage the economy neither efficiently nor fairly.

The interviewees were not critical of Labour solely because it had failed to improve their own standards of living, as the Luton team alleged. Individual consumer aspirations had not undermined their allegiance to Labour. Rather, they were disappointed at the way in which the party had failed to improve the material well-being of both their individual situation and the economic and social circumstances of the working class as a whole. Overall, however, the interviewees felt they could not vote any other way as members of the working class and, despite their dissatisfactions, they would vote Labour in the forthcoming General Election. This was not the case for the disillusioned Labour Party supporters.

Disillusioned Labour Party Supporters

An equal number of interviewees (twenty four) were disillusioned Labour Party supporters who would not vote Labour at the next General Election. These interviewees are, of course, the 'critical' group in the debate on class dealignment. Like the Labour supporters, they spontaneously associated the Labour Party with the working class. The Labour Party, it was argued, represented the working class and, theoretically, as members of the working class they should vote Labour. As Anthony Dodd suggested:

> I'd rather vote Labour because I come from a Labour upbringing. Everyone I know and work with is Labour as we're workingclass. I associate the working class with Labour.

Similarly, these interviewees looked to Labour to improve their standards of living, but they also had doubts about the promises which Labour made, along with the other political parties, to reverse the current economic climate and to achieve economic prosperity. Once again, a fatalism about the economic fortunes of the country informed their political persuasions. On the issue of unemployment, for example, Sandra Davis explained her feelings towards Labour:

> The Labour Party keeps telling me how it is going to create thousands of jobs. I do think this is a good thing for the children's future. If jobs keep disappearing my children will never have a job. It is a worry but I wonder if the Labour Party will do it.

The interviewees, therefore, were far from convinced that Labour's programme could achieve economic prosperity whereby they would also enjoy improved standards of living. For these interviewees, as Whiteley (1983: 151) also found, Labour did not offer them a credible economic policy.

Moreover, the interviewees expressed feelings of disbelief and alarm at the number of promises that Labour seemed to make to the electorate. Labour claimed it would turn round the economic fortunes of the country and reduce unemployment in a short period of time. It also claimed to increase public expenditure in the public sector to improve the health service, the education system, the stock of housing and so forth. However, it was not clear to the interviewees how Labour was going to secure economic prosperity and finance a variety of social programmes. How could the economy afford such social policies? What if they were unable to achieve economic growth? What would happen to their welfare policies if prosperity was not forthcoming? The interviewees, then, were not convinced of either the economic or the social policies of the Labour Party, and were perturbed at how much they were trying to offer. These comments highlight what Goldthorpe has described as Labour's 'continuing difficulties in presenting its economic and its social policies as being coherently related' (1987: 346).

The implications of this dissatisfaction on future voting among the disillusioned Labour Party supporters were diverse. Just under half (eleven) of these interviewees felt they would not vote. As Gerald Mills stated: 'I don't know if I'll vote next time. I might not bother. If I don't vote it's a vote of no confidence in the lot of them.' Four interviewees, while expressing very similar sentiments to the others, felt they might vote for the Liberal/SDP Alliance 'just to give them a chance to see if they could do any better'.[6]

However, nine interviewees had decided to vote for the Conservative Party at the next election and, once again, they referred to the same issues which were discussed by the other members of the sample. Concern was voiced about the 'winter of discontent' of 1978–9 and the less than harmonious relations between Labour and the trade unions over that period. Robert Edwards argued:

> It's selfish but the way I look at it at the moment if things stop the way they are I'm better off. If the other people got in I don't know what's going to happen. I think they'll just blow the lid off of everything. Inflation frightens me and I just don't want it back again. It was ridiculous. Everyone lost control.

It should be noted, of course, that the Conservative Party has constantly referred to the 'winter of discontent' of 1978–9 in its electioneering and it appears to have been successful in keeping the issue on the political agenda. The Labour Party supporters or disillusioned supporters did not detract from this view of past political events. The interviewees were fearful of what a Labour victory would mean, while voting for the Conservative Party meant, at the very least, that things would remain the same. In this respect, it was a damning evaluation of Labour even if it was not a positive endorsement of the Conservative Party's economic policies.

The sole Conservative Party policy which was mentioned with any enthusiasm was home ownership. Anthony Dodd, a home owner, suggested: 'Thatcher has done a lot for the home owner and council tenants.

She has given us self-respect and independence. She's taken us up a peg.' Similarly, Sheila Ibbotson felt that 'the Conservatives were all for the common person buying their own place'. It was seen as a policy which gave people another opportunity to 'better themselves' which, it will be remembered, was not usually associated with the Conservative Party. On this issue at least, it was the Conservative Party rather than the Labour Party which was offering people the opportunity to improve their standards of living. It is a good example of the ways in which interests can be defined and discussed in different ways to a party's advantage, and the role which the political parties play in such debates.

Why these nine disillusioned Labour Party supporters decided to vote for the Conservative Party and against the Labour Party rather than abstain is difficult to ascertain. They were not distinctive from other members of the sample in any notable sense.[7] They were not any more individualistic than the other interviewees. Nor were their evaluations of the political parties any different from other disillusioned supporters of the Labour Party or even, for that matter, from those interviewees who intended to remain loyal to Labour. Finally, like the other interviewees, they did not hold political parties or politicians in high regard, noting with cynicism the various promises which all of the political parties made while their daily lives continued unchanged.

Bearing this in mind, the interviewees did not appear to attach great importance to their vote. As individuals, they did not feel that they had a great impact on the electoral fortunes of the country. They did not perceive voting to be a political power but noted their political impotence instead, as Lane (1962) also found in his wide-ranging study of political attitudes. It may be that having decided that Labour had very little chance of winning the forthcoming election according to their evaluation, placing their votes with the Conservatives would not rob Labour of victory anyway. If the Labour Party's standing in the polls were better, they would not deny them a vote to facilitate a win, but these circumstances did not exist in the mid-1980s. The interviewees shared a body of ideas but the reasons for acting as they did disguised their similar attitudes and opinions.

Non-Labour Voters

Fourteen members of the sample aligned themselves with the Conservative Party at the time of the interview, although four of them had voted for the Liberal Party in the past. This finding is not surprising since it is well known that a large minority of the working class has always voted against their so-called 'natural' class interests (Robertson 1984: 6). Like the other interviewees, they cited their parents' political allegiances as a major influence on their own voting behaviour. As Brenda Richards stated: 'I voted as my Dad did. I tended to think that everything that he did was right.' Similarly, the interviewees could not explicitly state the reasons behind their parents or their own allegiance to the Conservative Party.

The Conservative Party supporters also associated the political parties with different classes. They saw themselves as 'ordinary working people' who, according to some, should vote for the Labour Party. They also saw the Conservative Party as largely constituting and representing the 'rich'. However, the Conservative Party was not seen to act against the working class. As John Hills noted:

> I know working people are supposed to vote Labour but I don't feel the same. I felt in the past that the working class did better under the Conservatives when business was better. Business doing better means better things for the workers overall.

Dorothy Atkinson said 'I have respect for the Tory Government because the money is there.' Thus, while there was a sense of the Conservative Party representing the rich, the working class were also seen to benefit when they were in power. In this respect, the Conservative Party was seen to represent everyone in Britain in a more patriotic way than did the Labour Party.

The issue of patriotism led the Conservative Party supporters to discuss the issue of immigration as another reason for their political allegiances. They believed, very strongly, that immigration should be restricted, and they disagreed with what they perceived to be the Labour Party's liberal stand on the issue. Referring to conflict over the distribution of resources, a long-standing Conservative Party supporter remarked: 'I agree that we shouldn't allow more immigrants in. The Labour Party would let more in. We have youngsters of our own who want jobs. It gets harder for those here.'

Given that the majority of the interviewees felt very strongly about immigration (concurring with Sarlvik and Crewe's (1983: 242) finding that those who think they live in a 'high immigrant area' are more likely to feel very strongly about the issue than those who do not), it was somewhat surprising that the other interviewees did not mention the issue of immigration as well. After all, Luton's two MPs – John Carlisle and Graham Bright – are well known for their tough stands on immigration. However, the Labour Party supporters and disillusioned Labour Party suppporters justified their present or past party choice on a class basis. Their national identity did not translate into party choice, remaining, instead, a 'dormant' frame of reference in the political arena (Devine 1992a). It may be that the Labour Party's less than liberal immigration policy is a way of avoiding losses to the Conservative Party on this issue. Only the Conservative Party supporters cited the issue of immigration as a justification for their political proclivities.

Like the other interviewees, however, the Conservative Party supporters' allegiance was not total for they were critical as well. They had misgivings about the economy, unemployment and the problems of

funding the public services. Again, the ill health of the economy was seen
as an intractable problem which none of the political parties could overcome. As Angela Stone said: 'I think it's awful all this unemployment but
it's world wide you see. Everyone says it's her [Mrs Thatcher's] fault but
it is a world wide thing.' Other political parties were not seen to offer any
solutions. As she went on to say: 'I can't see anybody any better, this is
the thing and this is what most people feel. I mean most people go on
about Thatcher but they just don't stand up to her. She's a powerful
woman.' Not surprisingly, the Conservative Party supporters were
highly critical of the Labour Party and their views and, like the other
interviewees, they focused on a similar range of economic issues. Again,
the 'winter of discontent' of 1978–9 was frequently mentioned as a poor
example of how Labour had run the economy. They were not convinced
that such events would not happen again. Peter Ibbotson, who was a
shop steward, noted:

> With Labour we would have to have a ceiling as everything would
> go stupid but then my position would go down. I don't know. The
> wage rises have been OK. Under Labour there was a wage freeze
> and we weren't allowed anything over 5 per cent. With free collec-
> tive bargaining I can definitely feel the difference. It is good for me
> personally although if everything goes up it's not.

The interviewees were, therefore, not entirely content with the present
government which they had voted into office. High unemployment, cuts
in the National Health Service and other welfare services came under
criticism. Thus, they were unhappy with the government's record on
economic and social policies but they could see no alternative. In total,
seven interviewees felt they would vote for the Conservative Party, three
were undecided and one would abstain because of her present misgivings. Finally, three interviewees felt they would vote for the Alliance
parties to give them an opportunity of power. None of the interviewees
in this group considered voting for the Labour Party at the next General
Election. There appeared, then, to be volatility among these interviewees
as there did among the disillusioned Labour Party supporters.

CONCLUSION

The majority of the interviewees looked either to the trade unions or to
the Labour Party to defend and promote their interests collectively as
members of the working class. Invariably, the interviewees referred specifically to improvements in the economic and social circumstances of
themselves and other working-class families. In other words, the desire
for material well-being certainly shaped and informed their industrial
and political perspectives. These findings concur with Goldthorpe's and
his colleagues' data. However, in contrast to the Luton team's findings,
the interviewees' consumer aspirations were not couched in purely individual terms but embraced collective gains for the working class as a

whole. Nor did their material aspirations preclude wider ideals for a fairer and more just democratic society than existed at present. Once again, the Luton team's dichotomy between the highly-idealised 'traditional' working class and the 'new' working class has been less than robust.

Similarily, as the Luton team found among their respondents, the interviewees of this research were not unswervingly loyal to the trade unions and the Labour Party. They were critical of both vehicles of working-class support. In opposition to the Luton team's view, however, the interviewees were not critical of the trade unions and Labour simply because they had failed to deliver improvements in their individual standards of living. Rather, their critical evaluations of both organisations centred on their failure to improve the economic and social circumstances of themselves, their families and other working-class families in British society. Once again, their comments embraced both individual and collective concerns.

This chapter, as with previous chapters, has highlighted some of the ambiguities in the concept of working-class instrumentalism. The problems and difficulties surrounding the distinction between the instrumental collectivism of the 'new' working class and the 'proletarian solidarism' of the 'traditional' working class have also been raised. In other words, the Luton team's account of the impact of economic, social and political changes on the working class in the second half of the twentieth century, and the importance which they attached to instrumentalism as the major catalyst for change, has been found wanting. The implications of these ambiguities for our understanding of the working class and how it may or may not have changed over the twentieth century as a whole are considered further in the concluding chapter.

NOTES

1. Like Butler and Stokes (1969), the Luton team emphasised the importance of early political socialisation on political perspectives. They also employed two other arguments to explain the political attitudes of their respondents. First, in their discussion of deviant voters, identified as the downwardly mobile middle class who still had bridges into a middle-class world, the Luton team drew attention to the changing occupational structure and its implications for class identity and political proclivities (Goldthorpe *et al.* 1968b: Chapter 4). These issues are still widely discussed by political commentators (Crewe 1983, 1985, 1987, 1989; Franklin 1985; Heath *et al.* 1985, 1991; Himmelweit *et al.* 1985). Secondly, in the last few pages of the final volume in the *Affluent Worker* trilogy, the Luton team briefly acknowledged the role of political events on the formation of political attitudes – namely, the performance of Labour in government and the nature of appeals for working-class support (Goldthorpe *et al.* 1969: 189–95). This last argument is given heightened emphasis

by Marshall and his colleagues (1988) in their account of political proclivities in the 1980s.

2. The interviews were conducted between September 1986 and March 1987, when there was considerable speculation about the date of the forthcoming General Election. The election was eventually called for 11 June 1987 and the Conservative Party was returned to power with 42.2 per cent of the vote. The Labour Party received 30.8 per cent of the vote and the Liberal/SDP Alliance 22.6 per cent (Crewe 1987).

The two sitting MPs for Luton – John Carlisle and Graham Bright – were returned with increased majorities. Both MPs were narrowly elected to represent Luton in 1979, overturning slim Labour majorities. In the subsequent election of 1983, they secured their hold on the two Luton constituencies. The extent to which they increased their majorities by winning support from members of the working class is difficult to ascertain since the constituency boundaries were changed in the intervening period. After the 1987 election, Bright's seat remains marginal with a majority of 5, 115, while Carlisle now occupies a safe Conservative seat, having increased his 1979 majority of just 246 in 1979 (for Luton West) into a 15,424 lead over Labour in 1987 (for Luton North) *(The Times Guide to the House of Commons)*.

3. These limited perceptions of the ways in which Labour stood for the working class were also voiced by Willmott's (1963: 106) respondents living on a working-class housing estate in Dagenham.

4. The social and political influences on the interviewees' political perspectives have been separated in a somewhat simplistic fashion in this chapter, while, of course, people's daily lives and wider political events are meshed much more closely through their lives.

5. These remarks are similar to the interviewees' comments on the trade unions and whether it was the union or its members or both who were to 'blame' for the failure to achieve collective action.

6. Somewhat surprisingly, the majority of the interviewees made little reference to the Liberal/SDP Alliance in the conversations on politics.

7. These findings raise the question of whether the disillusioned Labour Party supporters who intended to vote Conservative occupied a distinctive sectoral location. Did 'new' consumer cleavages such as housing tenure, as some have argued (Dunleavy 1980; Dunleavy and Husbands 1985; Saunders 1990a), fragment the sample? The answer is 'no', since all of the disillusioned Labour Party supporters were, and had always been, home owners so the policy did not affect them directly.

Five families in the sample – Mr and Mrs Kasim, Mr and Mrs Burgess, Mr and Mrs Mills, Mr and Mrs Farrell, and Mr and Mrs Knight – lived in council houses, and all of them were loyal Labour Party supporters even though they agreed with the Conservative Party's policy of selling council houses. Two of the families – Mrs and Mrs Kasim and Mr and Mrs Knight talked of buying their homes in the future. This finding concurs with Saunders's (1990: 233) three towns survey, since he found that 'while council tenants are overwhelmingly Labour, owner occupiers are divided across all parties, and it is partly because unskilled and (to a lesser extent) semi-skilled manual working-class households remain solidly supportive of the Labour Party even if they own a house.'

Three families had been council tenants in the past before buying their own homes, and all members of these households were long-standing Conservative Party supporters. Two of these families – Mr and Mrs Hills and Mr and Mrs Foulds – were older members of the sample who had bought their houses in the 1950s when there was an extensive programme of house building at relatively cheap prices in Luton. One only family – Mr and Mrs Stone – had actually bought their council house which they did at the first opportunity in 1980. In this instance, as Heath and his colleagues (1985: 49) claim, it appeared that conservatism went hand in hand with the desire for home ownership rather than home ownership leading to conservatism.

11

CONCLUSION

Despite the attention that the *Affluent Worker* series has enjoyed, the key finding of privatism attracted almost no subsequent debate in the field of class analysis. It is only recently, as commentators have begun to re-evaluate accounts of changing working-class life-styles and associated norms and values from the vantage point of historical material on developments in the nineteenth-century, that the concept of privatism has been seriously contested. However, attempts to locate privatism among the nineteeth century working class have effectively drawn attention away from the question of whether the concept adequately describes working-class culture today. In other words, the Luton team's predictions about the working class as a socio-political entity in the late twentieth century continue to be ignored.

This study was undertaken to rectify the omission. The research set out to explore the extent to which working-class life-styles centre on the immediate family in the home. A further objective was to examine the ways in which such an existence may generate and sustain a set of norms and values disposed towards high levels of domestic comfort and material well-being in the home for the individual family. In other words, the overall aim of the research was to examine critically the interconnections between instrumentalism, privatism and individualism. In so doing, it has also tried to gain some insight into the degree to which working-class life-styles and values may have changed, and the processes of change in the second half of the twentieth century, as well as the nature of 'traditional' working-class culture in the first half of the century.

The research was designed to explore in depth the meaning which people attach to their home and family lives and their aspirations and values. Intensive interviews were conducted with a small number (sixty two) of men and women, and biographical details on the interviewees' geographical mobility and work histories were collected. Attention focused on patterns of sociability with kin, neighbours and colleagues from work to ascertain whether the interviewees' life-styles could be accurately described as family-centred. The degree to which their lives could be portrayed as home-centred was explored by focusing on the interviewees' domestic roles and patterns of leisure. The interviewees were also asked to discuss their aspirations, social perspectives, industrial attitudes and political proclivities to analyse the extent to which their values could be described as individualistic. With equal weight attached to the interviews with husbands and wives, the men and women interviewees were questioned on different aspects of their daily lives as well as their hopes, fears, plans and misgivings for the future.

Like the respondents of the *Affluent Worker* study, the interviewees worked and lived in Luton. Furthermore, like one-third of the Luton team's respondents, all thirty men worked in shop-floor jobs at the Vauxhall car factory. Six women also worked for the company, while a further eight of them had done so in the past. In sum, nearly three-quarters (forty four) of the sample had worked or worked for Vauxhall. Even though the company had remained the largest employer in the town throughout the 1960s, 1970s and 1980s, it operated on a much reduced workforce. While it employed over 22,000 workers from the locality in the mid-1960s, by the mid-1980s it had only 6,000 employees. Much of the company's workforce had been gradually discarded from the late 1960s onwards although substantial redundancies in the late 1970s and early 1980s accelerated a process already in train.

Conducting the research in Luton entailed 'revisiting' a town with a different economic and social structure from that previously described by Goldthorpe and his colleagues. In the intervening period between the Luton team's research in 1961–2 and this study in 1986–7, the town experienced economic restructuring – industrial and occupational shifts and their gendered and spatial consequences – as well as recession. These economic conditions were the context in which working-class cultural history was explored. Despite the difficult economic circumstances of the 1980s in comparison to the more buoyant economic climate of the 1960s, had the Luton team's predictions stood the test of time?

Revisiting Luton presented the opportunity of examining the motives, the processes and the consequences of geographical mobility. Like the respondents of the *Affluent Worker* study, the interviewees and their families were a highly mobile group. Just under half of the sample had moved to Luton from other parts of Britain, Eire and the New Commonwealth. Indeed, the majority of the parents of the 'native' Lutonians had moved into the town from elsewhere as well. That is, the predominantly young members of the sample who were 'natives' rather than 'migrants' were the second generation of geographically mobile families into Luton. The sample was not demographically mature, although the mobile interviewees were long-established rather than newly-arrived migrants to the town.

However, the interviewees' motives for mobility were much more complex than Goldthorpe and his colleagues supposed. The interviewees did not move simply in search of high wages and the prospect of relatively good standards of living. The overwhelming majority of the interviewees and their parents moved to escape from unemployment, job insecurity and/or the inability to afford private housing. The long-distance migrants from Scotland, Wales, Eire, the North of Britain and the New Commonwealth, for example, moved to get away from unemployment and the threat of redundancy. The short-distance migrants from London and the South East moved to Luton in search of private housing, which they could not afford in the capital and elsewhere. It was in the context of these constraints that the interviewees grasped the opportunities presented by the post-war period of prosperity to improve their economic and social circumstances. Push and pull factors shaped the interviewees' motives for moving to Luton. In other words, a more complicated picture of instrumentalism and individualism was in evidence than the Luton team portrayed.

Furthermore, many of the interviewees and their families followed, or were followed by, kin and friends to Luton. They invariably facilitated mobility by providing information on job opportunities and the availability of suitable housing in the town. Individual families did not usually move to Luton alone but 'regrouped' with their kin and friends in the new locale. Rather than move away from kin and friends, families helped each other in the search for improved standards of living. There was plenty of evidence of solidarity rather than individualism. The processes of geographical mobility were somewhat different from those described by Goldthorpe and his colleagues.

Finally, the consequences of mobility were rather different for the interviewees of this research in comparison to the Luton team's respondents. Goldthorpe and his colleagues found considerable enthusiasm about moving among their newly-arrived migrants. However, among the long-established migrants of this study, the context in which they decided to move to Luton and their subsequent experiences of the advantages and disadvantages of mobility had tempered any excitement which they might have felt. They had adapted to the situation in which they found themselves, their feelings about their circumstances taking a secondary importance in their daily lives.

With little firm evidence of a singularly instrumental pursuit of improved standards of living as the catalyst for geographical mobility, there was no inevitable interconnection between instrumentalism and privatism. The interviewees' lives were not exclusively family-centred. While their daily routine centred on the work, both paid and unpaid, deemed necessary to sustain the livelihood and well-being of the household and its members, the interviewees were far from isolated from other people. They did not lead singular lives. On the contrary, they enjoyed the companionship and support of extended kin, neighbours and colleagues from work. It was found, for example, that the three-generation family continues to be an important source of companionship and support. Sociable contact between parents and children is invariably sustained throughout a lifetime and it is particularly important when care is needed, be it child-care or care of ageing parents. Geographical mobility obviously curtails frequent and casual, unplanned contact with kin, but the intimacy of relations is not necessarily undermined by physical distance.

Similarly, neighbours are often an important source of friendship, especially among women looking after their children full-time, who are usually confined to the home and immediate locality. There was plenty of evidence of neighbours giving practical support to those in need, like elderly neighbours who lived alone. Finally, men enjoyed the company of two or three fellow men in the locality, especially if they worked for Vauxhall as well. In other words, there was little indication of insularity among the interviewees of this research.

Finally, both the men and women interviewees enjoyed the company of their colleagues from work inside and outside the workplace. Their instrumental orientation towards paid work was a source of solidarity not schism at the workplace. Friendship and intimacy with particular colleagues from work often developed between those workers who knew each other in other roles – as kin, neighbours, old school friends or whatever – and if they shared the same stage in the family life-cycle. As with some of their kin and particular neighbours, they confided in work-mates with whom they enjoyed intimate relations, sharing their hopes, plans, fears and misgivings of their day-to-day lives.

If the interviewees' life-styles could not be described as exclusively family-centred nor could they be portrayed as entirely home-centred. While the husbands of the sample were certainly not aloof members of their households, they did not contribute as much, or in the same way, to the domestic routine as did their wives. Their partners remained primarily responsible for household chores and child-care tasks. Where men undertook these duties, their participation in the domestic routine was invariably the product of necessity rather than choice. That is, their asistance was necessary when their wives returned to formal employment and contributed to the household income. Of course, women's return to the labour market implies that their lives are not wholly home-centred either.

Neither were the men's and women's leisure patterns completely home-based. It was found that men continue to take pleasure in separate leisure activities – usually a sport or a drink in the local pub – outside the home and in the company of people beyond the immediate family. They could enjoy their time, free from the demands of paid and unpaid work, to a far greater extent than could their wives. Their partners' lives, on the other hand, were closely meshed with looking after their children. Pleasure was often derived from entertaining them. That said, the wives' leisure activities were not fully home-centred either. As they passed the most demanding stages of the family life-cycle and their children became independent, they could enjoy some leisure beyond the home. Keep-fit and socialising with other women were the most popular leisure pursuits of the women of the sample.

Now, this is not to suggest that the interviewees were engaged in extensive sociability with a large group of people beyond the immediate family. Nor did they participate greatly in leisure activities outside the home. If their life-styles could not be accurately described as privatised, nor could they be precisely portrayed as communal. They did not lead 'traditional' working-class life-styles. The work, be it paid or unpaid, involved in sustaining the livelihood and well-being of the household was the most important determinant of levels of sociability and the patterning of conjugal roles and leisure. It dictated the opportunities for, and the constraints on, sociable contact with people beyond the conjugal family and leisure activities outside the home. Work militated against the kind of communal existence associated with the 'traditional' working class. Domestic duties and child-care tasks, for example, limited the amount of time which the women could spend socialising with kin and neighbours. Similarly, paid work structured the time available for men to engage in leisure activities with fellow workers beyond the home. Paid and unpaid work clearly structured the interviewees' styles of life.

The different work roles which the husbands and wives performed in sustaining the household meant that the opportunities for, and the constraints on, levels of sociability and patterns of leisure varied between them. The opportunities and constraints which structured their daily lives were 'gendered'. For the most part, paid work was the major influence on the men's life-styles, while unpaid work primarily shaped the women's styles of life. That said, unpaid work also structured the men's existence since domestic chores and child-care tasks limited the amount of time which they could spend with other people beyond the home. Likewise, paid work effected the women's capacity to socialise with others outside the home. Their different paid and unpaid work roles shaped and patterned their daily lives in varied ways.

Moreover, the opportunities for, and constraints on, sociability and leisure were not constant but dynamic across the family life-cycle. This was most notably the case for women since domestic tasks and child-care duties were the dominant structuring influences on their life-styles. As they passed through the most demanding stages of the family life-cycle and their children became independent, they had the time and money to socialise with others and pursue leisure activities beyond the home. By the same token, as men surpassed the most demanding stage of the family life-cycle when there was financial pressure to work overtime, they could also enjoy more free time with the necessary resources available to take pleasure in socialising with others and engage in leisure activities. The ways in which work shaped the opportunities and constraints which in turn shaped the interviewees' daily lives were ever-changing.

Emphasis has been placed on the ways in which paid and unpaid work structured the opportunities for, and constraints on, sociability and leisure. Work militated against the communal life-styles associated with the 'traditional' working class although the interviewees' life-styles were not privatised either. The interviewees' values reinforced the structural factors which influenced their styles of life and, in turn, affected the ways in which those structural factors shaped their daily existence. Undoubtedly, the interviewees' aspirations centred on sustaining and improving upon the material comfort and well-being of the immediate family in the home. 'Bettering' themselves and their families was a dominant aspiration of all of the interviewees. In pursuit of this material end, the means – the paid and unpaid work perceived to be involved – curtailed contact with people beyond the immediate family and restricted their free time to the home. That is, the interviewees did not consciously choose a home- and family-centred existence but the value which they placed on 'bettering' themselves and their families meant that their life-styles were a consequence of the means available to them of achieving their ends.

However, the interviewees' values did not entirely legitimise the ways in which paid and unpaid work dominated their existence. It was a source of considerable grievance that the work perceived to be required to meet their aspirations shaped their styles of life. They did not have a strong preference for the life-styles which they led. While they valued their home and family lives, they would have liked some more time and money to socialise with other people and to enjoy a wider range of leisure activities than they did at present. This is not to say that the interviewees wanted a communal existence but they would have liked a somewhat fuller and more varied life-style than they lived. In this respect, any feelings which they had about the nature of their daily lives and how they would have liked them to be different were given secondary importance in relation to their consumer aspirations. However, as ordinary working people, the work required to achieve a degree of material comfort – the perceived brute facts of economic life – gave them very little choice about how they lived their lives.

The interviewees, therefore, proffered a materialistic account of their life-styles and values. This materialism was not surprising since the threat of redundancy and unemployment hung over many of their lives. They hoped to hold on to their jobs for as long as possible and carry on with their 'normal' day-to-day existence. This included striving for improved standards of living for themselves and their immediate family in the home. However, the interviewees did not look to general economic advancement for economic improvements, as the Luton team found. Rather, they expected to enjoy small, cumulative gains as the household moved through the family life-cycle. Given the economic climate of economic restructuring and recession, they did not share the optimism about economic prosperity of the Luton team's respondents, who enjoyed the post-war period of prosperity. Even so, their consumer aspirations were not fixed, for they would continue to strive to 'better themselves' despite the unfavourable economic climate in which they lived. While the interviewees aspired for improved levels of domestic comfort for themselves and their immediate family in the home, their values were not exclusively individualistic. On the contrary, their remarks were constantly framed with reference to the aspirations of other ordinary, respectable people who worked for a living. Sharing similar standards of living and striving for more improvements was an important dimension of class identity. In other words, the interviewees' individual family consumer aspirations were not necessarily the source of individualism or schism. They were an important dimension of class solidarity. The interviewees proffered a pecuniary model of the class structure. They identified themselves with a mass working/middle class, distancing themselves from the extremes of the very rich and the very poor. Money was a shorthand way of identifying the different material standards of living between people of different social classes and, more importantly, the means by which they had acquired the money and associated life-style. While their lives, and that of other ordinary working people, were dominated by instrumental, material concerns, the rich enjoyed their wealth, life-style and freedom without the work which dominated working people's daily lives. This fact was a source of grievance to the interviewees. It was on this basis that they aspired for a more equitable distribution of resources in society as it stood, and, by implication, a more equal, free and democratic society in which people would be justly and fairly rewarded than existed at present. In other words, their aspirations lay inside and outside the capitalist society in which they lived.

Finally, it was found that the interviewees viewed the trade unions and the Labour Party as collective means of securing both individual and collective ends. They looked to both organisations to improve their individual family circumstances but, again, not in a singularly individualistic fashion, as the Luton team alleged. Rather, they inextricably linked individual family and collective working-class aspirations. Their class identity was especially salient in the political domain. Likewise, support for the trade unions and the Labour Party was not conditional upon individual material well-being alone. While the interviewees were critical of both organisations, their criticisms were voiced not simply because both organisations had failed to deliver improvement in their individual standards of living. On the contrary, their critical evaluations of the trade unions and the Labour Party arose out of disappointment with both organisations to improve the economic and social circumstances of themselves, their families and other working-class families in Britain. They had failed to redistribute resources more equitably in society and, by implication, they had been unsuccessful in creating a more just and fair society than existed at present. Thus, neither the interviewees' industrial perspectives nor their political proclivities were exclusively individualistic.

These conclusions do not sit comfortably alongside the Luton team's key findings on changing working-class life-styles and values in the twentieth century and their predictions for the future. The interviewees were not singularly instrumental in their motives for mobility. Nor did they lead exclusively privatised styles of life. Lastly, their aspirations and socio-political values were not entirely individualistic. The links in the chain between instrumentalism, privatism and individualism have been broken. The voluntarism of their account of the interconnection between instrumentalism and privatism has been found wanting, as has their deterministic description of the interconnection between privatism and individualism.

Overall, the findings of this research suggest that working-class life-styles and values have not changed as much as the Luton team suggested. Uncritically relying on notions of a 'traditional' working-class culture, they exaggerated the extent of change in working-class life-styles and values between the first and second halves of the twentieth century. Furthermore, they incorrectly gave primacy to changing working-class norms and values in their account of the processes of change, neglecting the many structural factors, like changing patterns of work, which shape and patttern people's lives and values and are, in turn, shaped by them. That is, the criticisms which the Luton team levelled against the embourgeoisement theorists can also be employed against their description and explanation of social change. The Luton team's caution may explain the continued popularity of the embourgeoisement thesis over a considerable period of time and, indeed, the way in which their key findings have been incorporated into a wide-ranging theory of economic, social and political change since the Second World War. Despite evidence to the contrary (Abercrombie *et al.* 1986), the interconnection between individualism and capitalism is still widely accepted by sociologists and political scientists alike.

These conclusions provide an interesting insight into the wider issues of the failure of the working class to overthrow the capitalist system as Marx predicted, the incorporation of the working class into the system and the social cohesion of advanced capitalist societies. The findings of this study are an empirical illustration of the arguments espoused by Abercrombie and his colleagues (1980) in *The Dominant Ideology Thesis*. Challenging the notion that the working class has been incorporated into capitalist society by an all-embracing dominant ideology, as both Marxists and functionalists have argued, they insist instead that it is the everyday economic realities of people's lives which shape their aspirations and social and political perspectives. Despite improved standards of living, the economic interdependence of people and the system acts as a powerful constraint on people doing anything other than accept their circumstances. As they argued:

> Compulsion is most obviously founded in the economic relations which oblige people to behave in ways which support the status quo and to defer to the decisions of the powerful if they are to continue to work and to live (Abercrombie *et al.* 1980: 154–55).

The 'iron cage' of people's everyday life, therefore, is an important influence on the form and nature of people's aspirations and social and political perspectives.

However, the constraints which continue to shape people's lives imply that members of the working class do not normatively accept or endorse the prevailing system. As Abercrombie and his colleagues argue further:

> Workers may accept the economic order of capitalism and its class based social organisation at a factual level. This factual acceptance need not involve any signs of normative acceptance or indoctrination. Habituation and a realistic appreciation of the strength of the existing order do not add up to any form of commitment, nor even a decline in workers' awareness of alternative or more desireable systems (1980 *et al.* : 122).

Thus, while the working class has not overthrown the capitalist system, the distribution of rewards still lacks 'a moral order' as Marshall and his colleagues (1987) have also argued. The potential for conflict over the distribution of rewards remains.

The findings of this research also confirm the political argument espoused by Marshall and his colleagues (1988) and neglected by Abercrombie and his colleagues (Turner 1990). The interviewees of this study held a collective class identity. They described the class structure and their own position within it in terms of money and wealth. Many of them felt that the distribution of rewards was unfair and they supported the trade unions and the Labour Party in pursuit of justice. However, they had also critically evaluated both vehicles of collective working-class support in bringing about change and had found them wanting. As the Essex team also found, 'the failure of successive Labour governments to pursue a more generalised social justice by controlling union sectionalism' (Marshall *et al.* 1988: 268) had led some of the interviewees to withhold their support. In the 1980s at least, the lack of collective action was the product of 'institutional and organisational' failures, and was not the outcome of increased individualism among the working class.

These issues go beyond the findings of this research. However, they highlight an important methodological point. If aspirations and sociopolitical attitudes are shaped and informed by an individual's daily life, then it is important to consider people's hopes, plans, fears and disappointments in an economic, social and political context. Highly structured questionnaires, such as the questionnaire employed by the Luton team, do not allow the researcher to consider individual biographies in any depth. The *Affluent Worker* study, for example, contained very little information on the respondents' work histories before their employment at Vauxhall, and the varied circumstances in which the men and women came to live and work in Luton. The findings presented here highlighted the diverse circumstances in which some of the interviewees chose, within certain constraints, to move to Luton, and questioned the notion that they were motivated by the individualistic desire for material well-being.

One final point must be made. This study focuses on thirty-two families living in a particular place at a particular point in time. The sample was a small one and the data gathered from the interviews were analysed by looking at the similarities and differences in the life-styles, aspirations, social perspectives, industrial attitudes and political proclivities of the sixty-two interviewees. While the families comprised a diverse group of people, they were not representative of working-class families in Britain. The findings of this study, therefore, are not typical of all working-class life-styles and values in the 1980s. Nor may the findings be considered a simple refutation of the earlier findings of the Luton team, since they interviewed a different group of people at a different time. What the findings do provide, however, is some insight into the life-styles and values of a small group of people. In so doing, they have engaged with a number of sociological debates on the working class as a cultural and socio-political entity in the field of class analysis. It cannot and does not, of course, claim definitively to resolve these debates.

APPENDIX: THE AIDE MEMOIRE

Name
Date of birth
Place of birth
How long have you been married?
Where did you get married?
Do you have any children?
How old are they?
Do they live at home or elsewhere?
What is their marital status?
Do they have children of their own?
Are your parents still alive?
Where do they live?
Do you have any brothers and sisters?
Are they married with children?
Where do they live?
Are your grandparents still alive?
Where do they live?
Do you have aunts, uncles and cousins?
Where do they live?

GEOGRAPHICAL HISTORY

Where did you grow up?
Were your parents and their families originally from…?
Did you live anywhere else before you were married?
Why did you move?
How long did you live there?
Where have you lived since you married?
Why did you move?
How long have you lived there?
Have you been happy/unhappy about the moves to the different places
    that you have made?
Do you think you will move out of Luton in the future?
How long have you lived in this house?

How did you come to live here?
Have you lived in other houses in Luton?
Why did you move?
Have you been happy/unhappy with the moves to different houses that
  you have made?
Do you have any plans to move house again in the future?
How do you feel/did you feel about your children moving within/
  outside Luton?

WORK HISTORY

Husband

What is your job title?
What do you actually do?
How do you feel about your job?
Do you like/dislike parts/all of your job?
Which block/department do you work in?
Do you work alongside many other people?
How long have you worked at Vauxhall?
How did you come to work at Vauxhall?
What other main jobs did you have before working at Vauxhall?
Were you ever unemployed?
Do you expect to stay at Vauxhall for the future
Does your wife work?
How do you feel about women working?

Wife

Do you work?
If no, how long have you not worked?
If yes, what is your job title?
What do you actually do?
What hours do you work?
How do your feel about your job?
Do you like/dislike parts/all of your job?
Do you work alongside many other people?
How long have you worked for...?
How did you come to work for them?
What other jobs have you had before working here?
Were they full- or part-time jobs?
Have you ever been unemployed?
Have you spent any time away from work looking after the children full-
  time?
Do you expect to stay in the same job in the future?
How do you feel about women going out to work?
How does your husband feel about women going out to work?

SOCIABILITY WITH KIN

Do you see very much of your own married children, parents, brothers
and sister and wider kin?
Has that always been the case?
What has changed?
Why do you see more of...?
Do you feel you can turn to them for help and support?
Have you done so?
Would you like/have liked to have seen more of them?
Overall, have you been happy/unhappy about the level of contact with
married children, parents, siblings and wider kin?

SOCIABILITY WITH NEIGHBOURS

Do you see very much of your neighbours?
Has that always been the case?
What has changed?
Do you know some of your neighbours better than others?
How have you come to know some neighbours better than others?
Do you feel you can turn to them for help and support?
Have you done so?
Overall, you would like to see more/less of your neighbours?
Have there been many changes of neighbours since you've lived here?
Did you see very much of any of your previous neighbours?
Did you get to know any of them well?
Have you kept in contact?
What do you think of as a good/bad neighbour?
Do you know many other people in the area, other than your immediate
neighbours?
How much do you see of them?
How did you come to know them?

Overall, do you feel that you know people (well) in the area?
Do you have a sense of belonging?
Has that always been the case?
How would you describe the area in which you live?
How would you describe the people who live around here?
Has the area changed since you've lived here?
In what ways has it changed?

SOCIABILITY WITH FELLOW WORKERS

Do you get on well with the people with whom you work?
Have you got to know some colleagues better than others?
Do you feel you can turn to them for help and support?
Have you done so?
Do you see any of your fellow workers outside work?

Would you like to see more/less of them?
Overall, are you satisfied/dissatified with how much you have seen of
    fellow workers outside work?
Have you kept in contact or see any of your fellow workers from other
    jobs?
Do you know your husband's/wife's colleagues from work at all?
Do you see them?

FRIENDS

Do you have any other friends that you see?
How did you get to know them well?
Do you have other friends which you don't see?
How did you get to know them well?
Why don't you see very much of them now?

CONJUGAL ROLES

How do you organise your domestic work between yourself and your
    husband/wife?
What sort of things do you generally do on your own which are your
    responsibility?
What sort of things does your husband/wife usually do on his/her own
    which you consider their responsibility?
What sort of things do you generally do together?
Are you/have you been happy with the way you organised things?
Have you been satisfied with the amount of work your partner has done?
Are you happy with the amount of work you contribute?

How do/did you organise looking after the children between yourself
    and your husband/wife?
What sort of things do/did you do generally on your own?
What sort of things do/did you generally do together?
Are you/have you been satisfied with the way you organised things?
Have you been satisfied with the amount of child-care your partner has
    done?
Have you been happy with the amount of work you contribute?
What do you think makes a marriage work?
Do you feel that you have achieved those things?

LEISURE

When do you consider your free time starts in the day/evenings/
    weekends?
Does your free time vary at all?
What kinds of things do you generally do?
Do you have any particular hobbies?
How did you take your hobby up?

What do you enjoy about it/them?

Are you satisfied with the amount of free time you have and what you do with it?

Is your husband/wife satisfied with the amount of free time they enjoy and their hobbies?

Are there other things which you would have liked to have done in the past/like to do now/ like to do in the future?

Do you belong to any clubs or organisations?

How did you come to belong to it?

What do you actually do within the organisation?

Is there anything else that you do in your spare time?

ASPIRATIONS

How much do you earn, approximately, from your job?

Are you satisfied/dissatisfied with your pay?

What sorts of things do you spend your income on?

What have you spent it on over the years?

Have you/do make plans and save for different items?

Do you have any plans at the moment?

Have you/do you generally discuss how and what you spend your money on with your husband/wife?

What do you consider are your major achievements?

What sort of things would you have liked to have done?

What hopes and plans have you had/do you have for your children?

What sort of job would you like them to have?

Are you happy/unhappy with the way things have turned out for them?

How would you describe your standard of living at the moment?

Are you satisfied/dissatified with your current standard of living?

Has it changed over the years?

Why has it changed?

Overall, have you been happy/unhappy about your standard of living over the years?

Do you expect it to change in the future?

How do you feel about your standard of living in the future?

Do you feel your job is secure at the moment/future?

Do you feel your husband's/wife's job is secure?

Is it a source of worry?

How has it affected your hopes and plans?

How would redundancy affect your lives?

Is there anything you could do to overcome the situation?

SOCIAL PERSPECTIVES

Do you think there are different classes?

What are they?

What size are the different classes?
What types of people are in the different classes?
How do people come to be in different classes?
What class do you think you are in?
Why do you think you are in that class?
What class would you place the people in that we have talked about – family, neighbours, fellow workers and friends?
How do you judge a person's class position?
Do you think class is important? Does it affect your life?
Has that always been the case?
What has changed?
How do you feel about the different classes? Are they a good or a bad thing?

INDUSTRIAL AND POLITICAL PERSPECTIVES

Do you belong to a trade union?
How/why did you join?
What is the role of the union?
What sorts of issues should a union be concerned with?
What issues should it not be concerned with?
Overall, do you think they have been successful or unsuccessful on those issues?
Do you think the union could or should take any action over redundancies?
Do you attend branch or other meetings?
Have you ever held any positions within the union?

Do you take an interest in politics and follow what the political parties are saying?
Do you support any particular party and vote for them?
Have you always supported them?
Why do you support and vote for them?
What'do you think of the other political parties?
Why do you not support and vote for them?
Which way do you think you will be voting in the future?
Overall, have the political parties been successful in their aims and objectives?
Where do your allegiances come from?
Did anyone influence your early political opinions?
Do you share the same political views as the people we talked about – family, neighbours, fellow workers and friends?
Do you discuss politics with any of them?
Are you a member of a political party?
Do you attend party meetings?
Have you ever or do you hold any positions within the party?
How did you come to be active?

REFERENCES

Abercrombie, N., Hill, S. and Turner, B.S. (1980) *The Dominant Ideology Thesis*, London: George Allen and Unwin.

Abercrombie, N., Hill, S. and Turner, B.S. (1986) *Sovereign Individuals of Capitalism*, London: Allen and Unwin.

Abrams, M., Rose, R. and Hinden, M. (1960) *Must Labour Lose?* Harmondsworth: Penguin.

Alexander, S. (1976) 'Women's Work in Nineteenth-Century London: A Study of the Years 1820–1850' in J. Mitchell and A. Oakley, (eds), *The Rights and Wrongs of Women*, Harmondsworth: Penguin.

Allan, G. (1979) *A Sociology of Friendship and Kinship*, London: George Allen and Unwin.

Allan, G. (1985) *Family Life*, Oxford: Basil Blackwell.

Allan, G. and Crow, G. (1991) 'Privatization, Home-Centredness and Leisure', *Leisure Studies*, 10, 19–32.

Allcorn, D.H. and Marsh, C.M. (1975) 'Occupational Communities – Communities of What?' in M. Bulmer (ed.), *Working-Class Images of Society*, London: Routledge and Kegan Paul, 206–18.

Alt, J.E. (1979) *The Politics of Economic Decline*, Cambridge: Cambridge University Press.

Anderson, M. (1971) *Family Structure in Nineteenth-Century Lancashire*, Cambridge: Cambridge University Press.

Anderson, M. (ed.) (1975) *The Sociology of the Family*, Harmondsworth: Penguin.

Argyris, C. (1972) *The Applicability of Organisational Sociology*, Cambridge: Cambridge University Press.

Ayers, P. and Lambertz, J. (1986) 'Marriage Relations, Money and Domestic Violence in Working-Class Liverpool, 1919–39' in J. Lewis (ed.), *Labour and Love: Women's Experience of Home and Family, 1850–1940*, Oxford: Oxford University Press.

Backett, K.C. (1982) *Mothers and Fathers*, London: Macmillan.

Bailey, P. (1978) *Leisure and Class in Victorian England*, London: Routledge and Kegan Paul.

Bain, G.S, and Elias, P. (1985) 'Trade Union Membership in Great Britain: An Individual-Level Analysis', *British Journal of Industrial Relations*, 23 (1), March, 70–92.

Batstone, E. (1975) 'Deference and the Ethos of Small-Town Capitalism' in M. Bulmer (ed.), *Working-Class Images of Society*, London: Routledge and Kegan Paul.

Beechey, V. and Perkins, T. (1987) *A Matter of Hours*, Cambridge: Polity Press.

Bell, C. (1968) *Middle-Class Families*, London: Routledge and Kegan Paul.

Bell, C. (1990) 'Middle-Class Families. 1964–1989' in C.C. Harris (ed.), *Family, Economy and Community*, Cardiff: University of Wales Press.

Bell, C. and Healey, P. (1973) 'The Family and Leisure' in M.A. Smith, S. Parker and C.S. Smith (eds), *Leisure and Society in Britain*, London: Allen Lane.

Bell, C. and Newby, H. (1971) *Community Studies*, London: Unwin Hyman.

Bell, C. and Newby, H. (1975) 'The Sources of Variation in Agricultural Workers' Images of Society' in M. Bulmer (ed.), *Working-Class Images of Society*, London: Routledge and Kegan Paul.

Benson, L. (1978) *Proletarians and Parties*, London: Tavistock Publications.

Beynon, H. (1980) *Working for Ford*, Wakefield: EP Publishing.

Beynon, H. and Blackburn, R.M. (1972) *Perceptions of Work*, Cambridge: Cambridge University Press.

Black, E.I. and Simey, T.S. (eds), (1954) *Neighbourhood and Community*, Liverpool: Liverpool University Press.

Blackburn, R.M. and Mann, M. (1975) 'Ideology in the Non-Skilled Working Class' in M. Bulmer (ed.), *Working-Class Images of Society*, London: Routledge and Kegan Paul.

Blackburn, R.M. and Mann, M. (1979) *The Working Class in the Labour Market*, London: Macmillan.

Blauner, R. (1964) *Alienation and Freedom*, London: The University of Chicago Press.

Bose, C. (1982) 'Technology and Changes in the Division of Labour in the American House' in E. Whitelegg (ed.), *The Changing Experience of Women*, Oxford: Martin Robertson.

Bott, E. (1957) *Family and Social Network*, London: Tavistock Publications.

Bowlby, J. (1953) *Child-care and the Growth of Love*, Harmondsworth: Penguin.

Bowlby, J. (1969) *Attachment and Loss*, Volume 1, London: Hogarth.

Brown, R. (1973) 'Sources of Objectives in Work and Employment' in J. Child (ed.), *Man and Organisation*, London: George Allen and Unwin.

Brown, R., Brannan, P., Cousins, J. and Samphier, M. (1973) 'Leisure in Work: The "Occupational Culture" of Shipbuilding Workers', in M.A. Smith, S. Parker and C.S. Smith (eds), *Leisure and Society in Britain*, London: Allen Lane.

Brown, R. Curran, M. and Cousins, J. (1983) 'Changing Attitudes to Employment?', *Department of Employment Research Paper 40*, London: Department of Employment.

Brown, R.K. (1988) 'Employment Relationships in Sociological Theory' in D. Gallie (ed.), *Employment in Britain*, Oxford: Basil Blackwell.

Bulmer, M. (1975) 'Some Problems of Research into Class Imagery' in M. Bulmer (ed.), *Working-Class Images of Society*, London: Routledge and Kegan Paul.

Bulmer, M. (ed.), (1985) *Essays on the History of British Sociological Research*, Cambridge: Cambridge University Press.

Bulmer, M. (1986) *Neighbours: The Work of Philip Abrams*, Cambridge: Cambridge University Press.

Bulmer, M. (1990) 'Successful Applications of Sociology' in C.G.A. Bryant and H.A. Becker (eds), *What Has Sociology Achieved?*, London: Macmillan.

Burgess, R.G. (ed.), (1982) *Field Research: A Sourcebook and Field Manual*, London: Allen and Unwin.

Burgess, R.G. (1984) *In the Field*, London: Allen and Unwin.

Burns, T. (1973) 'Leisure in Industrial Society' in M.A. Smith, S. Parker and C.S. Smith (eds), *Leisure and Society in Britain*, London: Allen Lane.

Butler, D. and Kavanagh, D. (1984) *The British General Election of 1983*, London: Macmillan.

Butler, D. and Rose, R. (1960) *The British General Election of 1959*, London: Macmillan.

Butler, D. and Stokes, D. (1969) *Political Change in Britain*, London: Macmillan.

Cavendish, R. (1982) *Women on the Line*, London: Routledge and Kegan Paul.

Chinoy, Ely (1955), *Automobile Workers and the American Dream*, New York: Doubleday and Company.

Collins, R. (1985) 'Ideology and the Domestic Division of Labour' in P. Close and R. Collins (eds), *Family and Economy in Modern Society*, London: Macmillan.

Comer, L. (1974) *Wedlocked Women*, Leeds: Feminist Books.

Cornwell, J. (1984) *Hard-Earned Lives*, London: Tavistock Publications.

Cotgrove, S. and Parker, S. (1963) 'Work and Non-Work', *New Society*, 2 (41), 18–9.

Cousins, J. and Brown, R. (1975) 'Patterns of Paradox: Shipbuilding Workers' Images of Society' in M. Bulmer (ed.), *Working-Class Images of Society*, London: Routledge and Kegan Paul.

Coyle, A. (1984) *Redundant Women*, London: The Women's Press.

Crewe, I. (1973) 'The Politics of "Affluent" and "Traditional" Workers in Britain: An Aggregate Data Analysis', *British Journal of Political Science*, 3, 29–52.

Crewe, I. (1983) 'The Electorate: Partisan Dealignment Ten Years On', *West European Politics* 6, 183–215.

Crewe, I. (1985) 'Electoral Change in Western Democracy: A Framework for Analysis' in I. Crewe and D. Denver (eds), *Electoral Change in Western Democracy*, London: Croom Helm.

Crewe, I. (1986) 'On the Death and Resurrection of Class Voting: Some Comments on How Britain Votes', *Political Studies*, 34, 620–38.

Crewe, I. (1987) 'Why Mrs Thatcher was Returned with a Landslide', *Social Studies Review*, 3 (1), September, 2–9.

Crewe, I. (1989) 'The Decline of labour and the Decline of Labour': Social and Electoral Trends in Post-War Britain', *Essex Papers in Government and Politics*, 65, September.

Cronin, J.E. (1984) *Labour and Society in Britain, 1918–1979*, London: Batsford.

Crossick, G.J. (1978) *An Artisan Elite in Victorian Society: Kentish London 1840–1880*, London: Croom Helm.

Crow, G. and Allan, G. (1990) 'Constructing the Domestic Sphere: The Emergence of the Home in Post-War Britain' in H. Corr and L. Jamieson (eds), *Politics of Everyday Life: Continuity and Change in Work, Labour and the Family*, London: Macmillan.

Daniel, W.W. (1969) 'Industrial Behaviour and Orientation to Work – A Critique', *Journal of Management Studies*, 6, 366–75.

Daniel, W.W. (1971) 'Productivity Bargaining and Orientation to Work – a Rejoinder to Goldthorpe', *Journal of Management Studies*, 8, 329–35.

Davies, A. (1992) *Leisure, Gender and Poverty: Working-Class Culture in Salford and Manchester, 1900-39*, Buckingham: Open University Press.

Davis, R.L. and Cousins, J. (1975), 'The "New Working Class" and the Old' in M. Bulmer (ed.), *Working-Class Images of Society*, London: Routledge and Kegan Paul.

Davison, Cannon W. (1977) 'Memories and Reminisences of Luton: 1933-61', *Bedfordshire Magazine*, Winter.

DeAngelis, R. (1982) *Blue-Collar Workers and Politics*, London: Croom Helm.

Deem, R. (1985) 'Leisure, Work and Unemployment: Old Traditions and New Boundaries' in R. Deem and G. Salaman (eds), *Work, Culture and Society*, Milton Keynes: Open University Press.

Deem, R. (1986) *All Work and No Play?*, Milton Keynes: Open University Press.

Dennis, N., Henriques, F. and Slaughter, C. (1956) *Coal is our Life*, London: Eyre and Spottiswoode.

Devine, F. (1989) 'Privatised Families and their Homes' in G. Allan and G. Crow (eds) *Home and Family: Creating the Domestic Sphere*, London: Macmillan.

Devine, F. (1992a) 'Working-Class Evaluations of the Labour Party' in I. Crewe, P. Norris, D. Denver and D, Broughton (eds) *British Elections and Parties Yearbook 1991*, Hemel Hempstead: Harvester Wheatsheaf.

Devine, F. (1992b) 'Social Identities, Class Identity and Political Perspectives', *Sociological Review*, 40, (2), 229–252.

Dex, S. (1984) 'Women's Work Histories: An Analysis of the Women and Employment Survey', *Department of Employment Research Paper No. 46*, London: Department of Employment.'

Dex, S. (1985) *The Sexual Division of Work*, Sussex: Wheatsheaf.

Dex, S. (1988) 'Gender and the Labour Market' in D. Gallie (ed.), *Employment in Britain*, Oxford: Basil Blackwell.

Dhooge, Y. (1982) 'Local Involvement' in S. Wallman, I.H. Buchanan, Y. Dhooge, J.I. Gershuny and B.A. Kasmin (eds.), *Living in South London*, Aldershot: Gower.

Dubin, R. (1956) 'Industrial Workers" Worlds: A Study of the "Central Life Interests" of Industrial Workers', *Social Problems*, 3 (1), 131–41.

Dunleavy, P. (1980) *Urban Political Analysis*, London: Macmillan.

Dunleavy, P. and Husbands, C.T. (1985) *British Democracy at the Crossroads*, London: George Allan and Unwin.

Edgell, S. (1980) *Middle-Class Couples*, London: George Allen and Unwin.

Eldridge, J. (1990) 'Sociology in Britain: A Going Concern' in C.G.A. Bryant and H.A. Becker (eds), *What Has Sociology Achieved?*, London: Macmillan.

Finch, J. (1989a) *Family Obligations and Social Change*, Oxford: Polity Press.

Finch, J. (1989b) 'Kinship and Friendship' in R. Jowell, S. Witherspoon and L. Brook (eds), *British Social Attitudes: Special International Report*, Aldershot: SCPR/Gower.

Finch, J. and Groves, D. (eds), (1983) *A Labour of Love: Women, Work and Caring*, London: Routledge and Kegan Paul.

Foster, J. (1974) *Class Struggle and the Industrial Revolution*, London: Methuen.

Franklin, A. (1989) 'Working-Class Privatism: An Historical Case Study of Bedminster, Bristol', *Society and Space*, 7, 93–113.

Franklin, M.N. (1985) *The Decline of Class Voting in Britain*, Oxford: Claredon Press.

Gallie, D. (1983) *Social Inequality and Class Radicalism in France and Britain*, Cambridge: Cambridge University Press.

Gallie, D. (1988) 'Introduction' in D. Gallie (ed.), *Employment in Britain*, Oxford: Basil Blackwell.

Gamble, A. (1990) *Britain in Decline*, London: Macmillan.

Gavron, H. (1966) *The Captive Wife*, London: Routledge and Kegan Paul.

Gershuny, J. (1983) *Social Innovation and the Division of Labour*, Oxford: Oxford University Press.

Gershuny, J. and Jones, S. (1987) 'The Changing Work/Leisure Balance in Britain: 1961–1984', in J. Horne, D. Jary and A. Tomlinson (eds), *Sport, Leisure and Social Relations*, Sociological Review Monograph 33, London: Routledge and Kegan Paul.

Giddens, A. (1973) *The Class Structure of the Advanced Societies*, London: Hutchinson.

Giddens, A. (1984) *The Constitution of Society*, Cambridge: Polity Press.

Gittins, D. (1982) *Fair Sex*, London: Hutchinson.

Gittins, D. (1985) *The Family in Question: Changing Households and Familiar Ideologies*, London: Macmillan.

Goldthorpe, J.H. (1970) 'The Social Action Approach to Industrial Sociology: A Reply to Daniel', *Journal of Management Studies*, 7, 199–208.

Goldthorpe, J.H. (1972) 'Daniel on Orientations to Work: A Final Comment,' *Journal of Management Studies*, 9, 266–73.

Goldthorpe, J.H. (1978) 'The Current Inflation: Towards a Sociological Account' in F. Hirsch and J.H. Goldthorpe (eds.), *The Political Economy of Inflation*, London: Martin Robertson.

Goldthorpe, J.H. in collaboration with C. Llewellyn and C. Payne (1980) *Social Mobility and Class Structure in Modern Britain*, Oxford: Clarendon Press.

Goldthorpe, J.H. and Lockwood, D. (1963) 'Affluence and the British Class Structure', *Sociological Review*, 11, (2), 133-63.

Goldthorpe, J.H., Lockwood, D., Bechhofer, F. and Platt, J. (1968a) *The Affluent Worker: Industrial Attitudes and Behaviour*, Cambridge: Cambridge University Press.

Goldthorpe, J.H., Lockwood, D., Bechhofer, F. and Platt, J. (1968b) *The Affluent Worker: Political Attitudes and Behaviour*, Cambridge: Cambridge University Press.

Goldthorpe, J.H., Lockwood, D., Bechhofer, F. and Platt, J. (1969) *The Affluent Worker in the Class Structure*, Cambridge: Cambridge University Press.

Goldthorpe, J. H. and Payne, C. (1986) ' On the Class Mobility of Women: Results from Different Approaches to the Analysis of Recent British Data', *Sociology*, 20, 531-55.

Goldthorpe, J.H. in collaboration with Catriona Llewellyn and C. Payne (1987) *Social Mobility and Class Structure in Modern Britain: Second Edition*, Oxford: Clarendon Press.

Gouldner, A.W. (1965) *Wildcat Strike*, New York: Harper and Row.

Gray, R.Q. (1976) *The Labour Aristocracy in Victorian Edinburgh*, Oxford: Oxford University Press.

Green, F. (1989) *The Restructuring of the UK Economy*, Hemel Hempstead: Harvester Wheatsheaf.

Grieco, M. (1981) 'The Shaping of a Workforce: A Critique of the *Affluent Worker* Study', *International Journal of Sociology and Social Policy*, 1 (1), 62–88.

Grieco, M. (1987) *Keeping it in the Family: Social Networks and Employment Change*, London: Tavistock Publications.

Grint, K. (1991) *The Sociology of Work: An Introduction*, Cambridge: Polity Press.

Gullestad, M. (1984) *Kitchen-Table Society: A Case Study of the Family Life and Friendships of Young Working-Class Mothers in Urban Norway*, Oslo: Universitetsforlaget.

The *Guardian*.

Hakim, C. (1979) 'Occupational Segregation: A Comparative Study of the Degree and Pattern of the Differentiation between Men and Women's Work in Britain, the US and Other Countries', *Department of Employment Research Paper No. 9*, London: Department of Employment.

Hareven, T.K. (1982) *Family Life and Industrial Time*, Cambridge: Cambridge University Press.

Harloe, M. (1984) 'Sector and Class: A Critical Comment', *International Journal of Urban and Regional Research*, 8 (2), 228–37.

Harris, C.C. (1969) *The Family: An Introduction*, London: Allen and Unwin.

Hart, N. (1976) *When Marriage Ends*, London: Tavistock Publications.

Heath, A., Jowell, R. and Curtice, J. (1985) *How Britain Votes*, Oxford: Pergamon Press.

Heath, A., Jowell, R. and Curtice, J. (1987) 'Trendless Fluctuation: A Reply to Crewe', *Political Studies*, 35, 256–77.

Heath, A., Jowell, R., Curtice, J., Evans, G., Field, J. and Witherspoon, S. (1991) *Understanding Political Change: The British Voter 1964–1987*, Oxford: Pergamon Press.

The *Herald*

Hill, S. (1976) *The Dockers*, London: Heinemann.

Hill, S. (1990) 'Britain: The Dominant Ideology Thesis after a Decade' in N. Abercrombie, S. Hill and B.S. Turner (eds), *Dominant Ideologies*, London: Unwin Hyman.

Himmelweit, H.T., Humphreys, P., Jaeger, M. and Katz, M. (1985) *How Voters Decide*, Milton Keynes: Open University Press.

Hinton, J. (1983) *A History of the Labour Movement, 1967–1974*, Brighton: Harvester.

Hobson, D. (1978) 'Housewives: Isolation as Oppression' in Women's Studies Group, Centre for Contemporary Cultural Research (eds), *Women Take Issue*, London: Hutchinson.

Hoggart, R. (1957) *The Uses of Literacy*, Harmondsworth: Penguin.

Holden, L.T. (1983), 'A History of Vauxhall Motors to 1950: Industry, Development and Local Impact on the Luton Economy' Unpublished M. Phil Thesis, Open University.

Holme, A. (1985) *Housing and Young Families in East London*, London: Routledge and Kegan Paul.
Horne, J. and Jary, D. (eds)(1987) *Sport, Leisure and Social Relations*, London: Routledge and Kegan Paul.
Hubert, J. (1965) 'Kinship and Geographical Mobility in a Sample from a London Middle-Class Area', *International Journal of Comparative Sociology*, 6, 61–80.
Hunt, J. (1982) 'A Woman's Place is in Her Union' in J. West (ed.), *Work, Women and the Labour Market*, London: Routledge and Kegan Paul.
Hunt, P. (1980) *Gender and Class Consciousness*, London: Macmillan.

IDS Report 513/January 1988.
The *Independent*.
The *Independent on Sunday*.

Jennings, H. (1962) *Societies in the Making*, London: Allen and Unwin.
Joyce, P. (1980) *Work, Society and Politics*, London: Macmillan.

Keller, S. (1968) *The Urban Neighbourhood: A Sociological Perspective*, New York: Random House.
Kemeny, P.J. (1972) 'The Affluent Worker Project: Some Criticisms and a Derivative Study', *Sociological Review*, 20 (3), 373–89.
Kent, R.A. (1981) *A History of British Empiricial Sociology*, Aldershot: Gower.
Kerr, M. (1958) *The People of Ship Street*, London: Routledge and Kegan Paul.
Kirk, N. (1991) '"Traditional" Working-Class Culture and "the Rise of Labour": Some Preliminary Questions and Observations', *Social History*, 16, (2), 203–16.
Klein, J. (1965) *Samples From English Culture*, Volume 1, London: Routledge and Kegan Paul.
Kuper, L. (ed.), (1953) *Living in Towns*, London: The Cresset Press.

Laczko, F. and Phillipson, C. (1991) *Changing Work and Retirement: Social Policy and the Older Worker*, Milton Keynes: Open University Press.
Laing, S. (1986) *Representations of Working-Class Life 1957-1964*, London: Macmillan.
Lane, R.E. (1962) *Political Ideology*, New York: The Free Press.
Lane, T. and Roberts, K. (1971) *Strike at Pilkingtons*, London: Fontana.
Leaver, G.G. (1987) 'Getting by Without Employment' in C.C. Harris and The Redundancy and Unemployment Research Group (eds), *Redundancy and Recession in South Wales*, Oxford: Basil Blackwell.
Leonard, D. (1980) *Sex and Generation*, London: Tavistock Publications.
Lockwood, D. (1966) 'Sources in Variation in Working-Class Images of Society', *Sociological Review*, 14, (3), 249-67.
Lockwood, D. (1975), 'In Search of the Traditional Worker' in M. Bulmer (ed.), *Working-Class Images of Society*, London: Routledge and Kegan Paul.
Luton District Citizen.
Luton Gazette.
The *Luton News*.
Luton Official Guide 1991

MacKenzie, G. (1974) 'The "Affluent Worker" Study: An Evaluation and Critique' in F. Parkin (ed.), *The Social Analysis of Class Structure*, London: Tavistock Publications.

MacKinnon, M.H. (1980) 'Work Instrumentalism Reconsidered', *British Journal of Sociology*, 31, 339–74.

McKee, L. and Bell, C. (1986) 'His Unemployment: Her Problem' in S. Allen,A. Watson, K. Parcell and S. Wood (eds), *The Experience of Unemployment*, London: Macmillan.

McLennan, G. (1981) "The Labour Aristocracy" and "Incorporation": Notes on Some Terms in the Social History of the Working Class', *Social History*, 6, 71–81.

McRae, S. (1986) *Cross-Class Families*, Oxford: Clarendon Press.

Mallet, S. (translated by A. and B. Shephard), (1975) *The New Working Class*, Nottingham: Spokesman Books.

Mann, M. (1970) 'The Social Cohesion of Liberal Democracy', *American Sociological Review*, 35 (3), 423–31.

Mann, M. (1973a) *Consciousness and Action Amongst The Western Working Class*, London: Macmillan.

Mann, M. (1973b) *Workers on the Move*, Cambridge: Cambridge University Press.

Mansfield, P. and Collard, J. (1988) *The Beginning of the Rest of Your Life: A Portrait of Newly-Wed Marriage*, London: Macmillan.

Marcuse, H. (1964) *One Dimensional Man*, London: Sphere.

Mark-Lawson, J. (1988) 'Occupational Segregation and Women's Politics' in S. Walby (ed.), *Gender Segregation at Work*, Milton Keynes: Open University Press.

Marsden, D., Morris, T., Willman, P. and Wood, S. (1985) *The Car Industry: Labour Relations and Industrial Adjustment*, London: Tavistock Publications.

Marsh, C. (1991) *Hours of Work of Women and Men in Britain*, London: Her Majesty's Stationery Office.

Marshall, G. (1990) *In Praise of Sociology*, London: Unwin Hyman.

Marshall, G. (1986) 'The Workplace Culture of a Licenced Restaurant', *Theory, Culture and Society*, 3 (1), 33–47.

Marshall, G. (1988) 'Some Remarks on the Study of Working-Class Consciousness' in D. Rose (ed.) *Social Stratification and Economic Change*, London: Hutchinson.

Marshall, G., Rose, D., Vogler, C. and Newby, H. (1985) 'Class, Citizenship and Distributional Justice in Modern Britain' *British Journal of Sociology*, 36 (2), 259–84.

Marshall, G., Vogler, C., Rose, D. and Newby, H. (1987) 'Distributional Struggle and Moral Order in a Market Society', *Sociology*, 21, (1), 55-73.

Marshall, G., Newby, H., Rose, D. and Vogler, C. (1988) *Social Class in Modern Britain*, London: Hutchinson.

Marshall, T.H. (1970) 'Review of "The Affluent Worker in the Class Structure"', *Economic Journal*, 80 (2), 415–17.

Martin, F.M. (1954) 'Some Subjective Aspects of Social Stratification' in D.V. Glass (ed.), *Social Mobility in Britain*, London: Routledge and Kegan Paul.

Martin, J. and Roberts, C. (1984) *Women and Employment: A Lifetime Perspective*, London: Her Majesty's Stationery Office.

Maynard, M. (1985) 'Houseworkers and their Work', in R. Deem and G. Salaman (eds), *Work, Culture and Society*, Milton Keynes: Open University Press.

Millward, N. and Stevens, M. (1986) *British Workplace Industrial Relations 1980–1984: The DE/ESRC/PSI/ACAS Surveys*, London: Gower.

Mogey, J.M. (1956) *Family and Neighbourhood: Two Studies in Oxford*, London: Oxford University Press.

Moore, R.S. (1975) 'Religion as a Source of Variation in Working-Class Images of Society' in M. Bulmer (ed.), *Working-Class Images of Society*, London: Routledge and Kegan Paul.

Moorhouse, H.F. (1978) 'The Marxist Theory of the Labour Aristocracy', *Social History*, 4, 481–90.

Moorhouse, H.F. (1979) 'History, Sociology and the Quiescence of the British Working Class', *Social History*, 4, 229–33.

Moorhouse, H.F. (1981) 'The Significance of the Labour Aristocracy', *Social History*, 6, 229–33.

Moorhouse, H.F. (1983) 'American Automobiles and Workers' Dreams', *Sociological Review*, 31, 403–26.

Moorhouse, H.F. (1989) 'Models of Work, Models of Leisure' in C. Rojek (ed.), *Leisure for Leisure*, London: Macmillan.

Morgan, D.H.J. (1975) *Social Theory and the Family*, London: Routledge and Kegan Paul.

Morgan, D.H.J. (1985) *Social Theory, Politics and the Family*, London: Routledge and Kegan Paul.

Newby, H. (1977) *The Deferential Worker*, London: Allen Lane.

Newby, H. (1982) *The State of Research into Social Stratification in Britain*, London: Economic and Social Research Council.

Newby, H. Vogler, C. Marshall, G. and Rose, D. (1985) 'From Class Structure to Class Action: British Working-Class Politics in the 1980s' in B. Roberts, R. Finnegan and D. Gallie (eds), *New Approaches to Economic Life*, Manchester: Manchester University Press.

Newson, J. and Newson, E. (1963) *Patterns of Infant Care in an Urban Community*, Harmondsworth: Penguin.

Oakley, A. (1972) *Sex, Gender and Society*, London: Temple Smith.

Oakley, A. (1974) *The Sociology of Housework*, New York: Pantheon Books.

Oakley, A. (1981) *Subject Women*, Oxford: Martin Robertson.

Oakley, A. and Rajan, L. (1991) 'Social Class and Social Support: The Same or Different', *Sociology*, 25 (1), 31–59.

OECD, (1983), *Long Term Outlook for the World Automobile Industry*, Paris: OECD.

Pahl, J.M. and Pahl, R.E. (1971) *Managers and their Wives*, Harmondsworth: Penguin.

Pahl, R.E. (1984) *Divisions of Labour*, Oxford: Basil Blackwell.

Pahl, R.E. and Wallace, C. (1988) 'Neither Angels in Marble Nor Rebels in Red: Privatization and Working-Class Consciousness' in D. Rose (ed.), *Social Stratification and Economic Change*, London: Hutchinson.

Parker, S.R. (1964) 'Types of Work, Friendship Patterns and Leisure *Human Relations*, 17 (3), 215–19.

Parker, S.R. (1965) 'Work and Non-Work in Three Occupations', *Sociological Review*, 13 (1), 65–75.

Parker, S. (1976) *The Sociology of Leisure*, London: George Allen and Unwin.

Parkin, F. (1972) *Class Inequality and Political Order*, London: Paladin.
Pilgrim Trust, (1938) *Men Without Work*, Cambridge: Cambridge University Press.
Platt, J. (1969) 'Some Problems in Measuring the Jointness of Conjugal Role-Relationships', *Sociology*, 3 (3), 287–95.
Platt, J. (1971) 'Variations in Answers to Different Questions on Perceptions of Class', *Sociological Review*, 19, 409–19.
Platt, J. (1984) 'The Affluent Worker Re-visited', in C. Bell and H. Roberts (eds.), *Social Researching: Politics, Problems, Practice*, London: Routledge and Kegan Paul.
Pollert, A. (1981) *Girls, Wives, Factory Lives*, London: Macmillan.
Proctor, I. (1990) 'The Privatisation of Working-Class Life: A Dissenting View', *British Journal of Sociology*, 41 (2), 158–80.

Rapoport, R., Rapoport, R.N. with the collaboration of Strelitz, Z. (1975) *Leisure and the Family Life-Cycle*, London: Routledge and Kegan Paul.
Regional Trends 26, (1991) London: Central Statistical Office/Her Majesty's Stationery Office.
Reid, A. (1978) 'Politics and Economics in the Formation of the British Working Class', *Social History*, 3, 347–61.
Reid, A. (1986) 'Intelligent Artisans and Aristocrats of Labour: The Essays of Thomas Wright' in J. Winter (ed.), *The Working Class in Modern British History*, Cambridge: Cambridge University Press.
Report of the County Secretary: Luton Law Centre.
Rich, D. (1953) 'Spare Time in the Black Country' in L. Kuper (ed.), *Living in Towns*, London: The Cresset Press.
Roberts, E. (1984) *A Woman's Place: An Oral History of Working-Class Women 1890–1940*, Oxford: Basil Blackwell.
Roberts, K. (1970) *Leisure*, London: Longman.
Roberts, K., Cook, F.G., Clark, S.C. and Semeonoff, E. (1977) *The Fragmentary Class Structure*, London: Heinemann.
Roberts, R. (1974) *The Classic Slum*, Harmondsworth: Penguin.
Robertson, D. (1984) *Class and the British Electorate*, Oxford: Basil Blackwell.
Robertson Elliot, F. (1986) *The Family: Change or Continuity?*, London: Macmillan.
Rojek, C. (ed.) (1989) *Leisure for Leisure*, London: Macmillan.
Rose, D., Marshall, G. Newby, H. and Vogler, C. (1984) Economic Restructuring: the British Experience', *Annals of the American Academy of Political and Social Science*, 475, 137–57.
Rose, G. (1982) *Deciphering Sociological Research*, London: Macmillan.

Salaman, G. (1974) *Community and Occupation*, Cambridge: Cambridge University Press.
Salaman, G. (1975) 'Occupations, Community and Consciousness' in M. Bulmer (ed.), *Working-Class Images of Society*, London: Routledge and Kegan Paul.
Sarlvik, B. and Crewe, I. (1983) *Decade of Dealignment*, Cambridge: Cambridge University Press.
Saunders, P. (1984) 'Beyond Housing Classes', *International Journal of Urban and Regional Research*, 8 (2), 202–27.
Saunders, P. (1990a) *A Nation of Home Owners*, London: Unwin Hyman.
Saunders, P. (1990b) *Social Class and Stratification*, London: Tavistock.

Scase, R. (1974) 'Conceptions of the Class Structure and Political Ideology: Some Observations on Attitudes in England and Sweden' in F. Parkin (ed.), *The Social Analysis of Class Structure*, London: Tavistock Publications.

Silverman, D. (1985) *Qualitative Methodology and Sociology*, Aldershot: Gower.

Slater, E.T.O. and Woodside, M. (1951) *Patterns of Marriage*, London: Cassell and Company.

Smith, C.A. (1973) 'Leisure in the Life-Cycle' in M.A. Smith, S. Parker and C.S. Smith (eds), *Leisure and Society in Britain*, London: Allen Lane.

Smith, J. (1987) 'Men and Women at Play: Gender, Life-Cycle and Leisure' in J. Horne, D. Jary and A. Tomlinson (eds), *Sport, Leisure and Social Relations*, Sociological Review Monograph 33, London: Routledge and Kegan Paul.

Smith, M., Parker, S. and Smith, C. (eds) (1973) *Leisure and Society in Britain*, London: Allen Lane

Spring Rice, M. (1981) *Working-Class Wives*, London: Virago.

Stacey, M. (1960), *Tradition and Change: A Study of Banbury*, Oxford: Oxford University Press.

Stacey, M. (1969) 'The Myth of Community Studies', *British Journal of Sociology*, 20, 134–48.

Talbot, M. (1979) *Women and Leisure*, London: Social Science Research Council/Sports Council.

The Times Guide to the House of Commons.

Tunstall, J. (1962) *The Fisherman*, London: MacGibbon and Kee.

Turner, B.S. (1990) ''Conclusion: Peroration on Ideology' in N. Abercrombie, S. Hill and B.S. Turner (eds), *Dominant Ideologies*, London: Unwin Hyman.

Ungerson, C. (1987) *Policy is Personal; Sex, Gender and Informal Care*, London: Tavistock Publications.

Vauxhall Annual Report 1990.

Walker, C.R. (1950) *Steeltown*, New York: Harper and Row.

Walker, C.R. and Guest, R.H. (1952) *The Man on the Assembly Line*, Cambridge, Mass. Harvard University Press.

Wallman, S. (1982) *Living in South London*, Aldershot: Gower.

Wallman, S. (1984) *Eight London Households*, London: Tavistock Publications.

Westergaard, J.H. (1970) 'The Rediscovery of the Cash Nexus', in R. Miliband and J. Saville (eds.), *The Socialist Register 1970*, London: Merlin.

Whelan, C.T. (1976) 'Orientations to Work: Some Theoretical and Methodological Problems,' *British Journal of Industrial Relations*, 14 (2), 142–58.

White, H. (ed.), (1977) *Luton: Past and Present*, Luton: White Cresent Press.

White, J. (1986) *The Worst Street in North London: Campbell Bunk, Islington, Between the Wars*, London: Routledge and Kegan Paul.

Whiteley, P. (1983) *The Labour Party in Crisis*, London: Methuen.

Wilensky, H.L. (1960) 'Work, Careers and Social Integration', *International Social Science Journal*, 12, 543–60.

Willener, A. (1975) 'Images, Action, "Us and Them"', in M. Bulmer (ed.), *Working-Class Images of Society*, London: Routledge and Kegan Paul.

Willmott, P. (1963) *The Evolution of a Community*, London: Routledge and Kegan Paul.

Willmott, P. (1986) *Social Networks, Informal Care and Public Policy*, Research Report 655, London: Policy Studies Institute.

Wilson, E. (1980) *Only Halfway to Paradise*, London: Tavistock Publications.

Winchester, D. (1988) 'Sectoral Change and Trade Union Organisation' in D. Gallie (ed.), *Employment in Britain*, Oxford: Basil Blackwell.

Woodward, J. (1958) *Management and Technology*, London: Her Majesty's Stationery Office

Yeandle, S. (1984) *Women's Working Lives: Patterns and Strategies*, London: Tavistock Publications.

Young, M. and Willmott, P. (1957) *Family and Kinship in East London*, Harmondsworth: Penguin.

Young, M. and Willmott, P. (1975) *The Symmetrical Family*, Harmondsworth: Penguin.

Young, M. amd Willmott, P. (1983) *Family and Kinship in East London: Second Edition*, London: Routledge and Kegan Paul.

Zweig, F. (1952) *The British Worker*, Harmondsworth: Penguin.

Zweig, F. (1961) *The Worker in an Affluent Society*, London: Heinemann.

INDEX